CAMPAIGN FINANCE
IN STATE LEGISLATIVE ELECTIONS

CAMPAIGN FINANCE
IN STATE LEGISLATIVE ELECTIONS

Joel A. Thompson
Appalachian State University

Gary F. Moncrief
Boise State University

Foreword by Herbert E. Alexander
University of Southern California

Congressional Quarterly Inc.
Washington, D.C.

BKY 3137-2/2

Some data used in this report were gathered from material based upon work supported by the National Science Foundation under Grant No. SBR-9320673. Any opinions, findings, and conclusions or recommendations expressed in this material are those of the authors and do not necessarily reflect the views of the National Science Foundation.

Library of Congress Cataloging-in-Publication Data

Campaign finance in state legislative elections / [edited by] Joel A. Thompson, Gary F. Moncrief.
    p.   cm.
    Includes bibliographical references and index.
    ISBN 1-56802-148-8 (hc). — ISBN 1-56802-149-6 (pbk.)
        1. Campaign funds—United States—States.   2. Elections—United States—States. I. Thompson, Joel A. II. Moncrief, Gary F.
    III. Congressional Quarterly, inc.
    JK1991.C343   1997
    324.7'8'0973—dc21   97-42272

To
Calvin and Jane Thompson
La Verne Moncrief and the memory of Charles Moncrief

Table of Contents

List of Tables and Figures   ix

Foreword by Herbert Alexander   xiii

Preface   xv

Contributors   xix

I. **The Study of Campaign Finance**   1
    1. Exploring the "Lost World" of Campaign Finance   3
      Joel A. Thompson and Gary F. Moncrief

    2. A Framework for the Study of Campaign Finance   18
      Anthony Gierzynski

II. **Spending Patterns**   35
    3. Candidate Spending in State Legislative Races   37
      Gary F. Moncrief

    4. Variations in District-Level Campaign Spending in   59
    State Legislatures
      Robert E. Hogan and Keith E. Hamm

    5. Candidate Revenues and Expenditures in State   80
    Legislative Primaries
      David A. Breaux and Anthony Gierzynski

    6. Expenditures and Election Results   99
      William E. Cassie and David A. Breaux

III. **Contribution Patterns**   115
    7. Gender, Candidate Attributes, and Campaign   117
    Contributions
      Joel A. Thompson, Gary F. Moncrief, and
      Keith E. Hamm

8. Minorities and Campaign Contributions   139
     Robert E. Hogan and Joel A. Thompson

9. Patterns of PAC Contributions to State   158
     Legislative Candidates
     William E. Cassie and Joel A. Thompson

10. The Financing Role of Parties   185
     Anthony Gierzynski and David A. Breaux

IV Conclusion   207
11. Can the Legislative Campaign Finance System   209
     Be Reformed?
     Malcolm E. Jewell and William E. Cassie

Appendix: Data-Gathering Issues   233
     Anthony Gierzynski

Index   239

List of Tables and Figures

Table 1-1	Characteristics of the Campaign Finance Environment in Selected States	12
Table 1-2	Classifying the States: A Modification of Kurtz's Legislative Professionalization Measure	15
Figure 2-1	Model of Campaign Finance Systems	20
Figure 2-2	Power and Contributions in Political Systems	28
Table 3-1	Total Expenditures Per Candidate in Contested House Races, 1994	43
Figure 3-1	Median Spending by Candidates in Contested House Races, 1994	44
Table 3-2	Total Expenditures Per Candidate in Competitive House Races, 1994	45
Table 3-3	Increase in Candidate Spending in Contested House Races, 1986–1994	48
Figure 3-2	Inflation-Adjusted Spending in Contested House Races, 1986–1994	49
Figure 3-3	Increase in Candidate Spending in Contested House Races, 1988–1994	49
Figure 3-4	Median Spending in Contested Races for State Legislatures, 1986–1994	51
Table 3-4	Gubernatorial Electoral Cycles and the Increase in Median Spending over Previous Election in Contested House Races	52
Table 3-5	Median Net Expenditures by Challengers, as a Percentage of Median Expenditures by Incumbents in Contested House Races	54
Table 4-1	Average District-Level Spending by Candidates Running for the State Legislature	62
Figure 4-1	District-Level Spending Per Eligible Voter by Candidate for the Lower House	65

Figure 4-2   Range of the Standard Deviations of District-Level
             Spending Per Eligible Voter   66
Table 4-2   Effects of Electoral and Structural Factors on
             District-Level Spending Per Eligible Voter   69
Figure 4-3   District-Level Spending Per Eligible Voter
             by Legislative Professionalism and General
             Election Competition   73
Figure 4-4   District-Level Spending Per Eligible Voter by
             Level of Chamber Competition and
             General Election Competition   74
Figure 4-5   District-Level Spending Per Eligible Voter by
             Strictness of Campaign Finance Laws and
             General Election Competition   75
Table 4-3   System- and District-Level Factors Affecting
             Average Spending Per Eligible Voter   76
Table 5-1   Primary and General Election Revenues,
             All Candidates   83
Table 5-2   Primary Revenues Raised by Candidates in
             Contested Versus Uncontested Primaries   85
Table 5-3   The Incumbency Advantage: Average Revenue in
             Contested Races   87
Table 5-4   Charting the Incumbency Advantage,
             General Election Candidates   89
Table 5-5   Expenditures During Primary and
             General Elections   90
Table 5-6   Mean Primary Expenditures, by Party
             and Incumbency   92
Table 5-7   Average Expenditures in Primary Elections,
             by Outcome   93
Table 5-8   Expenditures by Candidates and Opponents
             Needed to Change Candidate's Vote by One
             Percentage Point   95
Table 5A-1   Regression Analysis Results   97
Figure 6-1   Winners Outspending Losers in Contested Races   102
Table 6-1   Incumbency Advantage in Election Victories and
             Spending in Contested Elections   103
Table 6-2   Ratio of Challenger to Incumbent Spending in
             Contested Races   105
Table 6-3   Competitive Challengers Categorized by Ratio of
             Challenger to Incumbent Spending   107
Table 6-4   The Cost of Competing as a Challenger   109
Figure 7-1   Median Total Revenue by Gender, All Candidates   122

Figure 7-2   Median Total Revenue by Gender, Challengers   124

Figure 7-3   Median Total Revenue by Gender,
Open-Seat Candidates   125

Figure 7-4   Median Total Revenue by Gender, Incumbents   127

Figure 7-5   Median Total Revenue by Gender, Female Versus
Male Contestants in General Elections   128

Figure 7-6   Median PAC Contributions by Gender,
All Candidates in Contested General Elections   131

Figure 7-7   Median PAC Contributions to Incumbents
by Gender, in Contested General Elections   133

Figure 7-8   Median Political Party Contributions by Gender,
All Candidates in Contested General Elections   134

Table 7A-1   Regression Analysis of Total Revenue,
All Candidates in Contested General Elections   136

Table 8-1   Mean and Median Revenue Raised,
by Race/Ethnicity   146

Table 8-2   Mean and Median Revenue Raised Per Eligible
Voter, by Race   148

Table 8-3   Mean and Median Revenue Raised Per Eligible
Voter, by Race and Candidate Type   149

Table 8-4   Mean and Median Revenue Raised Per Eligible
Voter, by Race, Candidate Type, and Degree of
District Competition   151

Table 8-5   Campaign Revenue Raised from Political Parties
and Interest Groups   153

Table 9-1   Average PAC Contribution and Percentage of
Funds from PACs, by Candidate Status   164

Figure 9-1   Average Incumbent PAC Revenue,
by Professionalism   165

Figure 9-2   Average Incumbent PAC Revenue,
by Total Non-PAC Revenue   167

Figure 9-3   Ratio of Incumbent-to-Challenger PAC Revenues   169

Table 9-2   Average PAC Contribution, by Competitiveness
and Incumbency   172

Table 9-3   Average PAC Contribution, by Political Party and
Incumbency   174

Table 9-4   Average Incumbent PAC Revenues, by Leadership   175

Table 9-5   Average PAC Contributions to Incumbents,
by Type of PAC and Party   177

Table 10-1   Total and Average Party Contributions   187

Figure 10-1   Candidate Revenues from Political Parties   189

Table 10-2   Candidate Revenues from Party Organizations,
              1986–1992   191
Figure 10-2   Party Contributions, by Party Organization   192
Table 10-3   Party Contributions, by Party Organization   194
Figure 10-3   Party Contributions, by Incumbency   195
Table 10-4   Average Party Contributions,
              by Candidate Status   197
Figure 10-4   Party Contributions, by Competitiveness
              of the Race   198
Table 10-5   Average Party Contributions, by Competitiveness
              of the Race   199
Table 10-6   Mean Contributions from Party Sources,
              by Incumbency   201
Table 10-7   Mean Contributions to Safe and Close Races,
              by Party Organization   203
Table A-1   Campaign Finance Recording Practices in
              Eighteen States   235

Foreword

Much has been said on the related subjects of political finance and campaign finance reform at the state level, but until this book very little comparative information or systematic data were available on which to base opinions. This notable book is truly comparative, not a compilation of state case studies. Rather, it compares and contrasts data and information from eighteen states, in depth over several election cycles.

Surely, the states are where the action is: in the years from 1994 to 1997, four state legislatures passed major campaign finance reform enactments; five states have had task forces or commissions studying the subject and making recommendations; and there have been ballot issues on campaign finance reform in five states in 1994 and in seven in 1996 (twice in Colorado and two issues in California). While not all these states are studied in this compilation, one senses that dramatic change is occurring in the states. Hence the timeliness and relevance of this volume.

This collection of empirical data has enabled Joel Thompson, Gary Moncrief, David Breaux, William Cassie, Anthony Gierzynski, Keith Hamm, Robert Hogan, and Malcolm Jewell to explore the most important aspects of candidate and party finance. The presentation—asking and answering many controversial questions relating to uses and abuses of money in politics and forms of regulation—represents a major step forward in our understanding of these subjects.

Campaign Finance in State Legislative Elections is the product of a series of studies undertaken by the Comparative State Legislative Campaign Finance Project. The chapters were originally presented as papers at annual political science meetings. The National Science Foundation supported this unique comparative project, led by Joel Thompson and Gary Moncrief. The editors are to be congratulated on their ability to gather together a group of innovative scholars who have searched the literature, asked the right questions, empirically answered many of them on the basis of their massive data set, and worked cooperatively to produce this volume. As a group, the authors exemplify the finest traditions of joint social science research. We are indebted to them for their perseverance and determination in collecting the data in the diverse systems of disclosure and under the varying conditions of state availability. The resulting book touches on all variables relating to state legislative campaigns, covering the multiple and interacting roles of candidates, parties, political action committees, member committee assignments, governmental and party leadership, size of districts and legal restrictions in settings of incumbency, and challenger and open-seat status. Special attention is paid to gender and minority status of candidates for state legislatures.

The authors demonstrate the great diversity and variability of the differing state political cultures, ranging from professional legislatures to hybrid and citizen legislatures. They address varying relationships of political spending to census and redistricting years, gubernatorial election years, and off-years.

Excellent surveys of the growing literature are provided throughout the volume, and chapter bibliographies supply relevant references. The internal references from one chapter to another are especially useful and bring cohesion, making the book much more than a mere collection of related articles. The tables and figures are especially revealing.

Campaign Finance in State Legislative Elections should be read for its important implications for public policy. All state legislators and reformers who write the proliferating ballot issues in the twenty-four states permitting them will benefit from the knowledge and insights this book imparts. The record on ballot issues is not good since most of them are being litigated on constitutional grounds; several, in Missouri and Oregon, have been struck down by the courts, while others are in process. Political scientists will prize this book as a model of relevance and joint workmanship. We can hope that the media will learn from it, too.

We all should hope that Joel Thompson, Gary Moncrief, and their team of contributors will continue to work diligently in this area of research and expand their data base by including more states and more years for trend lines. One encouraging fact: in 1997 at least eleven states enacted laws enhancing disclosure by either mandating or authorizing electronic filing of campaign finance disclosure reports, making the job of data gathering by the Comparative State Legislative Campaign Finance Project perhaps a bit easier.

Herbert E. Alexander
Director, Citizens' Research Foundation, and Professor of Political
Science, University of Southern California

Preface

This volume spotlights the convergence of an institution—the state legislature—and an issue of significant contemporary interest—campaign finance reform. Since the elections of 1996, no issue has dominated the national media on a regular basis more than campaign finance. Attention has been focused on stories of campaign irregularities, alleged abuses, and a great deal of rhetoric, but very little action has been taken toward reform.

Largely because of this attention, the public's perception of the campaign finance system has been shaped by the Washington scene. But things are different at the state level. Here we are presented with fifty campaign finance systems, derived from fifty executives, ninety-nine legislative bodies, and a variety of socioeconomic, political, cultural, and legal environments. The confluence of these forces has produced a variety of combinations that make the states true laboratories for those interested in campaign finance.

With the continuing devolution of power, the states are assuming a more prominent role in our federal system. The states must now deal with some of the most important issues in decades—education, welfare, regulation of business and the environment, medical care, and other controversial and complex matters. The institution that will bear the brunt of the political battles over these issues is the state legislature. In short, state legislatures are, and will continue to be, the key political battlegrounds in the states. As a result, they will draw the attention of policy advocates, armed with substantial quantities of data and dollars.

The idea for this project first took form in 1990, in a coffee shop on Mason Street in San Francisco. Several of us had adjourned to this coffee shop after presenting papers at a panel on state campaigns and elections at the annual meeting of the American Political Science Association. After discussion, we realized that we were pursuing similar research questions about campaign finances in state legislative races but that each of us was hampered by the limited data we could collect individually. The solution was to develop a scheme whereby we would each collect data for several states, but in a uniform manner so that we could eventually pool the data for use by all of us.

We developed a common set of variables and a standardized coding procedure, assigning each member of the group the responsibility for collecting the data for several states. Information on campaign contributions, expenditures, candidate characteristics, and electoral outcomes was collected for eleven states for the 1988 electoral cycle. The data were merged and a set of research papers were presented at the 1992 annual meeting of the American Political Science Association in Chicago. This project demonstrated to us and others the viability and the potential benefits of such a collective effort.

After that meeting, we were encouraged by several individuals, including Ron Weber, David Magleby, and Herbert Alexander, to seek funding for our "pilot project," as it was now called, so that the scope of our efforts could be expanded. In the spring of 1993 Gary Moncrief visited Boone, North Carolina, where the two of us spent many days putting together a proposal for the National Science Foundation (NSF). Funding was approved in 1994. With this financial support, the team began what can only be termed a massive data collection effort. This effort took us to state capitols, archives, county court houses, and other interesting places across the country. Since no two states collect data in the same way and since reporting requirements and legal restrictions vary from state to state, it was necessary to make a number of adjustments in our coding scheme during the project (see the Appendix for a discussion of some of these issues). For each state, we collected as many variables for as many years as was feasible. In some cases, the states simply do not require certain information to be reported. Some states keep records for only a few years and then destroy them. For these reasons, readers will note that some of the analyses in this volume use different combinations of states.

The state responsibilities were as follows: Joel Thompson and William Cassie collected the data for New Jersey, North Carolina, Pennsylvania, and Utah. Gary Moncrief collected the data for Idaho, Montana, Oregon, and Washington. Anthony Gierzynski was responsible for the data from California, Maine, Minnesota, and Wisconsin. Keith Hamm (along with Robert Hogan) contributed the data for Delaware, Illinois, Kansas, and Wyoming. David Breaux provided information from Mississippi and Missouri. For the most part, these data represent four electoral cycles between 1986 and 1992. Several of the team members provided additional data for 1994.

Acknowledgments

This book is a culmination of our data gathering and analytical efforts. Without the financial assistance of the NSF, this extensive and time-consuming project would not have been possible. Other institutions were generous in providing support—the "seed money" for the larger project. The Graduate School and Department of Political Science/Criminal Justice at Appalachian State University provided some financial support for Joel Thompson. Two students—Michael Brooks and Patrick Ellcessor—were very helpful in collecting and coding data. William Cassie is indebted to Robert K. Goidel for his assistance in collecting some Pennsylvania data. Gary Moncrief wishes to acknowledge the financial assistance of the Idaho State Board of Education and the Boise State University Faculty Research Grant program. Several students assisted him, including Jennifer Carrington, Mike Haddon, Jay Janousek, Christie Maywhor, Randi McDermott, Deidre Peirson, Derrin Robinson, and Leah Weathers. Anthony Gierzynski wishes to acknowledge the assistance of three undergraduates who helped with data entry: Andrew Pennell, David Steer, and Renee Limoge. In addition, several state agency personnel were especially helpful: Marilyn Canavan and Annette Jones at the Maine Commission on Governmental Ethics and Election Practices, and Mary Ann McCoy and Jeanne Olson at the Minnesota Ethical Practices Board. David Breaux was assisted by his wife, Darlene, and Ph.D. candidate Tom Wilson with data collection and entry. Also, he received a Mississippi State University Research Initiation Grant that provided some financial assistance with the pilot project. Keith Hamm and Robert Hogan wish to thank Maria Isabella Peguero and Amy McKay for work on coding and data entry. They are especially appreciative of the assistance provided by Nick O'Connell, whose patience in coding the Illinois data made its inclusion in the book possible. Additional funding for the project was provided by the Center for the Study of Institutions and Values at Rice University.

There are others whose contribution to this volume we must acknowledge. We are fortunate that Jeffrey Stonecash at Syracuse University and Clyde Wilcox at Georgetown University reviewed drafts of each chapter. Their comments and suggestions made valuable contributions to the final product. We owe special thanks to Herb Alexander, not only for contributing the foreword to this book but also for his continuing interest in, and support of, our campaign finance project. We would be remiss if we failed to recognize the guiding influence that Malcolm Jewell has provided, not only with these analyses and our larger project but with our careers as political scientists. Shana Wagger, our exceedingly patient editor at CQ, has been most helpful and under-standing during the course of this project. She has been a pleasure to work with. Kerry Kern, our copy editor, is simply the best we have ever encountered in this profession. Finally, the editors would like to acknowledge the lifelong support of their parents—Calvin and Jane Thompson and LaVerne and the late Charles Moncrief. To them we simply say thank you.

Joel A. Thompson
Gary F. Moncrief

Contributors

DAVID A. BREAUX is associate professor of political science at Mississippi State University. He received his Ph.D. from the University of Kentucky. His publications include journal articles and book chapters on state legislative elections and southern politics.

WILLIAM E. CASSIE is assistant professor of political science at Appalachian State University. He received his Ph.D. from the University of Kentucky. His research interests are in the areas of legislative behavior, southern politics, parties, and elections. He is the author of several articles on state legislatures and southern politics.

ANTHONY GIERZYNSKI is assistant professor of political science at the University of Vermont. He is the author of *Legislative Party Campaign Committees in the American States* and has written several articles on the role of political parties in legislative elections and the importance of money in election outcomes.

KEITH E. HAMM is professor of political science at Rice University. He has published numerous articles on state legislatures. He is currently coeditor of *Legislative Studies Quarterly.*

ROBERT E. HOGAN is a Ph.D. candidate in political science at Rice University. His current research interests include electoral politics and campaign finance in the state setting. His dissertation is entitled "The Role of Campaigns in State Legislative Elections."

MALCOLM E. JEWELL is professor emeritus of political science at the University of Kentucky. His research includes books and articles on state legislatures and legislative elections, state political parties and elections, and campaign finance.

GARY F. MONCRIEF is professor of political science at Boise State University. He has published more than thirty-five book chapters and articles on various aspects of subnational legislatures and is coeditor of *Changing Patterns in State Legislative Careers*. His most recent work compares legislative career patterns in Australia, Canada, and the United States.

JOEL A. THOMPSON is professor of political science and associate dean of the graduate school at Appalachian State University. In addition to this volume, he is coeditor of two books: *American Jails,* with Larry Mays, and *Changing Patterns in State Legislative Careers,* with Gary Moncrief. He is author or coauthor of articles that have appeared in the *Journal of Politics, Western Political Quarterly, Political Research Quarterly, Polity, Social Science Quarterly, Legislative Studies Quarterly, Justice Quarterly,* and other journals.

Part I

THE STUDY OF CAMPAIGN FINANCE

CHAPTER ONE

Exploring the "Lost World" of Campaign Finance

Joel A. Thompson and Gary F. Moncrief

Appalled by a meteoric increase in campaign spending this year, and maybe by the disappointing drop in voter turnout as well, state legislators have begun working on campaign-finance proposals.

Winston-Salem Journal, December 8, 1996

Although this is the lead sentence from an editorial in one of North Carolina's major daily newspapers, the sad truth is that the above quote could apply to virtually any state. Across the states, not only have expenditures risen dramatically, but questions have been raised about the sources of campaign funds and the motives of the contributors. To say that the public perception of the current state of campaign finance system is dreadful is an understatement.

Not only has the public watched as campaign costs have soared, but they have heard numerous stories of political action committees (PACs) giving large sums of money to candidates; seen media accounts of lobbyists "wining and dining" legislators at posh resorts; and read of instances where corporations, both domestic and international, have contributed large sums to political parties who then circumvent rules designed to limit campaign contributions by funneling the money to candidates. Is there any wonder that public confidence in the current system has eroded?

But upon what evidence are these perceptions based? To a large extent, the public's view of the campaign finance system is shaped by events at the national level—those affecting campaigns for president and Congress. Incidents surrounding recent campaigns for these offices have added much fuel to the public's ire: large contributions by foreign nationals to the Democratic party, much of which was funneled to the president's campaign; ethics charges and sanctions against the Speaker of the House for campaign irregularities; and the large sums given to and spent by incumbents who continue to win virtually every time they run for reelection.

At the less visible state and local level, the public's image is informed largely by media accounts of certain excesses (unusually large amounts raised and spent by particular candidates) or by irregularities or controversial tactics of some kind (e.g., corporate contributions funneled through party organizations or questionable expenditures). As the quote above suggests, North Carolina may represent a prime example of what is happening in many states. Throughout most of the twentieth century North Carolina has been a traditional one-party Democratic state. Until recently, its legislature was a part-time citizen institution, but the state has experienced growing pains of late, both political and socioeconomic. While North Carolina retains much of its rural heritage, it has grown to the eleventh most populous state, with three large urban areas and numerous small- to mid-size towns. Growth has forced the state to face many new and complex issues. As a result, the partisan landscape has changed: there is now intense competition for control of the legislature and clear movement toward a more professional legislature.

With these changes in partisanship and professionalism have come changes in political campaigns—and examples of excess and questionable practices. For example, in 1996 it was widely reported in the state's media that former state senator George Daniel spent almost $250,000 in a losing effort to regain his old seat. This is for a seat for which the annual salary is about $20,000! And this is not an isolated case. Candidates for two senate seats in the Raleigh area spent a total of $626,00 on their campaigns. Senate president pro tem Marc Basnight spent $428,835 *even though he had no opposition*. Most of Basnight's spending was in the form of transfers to other candidates and organizations, including a single contribution of $257,000 to a Democratic senate campaign committee.

In addition to examples of excess, there have been increasing instances of controversial practices in the state. One such practice is the end run made by corporations and wealthy donors around contribution limits or restrictions. North Carolina law limits individual contributions to $4,000 per election and bans corporate contributions. But take the case of Robin Hayes, the 1996 Republican nominee for governor and an heir to the Cannon Mills textile fortune. Trailing badly one month prior to the election, he paid a visit to an old friend who happened to be the vice chairman of First Union Bank. Hayes requested that the bank make a contribution to the Republican National Committee

(RNC). The bank responded with contributions totaling $100,000. The same day, another North Carolina corporation gave the RNC $12,000 at the request of the Hayes campaign. Two weeks later, Hayes contributed $100,000; the RNC netted a total of $212,000 from Hayes's efforts. Within days, the Republican National Committee sent the state GOP $213,450. That same day, the state party made a contribution of $213,450 to the Hayes campaign (Morrill 1997). In politics it may be called "soft money," but in any other endeavor this process is simply known as money laundering.

To conclude this example, Hayes's mother also contributed $500,000 to the RNC. Hayes "loaned" his campaign $1.6 million and "borrowed" an additional $2.2 million from his mother. He lost the election.

PUBLIC PERCEPTIONS

Examples like these, which can be found in virtually every state, have contributed to a number of perceptions about the current campaign finance system. One perception is that costs are skyrocketing and have simply gotten out of hand. Costs have, in fact, increased in many races, some quite dramatically. In our most visible political race, that for the presidency, candidate expenditures leaped from $311 million in 1992 to $800 million in just four years, an increase of over 250 percent in one election cycle.

Costs in congressional races have soared as well. Between 1974 and 1990 the average cost of winning a seat in the U.S. Senate rose from about $400,000 to $3 million, an increase of 750 percent. By 1994 the average cost of winning a seat in the U.S. House rose to $570,000. For freshmen, the average cost was nearly $625,000 (Goldstein 1995).

Although generally less visible, many state legislative races have experienced an abrupt increase in costs. Again, North Carolina provides a clear example. During the 1980s campaign costs doubled about every six years. Now costs are almost doubling every election. Total expenditures increased from $4.5 million in 1992, to $8 million in 1994, to $14.1 million in 1996. Between 1976 and 1996 the average cost for a state house seat increased from about $2,500 to more than $41,000, while the average cost of a state senate seat increased from $3,400 to more than $82,000 (Rice 1997).

It is clear that campaign costs have increased, but why so dramatically? Are the two changes—increased competition and growing professionalism—partly responsible? Are other states experiencing similar trends?

Another factor contributing to growing public dissatisfaction with campaign finance is the appearance that PACs are underwriting the lion's share of campaign costs, and that there is some political quid pro quo expected in return. Generally, lobbyists label this return "access," but it is more likely to be perceived by the public as "undue influence." Again there is considerable anecdotal evidence to support such claims. In 1994 the 3,954 PACs registered with the Federal Election Commission (FEC) contributed more than $189 million to congressional candidates. About 70 percent of PAC contributions go to incumbents (Goldstein 1995), with those sitting on strategically important committees receiving larger amounts.

Similar trends can be found for PAC contributions at the state level (see chapter 9). For example, PAC contributions to North Carolina candidates jumped 450 percent in the ten years between 1984 and 1994. Table 9-1 reports that PAC contributions constitute more than 40 percent of all funds raised by incumbents in twelve of the seventeen states in that analysis. By contrast, in only one state did challengers receive this large a percentage from PACs.

What are the trends relative to PAC contributions? To what extent are PAC contributions responsible for the soaring costs of campaigns? Do PAC contributions give some candidates (i.e., incumbents) an unfair advantage over others (i.e., challengers)?

Another perception is that PACs, corporations, unions, and other big donors circumvent rules designed to limit their influence and, as a result, are able to sway decisions on policies affecting their interests. The Federal Election Campaign Act of 1974 restricts individuals to maximum contributions of $1,000 to any federal candidate's primary and general election campaign (and an annual total contribution to all candidates of $25,000). PACs are limited to $5,000 contributions in each election. But since 1978, the Federal Elections Commission has allowed political parties to raise unlimited amounts of funds, ostensibly for "party-building" activities. As a result, the very contributors that the 1974 act was designed to limit—corporations, PACs, wealthy donors— may now contribute "soft money" to political parties without limit. And so was born the era of lunch with the Speaker, coffee with the president, a night in the Lincoln bedroom, and a flight on Air Force One. As a result, the Federal Election Commission reports that soft money contributions to the two major parties have escalated, tripling between 1992 and 1996.

Soft money has become a force in state campaigns as well. In the 1996 North Carolina elections, state Democratic party committees spent $7.1 million, of which $4 million came from the national party. Similarly, Republican committees spent $4.5 million, $2.7 of which came from the national party (Morrill 1997). As the case of Robin

Hayes demonstrates, quite often this money finds its way into individual campaigns.

What is the source of those funds? In a recent report from the Center for Responsive Politics, Paul Hendrie traces some of the money coming in to state party organizations and legislative caucuses (1997). Most noteworthy is the activity of corporations with specific policy interests. Tobacco companies, which are currently facing new government attempts at regulation, provide a good example. Hendrie found that in 1996, Philip Morris made $100,000 contributions to Democratic committees in New Mexico, Delaware, Missouri, and Nevada. R. J. Reynolds gave $50,000 to committees in New Jersey, Colorado, California, and Nevada.

Because of the influx of soft money, state party organizations now have funds available to distribute to their candidates. What are the patterns of party contributions across the states? What strategy is employed by party organizations to allocate funds? Do party funds help offset the incumbency bias of PAC contributions?

STATE CAMPAIGN FINANCE: PERCEPTIONS AND REALITY

In one sense it is unfortunate that the public's view of state campaign finance systems is based largely on the Washington scene, combined with anecdotal media reports of aberrant races and campaign irregularities at the subnational level. These negative perceptions can kindle feelings of alienation and apathy toward the system and ultimately lead to decline in participation—risky business for a democratic system. On the other hand, public disgust over the current state of affairs has led to calls for reform, like that noted at the outset of this chapter. But reform efforts must be informed by good comparative data, not by journalistic accounts and sensational anecdotes.

Another reason that it is unfortunate that public perceptions are formed largely from journalistic accounts is that they cloud the real picture of what is happening in the states. As will be shown in the following chapters, the states are characterized by great variation in many factors related to campaign finance. Are costs really soaring out of hand in every state? If not, which states and why? What happens to these numbers when we control for inflation? Should we expect campaign costs to increase like every other commodity in the United States? The states provide a fertile field in which to seek answers to these and other important questions.

Unfortunately, too little is known about the campaign finance systems in many states. Like our perceptions, for far too long our knowledge of the system has been based primarily on studies of Congress augmented with case studies at the state level. These studies have been valuable in identifying a number of factors that are important in explaining differences in particular states. But too little is known about general patterns and trends. For example, is there a relationship between election costs and legal restrictions on contributions? Do stricter limits lower the costs of elections? Do the strong party organizations found in some states take a more active role in campaign finance? Are they able to offset the incumbency bias of PACs? Primarily because there has been too little comparative research, state campaign finance remains, in the words of Frank Sorauf, "the 'lost world' of American campaign finance" (1988, 295).

Why should we care about the states? We submit that there are many reasons. First, the states are important political entities in the American system and they are becoming more important with the continued devolution of federal responsibilities. As a result, state decisionmakers are involved in many important issues, such as education, crime control, and welfare reform. Because they make decisions on matters of public policy, it is important that we know what factors influence their decision-making processes.

Because a state's policies matter in the lives of its citizens, state elections matter. Every two years, thousands of elections are held for legislative seats. Legislators are at the foci of decision making at the state level. Thus, it is important to know how they get elected and what role campaign finance plays in their election.

Since many of our perceptions of the campaign finance system are based upon national level events, we want to know if what has been learned at the national level applies to the states. State legislative elections differ from congressional elections in several ways. In most states, the districts are smaller and campaign expenditures are less. If they cost less, the amount spent may have less to do with outcomes. Candidates may be less dependent on PACs, and thus the incumbency advantage may not be as pronounced as in Congress. However, party organizations may be better positioned to affect outcomes at this level.

There are a number of reasons why the study of state campaign finance systems has lagged congressional studies. Gathering the necessary data is not an easy task. There is no state-level counterpart to the FEC, nor is there any organization that serves as a repository for state-level campaign finance data. Some states compile and/or publish campaign finance information or make it available on-line. Other states do not compile information, and researchers must visit state capitals, and in some cases county courthouses, to review the original individual reports filed by candidates.

Data collection is further confounded by other differences. Each state has its own itemization requirements and reporting timetables. Some states classify contributors, quite often differently, while others do not. Suffice it to say, no state collects campaign finance data for the convenience of the social scientist. For these and other reasons explained in the appendix, we were not able to collect data for all variables in all the sample states. For example, reporting requirements in some states made it impossible to separate revenues and expenditures in primary and general elections. As a result, the analysis in chapter 5 is limited to four to six states for which the appropriate data were available. Similarly, in some states we were able to use voter guides and media publications to determine the race of winning and losing candidates for the analysis in chapter 8. In general, the analyses in the following chapters represent our best efforts at collecting complete data for as many states as feasible.

FACTORS AFFECTING STATE-BY-STATE VARIATIONS

There are a number of factors that affect a state's campaign finance system. One is the political environment of the state, which is determined by variables such as political culture, legislative professionalism, interparty competition, and interest group strength. Another is the legal/electoral environment, which is defined by various campaign finance and election laws. Finally, the general socioeconomic environment of a state, especially wealth, is important in that it affects the pool of available money and, subsequently, the overall "costs" of campaigns and the price of doing political business in the state. These and other factors are examined in greater detail in chapter 2. Several of these factors were critical in determining which states were selected for our study.

Cost of Elections

One of the important variables to consider is the overall cost of elections. As the data in Table 3-1 show, California dwarfs the other states in our sample, and states in general, with an average expenditure for contested house seats of more than $275,000. Illinois, Oregon, Washington, and North Carolina also have relatively high expenditures per seat. In contrast, Montana, Wyoming, and Maine have average expenditures of less than $5,000 per seat. Several factors are related to costs, including (but not limited to) the size of the district, the level of competition, legislative professionalism, and various candidate characteristics.

Contribution and expenditure levels are important for several reasons. Viewed as a dependent variable, they may be influenced by the level of wealth, legal restrictions on giving, and the strength of political parties and interest groups within a given state. As an independent variable, they are important in determining the cost of doing political business (i.e., the average PAC contribution that is viewed as "acceptable" by an incumbent), the number and quality of challengers, and ultimately the outcome of elections.

Legislative Professionalism

The cost of elections may be related to the level of legislative professionalism in a state. More professional legislatures are characterized by higher salaries and greater institutional resources, making legislative service a more attractive vocation. Because these seats are more attractive, competition is greater, an additional factor in driving up the election costs. States with more professional legislatures invariably are states with large populations and, consequently, large state budgets. The state budget is a measure of policy priorities; the larger the budget, the greater the economic impact. The political stakes are simply higher under such circumstances, and those with a political interest will seek to influence the outcome of these "high-stakes" contest. Finally, professional legislatures are in wealthier states, those generally conceded to have a larger pool of political money.

Because of these factors, professionalism may play an important role in explaining variations in several aspects of campaign financing. First, it may help determine why legislative seats in some states cost several times more than seats in others. Second, it may be a factor in explaining variations in the increase in expenditures over time. Some citizen legislatures have moved toward becoming more professional, a fact that could help explain escalating costs in these states. Professionalism could also be a factor in explaining discrepancies between PAC contributions to incumbents and challengers, since members of professional bodies are more likely to want to hold on to their seats and have more at stake politically. In addition, professionalism may be related to other aspects of the campaign finance system.

Partisan Competition

In a similar vein to professionalism, partisan competition may be important in explaining a number of variations across the states. At the individual level, costs are almost certain to be higher in highly contested races compared to uncontested or nominally contested races. Open-seat races are likely to attract the financial attention of party organizations and PACs, especially when partisan control of the legislature is in question. Parties want a working majority and PACs want access to whomever is in power.

Campaign Finance Laws

There is wide variation in the laws regulating campaign finance practices across the states. Some states impose lower limits on individual and PAC contributions than others. Some allow unlimited PAC contributions. Others prohibit direct contributions from unions and corporations, while some allow such contributions. At the time of out analysis, two states—Minnesota and Wisconsin—provided some form of public financing for legislative races.[1] Clearly, it is possible that regulations can affect revenues and expenditures. However, given the innovative developments of soft money and independent expenditure practices, we do not know this for certain.

With these variables in mind, a sample of 18 states was selected. Some states were excluded either because the data were not available or their reporting requirements did not include the necessary information for our analyses. Table 1-1 presents an alphabetical listing of the states used in our study, the years for which data were obtained, their ranking on partisan competition and legislative professionalism, and information on their campaign finance laws. These states represent a good cross section of available states.

OUR APPROACH TO CLASSIFYING THE STATES

Because of the massive amount of data available for this analysis, one of the decisions we faced was how best to organize our analysis and present our results. Obviously, this depends on the particular topic to be studied and the specific variables to be analyzed. There are several possibilities—factor analyzing the variables in Table 1-1 or combining them in the form of an index. We chose a less complicated approach.

For most analyses, a four-fold classification of the states is employed as a way of organizing the presentations. This classification is a modified version of Karl Kurtz's legislative professionalism categories (Kurtz 1990). Kurtz originally classified state legislatures into three types: Type I are labeled "professional" legislatures, and they are characterized by higher salaries for legislators, more staffing, and longer legislative sessions. At the other end of the scale are Type III legislatures, which are often referred to as "citizen" legislatures. They are characterized by small staff, low pay for members, and short sessions. Type II legislatures are in between these two categories—not full-time, but not "amateur" or citizen either. This classification was first presented about eight years ago, and several states have moved from citizen to "hybrid" status since then (see Figure 5-2 in Patterson 1996).

Table 1-1 *Characteristics of the Campaign Finance Environment in Selected States*

| | | Electoral | Political | Legal | |
| | | | | | Corporate/ Unions |
State	Years	Legislative Party Competitiveness	Legislative Professionalism	Contribution Limits	Contributions Allowed
California	1986, 1988, 1990 1992, 1994	low	professional	none	yes
Delaware	1986, 1988, 1990 1992, 1994	low	hybrid	$600 per election, individuals and PACs	yes
Idaho	1986, 1988, 1990 1992, 1994	low	citizen	none	yes
Illinois	1986, 1988, 1990 1992, 1994	low	professional	none	yes
Kansas	1986, 1988 1990, 1992	moderate	hybrid	$500 per election, individuals and PACs	yes
Maine	1986, 1988, 1990 1992, 1994	moderate	citizen	$1,000 per election, individuals; $5,000, PACs and others	yes
Minnesota	1986, 1988, 1990 1992, 1994	high	hybrid	$3,750 total parties, $750 per election, others; state matching funds with expenditure limits	no
Mississippi	1987, 1991	low	citizen/hybrid	$1,000 per election, corporations; no limits on labor, PACs, or individuals	yes
Missouri	1986, 1988, 1990 1992, 1994	low	hybrid	none	yes
Montana	1986, 1988, 1990 1992, 1994	high	citizen	$300 per election, PACS; $250 per election, individuals	no corporate, $300 unions

State	Years	Professionalism	Type	Contribution limits	
New Jersey	1987, 1989, 1991	high	professional	none	yes
North Carolina	1988, 1990, 1992, 1994	moderate	citizen/hybrid	$4,000 per election PACs and individuals	no
Oregon	1986, 1988, 1990, 1992, 1994	high	hybrid	none	yes
Pennsylvania	1988, 1990, 1992	low	professional	none	no
Utah	1986, 1988, 1990, 1992, 1994	high	citizen	none	yes
Washington	1986, 1988, 1990, 1992, 1994	moderate	hybrid	none until 21 days before election[a]	yes
Wisconsin	1986, 1988, 1990, 1992, 1994	moderate	professional	$500 per election, individuals and PACs; public financing with expenditure limits	no
Wyoming	1986, 1988, 1990, 1992, 1994	moderate	citizen	$1,000 per election, individuals; none for PACs	no

Note: 1994 data is limited to total revenue and expenditures used in chapter 3.
[a] Contribution limits went into effect in Washington after the 1992 election.

One of the most useful aspects of this categorization is that professionalism, as noted in the previous section, is related to other characteristics of the campaign finance system. It is not surprising, for example, that the more professional state legislatures are generally found in the more populous states. It should also be obvious that states with larger populations are more likely to have a higher population-to-legislator ratio. If districts are more populous, then campaign costs are likely to be greater.

In a similar vein, states with greater populations have larger budgets. The larger the budget, the greater the "policy stakes." The greater the policy stakes, the more likely that interest groups and other political actors will seek to influence the policy-making institutions—especially, the state legislature.

Legislative professionalism can be thought of as a composite measure of many aspects of the state political environment. For this reason, this presentation will be used throughout the book where appropriate as a way to organize our data. The particular classification we use is shown in Table 1-2. Note that it generally follows Kurtz's categorization scheme, but California is broken out as a separate category. The reason should be clear: district population and budget size are much greater in California than any other state—even the other states normally classified as containing "professional" state legislatures. With the exception of California, however, the "professionalism" classification works well as a surrogate for other measures, such as district size and budget. It is not a perfect relationship, but a parsimonious one that captures the qualitative differences that exist among states.

SEARCHING FOR ANSWERS

Using this framework, we will explore a number of topics suggested by congressional studies, single state analyses, and our own previous research. Throughout the following chapters, we will be examining differences between the states. We will compare the larger, more professional states where campaigns are more expensive with the smaller, less professional ones where campaigns cost less. Where appropriate, we will be comparing the more competitive two-party states, where the party may play a more active role in legislative races, with less competitive ones. In a few chapters we will also look at differences within the states, such as districts with more or less party competition. In several chapters we will show what impact differences in state regulation of campaign finance have on the way money is raised and spent. In two chapters dealing with female and minority candidates, we will look at the impact of certain individual level characteristics.

Table 1-2   *Classifying the States: A Modification of Kurtz's Legislative Professionalization Measure*

Category	State	Squire's Index[a]	District Population[b] (thousands)	State Budget[c] (billions)
C	California	.625	375	$90.7
I. Professional	Illinois	.302	97	25.0
	New Jersey	.255	96	24.7
	Pennsylvania	.336	59	27.0
	Wisconsin	.280	49	14.0
II. Hybrid	Delaware	.192	16	2.4
	Kansas	.152	20	5.2
	Minnesota	.199	33	13.7
	Mississippi	.160	21	5.8
	Missouri	.287	31	10.0
	North Carolina	.203	55	15.3
	Oregon	.183	47	8.0
	Washington	.230	50	16.9
III. Citizen	Idaho	.119	14	2.5
	Maine	.161	8	3.2
	Montana	.110	8	2.4
	Utah	.082	23	4.3
	Wyoming	.056	7	2.0

[a] A composite score based on legislative salary, number of staff per legislator, and total days in session in 1988–1989. The score is relative to Congress (i.e., congressional professionalization would be 1.000).

[b] District population is from 1990 U.S. Census.

[c] State budget figures are for FY 91.

Sources: Adapted from Karl Kurtz, "The Changing State Legislature (Lobbyists Beware)," in *Leveraging State Government Relations* (Washington, D.C.: Public Affairs Council, 1990). Squire's Index is from Peverill Squire, "Legislative Professionalization and Membership Diversity in State Legislatures," *Legislative Studies Quarterly* 17 (1992): 69–79. District population is from the 1990 U.S. Census, U.S. Bureau of the Census (Washington, D.C.: U.S. Government Printing Office). Budget data are from *Book of the States, 1994–1995* (Lexington, Ky.: Council of State Governments), Table 6.8, p. 338.

Chapter 2 provides a theoretical scheme regarding legislative elections and their financing and discusses how variations in certain political, structural, electoral, and legal factors affect campaign finance behavior among the states. In the chapter we propose that two constants—the common purpose of money and the rational nature of participant decision making—help shape the system.

Part Two of this volume is devoted to exploring issues related to the cost of legislative elections. In chapter 3 data from the 1994 elections are used to show, state by state, how much it costs to campaign for the legislature and why this differs so much among the states. We show that the costs have been rising more rapidly in some states (particularly the larger, more professional ones) than in others and describe the spending advantage that incumbents enjoy in most of these states.

Chapter 4 explains why the cost of campaigning varies within states from one district to another. A number of candidate-level and contextual features are examined, including incumbency, number of candidates, district population, and the urban/rural character of the district. We find that costs are positively related to the number of potential voters within a district, a finding that may be important in explaining variations in costs across states.

If little is known about campaign finance in general elections, even less is known about financing state primary elections. In chapter 5 we examine patterns of raising and spending funds from a subset of the states for which primary and general election records can be separated. How much is raised and spent during the primary and how much during the general election? How much of an incumbency advantage in fund raising is due to the early start that incumbents get? And, do primary election expenditures affect the votes that candidates receive?

In chapter 6 one of the most difficult questions in the study of campaign finance is tackled: Does money buy elections? More specifically, do the candidates who spend the most money usually win, and if so, do they win because they spend the most? Under what conditions does money seem to be most crucial in determining the outcome of an election?

In Part Three the focus is on the pattern of contributions to legislative campaigns. Chapter 7 begins by examining how female candidates fare in raising campaign funds. Given their underrepresentation in state legislatures, one may assume this is partially attributable to bias in the campaign finance system. Is there a "good old boy" network of givers? Do PACs and party organizations contribute equitably to male and female candidates, all other factors being equal?

The analysis of female candidates is followed by an examination of minority candidates. Minority candidates share some similarities with females but differ in that many run in districts specifically created for them. What impact do individual and district characteristics have on the ability of minority candidates to raise revenue? Since minority districts are relatively safe districts, do candidates need to raise and spend as much money as minority candidates in other districts?

In chapters 9 and 10 the role that PACs and political parties play in campaign finance, and particularly the strategies that they follow, are compared. We examine contributions by party organizations at various levels as well as the role of Republican and Democratic organizations. Similarly, the role of PACs is explored. How much do PACs contribute, to whom do they give, and what effect does regulation of parties and PACs have on their activities?

Finally, in Part Four we examine the implications of our findings for campaign finance reform. Reformers have criticized state campaign financing on a number of grounds. Based on what we have learned about legislative campaign financing, are these criticisms accurate? What evidence is there that proposed reforms of campaign financing would accomplish their objectives? For example, does public financing of legislative races in the two states where it occurs make any difference?

In addition to making some contribution to the scholarly literature in the discipline, we hope to provide some hint toward answering important questions about our system of government: Does the current system operate in such a way that it distorts the representative process? Does it disadvantage certain groups, such as women, minorities, and perhaps challengers of any race or gender? Does the current system discourage accountability by giving incumbents too many advantages, especially financial advantages? Does it allow too much influence from PACs, corporations, and other large donors?

Public dissatisfaction with current practices across the states and in Washington has led to renewed demands for reforms. But it is difficult and risky to change something that we know little about. It is our desire to take advantage of the states as "laboratories of democracy" to provide a foundation for these efforts.

NOTE

1. Maine now has adopted limited public funding.

REFERENCES

Goldstein, J. 1995. "Class of '94: New Rhetoric, Old Money." *Capital Eye* 2 (February 15), 1, 6.

Hendrie, P. 1997. "Flying High Under the Radar." *Capital Eye* 4 (May 15), 1, 6.

Kurtz, Karl. 1990. "The Changing State Legislature (Lobbyists Beware)." *Leveraging State Government Relations.* Washington, D.C.: Public Affairs Council.

Morrill, J. 1997. "Soft Money Mocks Limits on Campaign Contributions." *Charlotte Observer* (June 1), 1A, 6A.

Patterson, S. 1996. "Legislative Politics in the States." In *Politics in the American States,* 6th ed., edited by V. Gray & H. Jacob. Washington, D.C.: CQ Press.

Rice, D. 1997. "Campaign Costs Spiral out of Reach." *Winston-Salem Journal* (May 17), A1, A4.

Sorauf, F. J. 1988. *Money in American Elections.* Glenview, Ill.: Scott, Foresman.

CHAPTER TWO

A Framework for the Study of Campaign Finance

Anthony Gierzynski

The study of campaign finance is the study of the behavior of those involved in what can be called "campaign finance systems." That behavior results in identifiable patterns in: the amounts of money raised and spent in elections, the distribution of campaign money among political candidates, the effect that campaign spending has on the vote, and the effect that campaign contributions have on governmental policy. Understanding campaign finance behavior in one system is not tantamount to understanding that behavior in all systems. Knowing, for example, that candidate spending has a certain impact on the vote in U.S. House races does not mean that we know what impact candidate spending will have on the vote in state house races, U.S. Senate races, or city elections, etc. The reason why knowing one is not the same as knowing the other is because the settings or environments in which these races take place affect campaign finance behavior. The length of the general election season, the wealth of an area, the laws that regulate campaign financing, the overlap between the electoral district and the reach of television and radio stations, and the size of the districts all are aspects of the setting that will influence campaign finance behavior. Consequently, to reach an understanding of campaign finance behavior that applies to many different settings one needs to conduct comparative research of campaign finance behavior in many different settings. That is why we endeavored to collect data on campaign finance behavior from eighteen states over four elections.

Before we can analyze these data and draw conclusions, we need to identify the aspects of the different settings in which campaign finance activity takes place that can have an effect on campaign finance behavior. We also need to identify the aspects of campaign finance behavior that will remain constant across all systems. That is, we need a framework or a theory that, by laying out these aspects, can act as a guide to our study.

CAMPAIGN FINANCE SYSTEMS

Campaign finance behavior takes place within different environments or settings in U.S. elections. U.S. Senate elections differ markedly from U.S. House races. Senate races attract more media attention, are higher profile, cost more, and have higher levels of competition than House races. The environment of Kentucky state house races is different from that of congressional races. Kentucky house races, for example, take place in a less competitive environment (legislative party politics are dominated by the Democratic party), have less visibility, and have different regulations for campaign finance practices than do U.S. House races. The environment of Vermont state house races is different from that of California Assembly races: Vermont house districts are smaller (with approximately 3,900 constituents as compared to 375,000 in California Assembly districts), some districts elect more than one member, campaign spending costs are less, the seats are in a less professional legislature, and the state does not limit the terms of its legislators. As is evident in these examples, each of these environments contains a different mix of factors that affect campaign finance behavior—either directly or indirectly, alone or in combination with other factors. The environmental factors, their interactions, and their effect on campaign finance behavior make up a campaign finance system.

A model of campaign finance systems is presented in Figure 2-1. The model depicts campaign finance behavior as being influenced by four categories of environmental factors: political, legal, structural, and electoral. While the discussion that follows of the individual factors in each category undoubtedly falls short of identifying all influences on campaign finance behavior, the classification scheme can act as a guide to identifying variables that need to be considered in any comparative study of campaign finance. Most of these factors will be evident in the chapters that follow.

Political Factors

Political factors are the nature of the political environment and institutions in campaign finance systems (for our purposes, the states). They include the level of party competition, political culture, legislative professionalism, interest group strength, party organization strength, the importance of elections, and the degree of decentralization in the

Figure 2-1   *Model of Campaign Finance Systems*

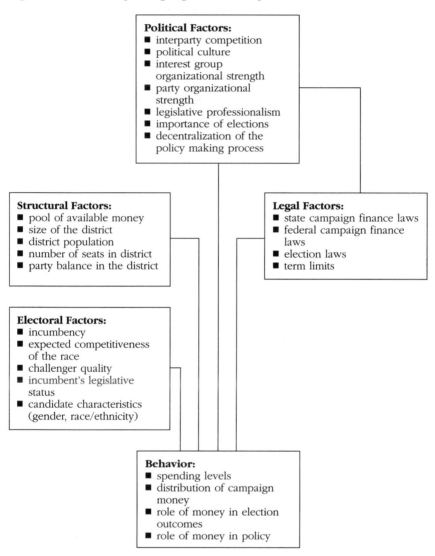

policy-making process. Such factors affect campaign finance behavior directly and indirectly.

The level of competition between the two major parties in a state should affect campaign spending levels. The more competitive the parties, the more active they will be in the electoral arena. In these days of cash campaigns, this means raising more money to support their candidates.

Since interest groups and political parties distribute their campaign resources differently, the relative strength of interest groups and political party organizations should affect the distribution of campaign money. Because of their desire for access to lawmakers, interest groups tend to contribute mainly to incumbents. Because of their desire to win political control of the government (which for legislatures means winning a majority of the seats in the legislature), parties tend to contribute to candidates in competitive races regardless of incumbency. So, systems in which interest groups are strong and political party organizations are weak should have a distribution of money skewed highly in favor of incumbents. In systems in which parties are strong, money should be distributed more equitably.

Systems with strong political parties may also be systems where money has less of an impact on elections and policymaking. When party organizations have the wherewithal to provide candidates with campaign workers and other campaign resources (such as phone banks, media consultants, and polling), candidates can win votes without spending a substantial amount of their own money. Such party activity makes what the candidates themselves spend in an election less important. When party organizations provide such resources, the effect of interest group money on policymaking will also be diminished: if candidates get a significant amount of help from their political party, then they will not need interest group money. Therefore, interest groups will have less leverage over legislators. Also, candidates who get help from the parties will have to spend less time raising money and will have more time to work on legislation.

The professionalism of the legislature should affect the amount of money raised and the financial advantage of incumbents. Professional legislatures (as compared with less professional citizen-type legislatures) have longer sessions, pay legislators more, and provide staff for legislators. This makes the value of the seat greater, so candidates will be willing to pay a higher price for the seat, thus increasing the cost of elections. Professionalism also means that those serving in the legislature—the incumbents in an election—have more individual power within the legislature (Rosenthal 1990) and greater advantages in an election (such as greater visibility and staff resources). Both of these translate to an incumbency advantage in fund raising. Special interests want access to those that have power, and incumbents in professional legislatures tend to have more power than citizen legislatures. Since such interests want access to actual lawmakers, supporting an incumbent is more of a sure bet in these systems.

Political factors also influence campaign finance behavior indirectly by affecting some of the legal factors in campaign finance systems. The political culture of a state, for example, is undoubtedly related to the strictness of campaign finance regulation in that state. Minnesota and Wisconsin, both with cultural norms that expect clean politics, have adopted tight regulations on campaign finance practices, including a system for public financing of state legislative races (Minnesota in 1994 tightened its limit on contributions from private, nonparty contributors to state house candidates to $100). Their neighbor, Illinois, with a culture more tolerant of back-room politics, has practically no limitations on campaign finance practices; this state even allows unlimited corporate contributions.

The strength of political parties and interest groups may also affect the "friendliness" of a system's campaign finance regulations regarding those groups. Where parties are strong they may create more freedom for their own fund-raising and contributing practices. Where interest groups are strong, they may have more freedom. (Discussion of the importance of elections and the decentralization of the policy-making process will be reserved for the next section.)

Legal Factors

Legal factors consist of the laws regulating campaign finance—including contribution limits, expenditure limits, public funding, and reporting requirements—and laws setting election practices—including the length of the general election season, term limits, and laws regulating party endorsements.

Campaign finance systems that do not limit contributions from corporations, political action committees (PACs), labor unions, trade associations, individuals, and political parties may see different campaign finance behavior than systems that ban and/or limit certain types of contributions. The absence of limits on contributions will foster higher levels of campaign spending since it is easier to raise campaign funds in larger increments.

The absence of contribution limits will also affect the distribution of campaign money. Evidence from research clearly demonstrates the superiority of incumbents in raising money from private, nonparty contributors (Gierzynski and Breaux 1994, Sorauf 1992, Thompson and Cassie 1992). This superiority comes from the desire of interests to have access to lawmakers and from aggressive fund raising by incumbent legislators (Sorauf 1992). In the absence of limits, private contributors can concentrate even more of their resources on incumbents, and incumbents will appeal for larger contributions, thus skewing the distribution of campaign revenues to favor incumbents even more than they would if contributors were legally forced to spread their contributions around (Box-Steffensmeier and Dow 1992).

Large contributions in systems without limits or with relatively high limits also increase the "debt" legislators owe to the interests behind those contributions. Because this gives the contributing interest some leverage, such debts have the potential for affecting public policy decisions by legislators. It may even be argued that the maldistribution of campaign funds in systems with no limits may affect public policy indirectly by contributing to low levels of competition in elections and reducing legislative turnover and the responsiveness of representatives to the electorate.

Legal limits on campaign expenditures (that is, those accompanying some sort of public funding) have an obvious effect on the levels of spending in elections. Such limits may also influence policymaking by affecting competition and turnover. Low expenditure limits may act as incumbency protection laws: challengers need to spend significant amounts of money in elections to overcome the advantages held by incumbents, such as the name recognition and familiarity that come from media attention and the use of various perquisites of office. With strict limits, nonincumbents are clearly at a disadvantage.

Public funding of elections (providing candidates with government-financed grants) can lead to more equity in the distribution of campaign funds by providing a floor of funding to challengers who traditionally have trouble raising money from private contributors. Public funding reduces candidates' dependence on private money, weakening the possible link between campaign contributions and policy decisions. Public funding can indirectly affect the levels of spending in a race by allowing governments to establish voluntary limits on candidate expenditures.

Election laws that have some bearing on campaign finance behavior include those that specify the date of the primary (and consequently the length of the general election season) and those that allow party endorsements. The length of the general election season can affect the importance of money in campaigns. Short election seasons make it difficult for nonincumbent candidates, especially those who have been in a divisive primary, to use door-to-door campaigning because they have less time to reach the voters. The need to reach voters quickly increases the value of media campaigns and the costs and importance of money in the election. Laws that allow party endorsements may affect the distribution of campaign money in primary elections by encouraging contributions to endorsed candidates and discouraging contributions to unendorsed candidates.

Term limits may increase the importance of money in elections because of the reduced effect of incumbency: there will be more open-seat contests, for which money is more important (see Electoral Factors), and less accumulation of the personal support that comes with incumbency.

Structural Factors

Structural factors are relatively stable factors (at least for the duration of one redistricting cycle) that set the context of legislative races from year to year in a campaign finance system. Included among these factors are: the pool of available money, district population, the geographic size of the district, the number of seats, and party history in the district.

The pool of available money in a campaign finance system—determined by the wealth of an area, including the wealth of the citizens and the wealth of interests willing to contribute—helps determine the amount of money raised and spent. It is unimaginable, for example, that the amount of money spent in races for the California Assembly could be raised in a less wealthy state, such as Mississippi.

The size of a district affects the nature of campaigns and, consequently, the importance of money and the cost of elections. Candidates in less populous districts, such as those that compose the New Hampshire and Vermont state houses (roughly 2,500 and 3,900, respectively) can campaign door to door, easily reaching all the districts' voters while spending little money in the process. Candidates in more populous districts, such as U.S. Senate and House races and California Assembly races (with approximately 375,000 constituents), will find door-to-door campaigning woefully insufficient for reaching all their districts' voters. Instead, they will need to run a campaign that utilizes the mass media and they will need to skillfully target their campaigns to focus on the voters in the districts that will most likely support them. This type of campaign involves costly purchases, including media and campaign consultants, air time, and computerized data files on the district. In such elections, money has a greater impact on election outcomes since candidates who have to rely on the less costly means of campaigning will be at an extreme disadvantage against a well-funded opponent.

The geographic size of a district, much like the population size, can be a factor in driving up costs and making campaign spending more important. In districts that cover a large amount of territory, the costs of reaching voters is high because the voters are far apart. This means extensive travel time or the use of mass media campaign techniques, both of which increase costs. In the largest districts, candidates are often required to purchase media time in several media markets in order to reach voters.

The number of seats in a district also affects the level of spending and the importance of money in elections. While voters in congressional districts elect only one representative per district, there are a number of states that have state legislative districts in which voters elect more than one candidate. These multimember districts take on a number of different forms. Some campaigns are free-for-alls in which all candidates are matched against each other and the top vote-getters win the seats. In Vermont voters in one state senate district (covering most of Chittenden County) cast votes for six candidates from a list of twelve or more candidates. The six candidates with the greatest number of votes win. Some multimember districts have what are known as post positions. Instead of all candidates competing for all seats, candidates face off against each other for specific seats within the district. Washington state uses such a system for its state house races.

In multimember districts candidates will likely be less well known and will be in more competition for voters' attention than candidates in single-member districts. This means they need to spend more money. By their very nature, multimember districts have larger constituencies, thus more voters to reach. Given these factors, multimember districts should not only have more expensive races than single-member districts but should also be districts in which campaign spending is a more important factor for winning.

Finally, the partisan nature of the district—the normal party vote in a district—will affect campaign finance behavior in a number of ways. Districts where voters are predominantly from one party will not be as competitive from year to year and consequently will be less expensive. Because such seats are safely in the column of one party, they will usually attract little in the way of party or ideological money. The impact money has on the vote will also be less in such lopsided districts since candidates from the minority party will be up against one of the strongest predispositions in voting behavior—voter's political party affiliation.

Electoral Factors

Electoral factors are the aspects of legislative races that can vary from race to race within a campaign finance system. Since they vary within campaign finance systems, these factors have received the most attention in the extant literature on campaign finance. Electoral factors include the incumbency status of the candidates, expected competitiveness of the race, quality of challengers, status of incumbents within the legislature, and demographic characteristics of the candidates (including, gender, race, and ethnicity).

The presence of an incumbent in a race has an impact on several aspects of campaign finance behavior. Incumbency is related to spending levels by affecting how much is raised and spent in a particular race. Candidates running against incumbents find it difficult to raise money because, with the close-to-perfect reelection success rates of incumbents, most contributors see challengers' campaigns as lost causes. Incumbents, though they have little trouble raising large sums of money, rarely have to spend it since their competition is often minimal. The rarity of races without incumbents and the greater uncertainty regarding the outcome of such races lead to higher spending levels in open-seat contests. The uncertainty attracts more money from contributors who see a rare chance to use their resources to affect the composition of the legislature. In terms of the candidates, the uncertainty insures that candidates will spend virtually every dollar that they raise.

Incumbency also affects the role of money in elections by reducing the impact of spending on the vote. Campaign spending is only one of a number of ways that candidates can win over voters. The extent to which other techniques for winning votes are used will reduce the impact of spending on the vote. Incumbents utilize the perquisites of their office in order to maintain and expand their support among the electorate; this makes campaign spending, which is used for the same purpose, less important. Furthermore, challengers, who use campaign money to sway voters to their side, face electorates with favorable predispositions about the incumbent. This makes it more difficult to win over voters than if voters were unfamiliar with both candidates. As a consequence of these predispositions, spending by challengers has less of an impact on a candidate's vote share than spending by open-seat candidates (Gierzynski and Breaux 1996).

The expected competitiveness of a race affects spending levels and the distribution of campaign money. Candidate viability is important to fund raising. Close races mean that both candidates are viable and both will be able to raise relatively large amounts of cash. Unlike safe incumbents, candidates in close races will spend almost all of what they raise. Races without incumbents or with strong challengers will be the most competitive and therefore the most expensive. The expected closeness of the race also affects the distribution of campaign money by affecting the way certain classes of contributors act. Party contributors tend to follow an electoral strategy. They attempt to affect change through the electoral process by concentrating their resources on close races. By contrast, PACs, individuals, labor unions, interest groups, and corporate contributors tend to follow a legislative strategy. They attempt to influence policy through the legislative process and thus are less likely to concentrate their resources on close races (Gierzynski and

Breaux 1994; Gierzynski 1992; Jones and Borris 1985; Sorauf 1992; Thompson, Cassie, and Jewell 1994).

The status of incumbents within the legislature influences the distribution of campaign money within a system. Legislators holding leadership or committee positions in their legislature attract more money because of their influence (Box-Steffensmeier and Dow 1992, Grier and Munger 1993). The surpluses of campaign funds created by this behavior have, in turn, allowed legislative leaders to create their own campaign committees for assisting legislative candidates and holding on to their leadership positions (Baker 1989, Box-Steffensmeier and Dow 1992, Clucas 1992, Gierzynski 1992).

The social and demographic groups candidates belong to affect contribution patterns, depending on the resources those groups can mobilize. Women candidates, for example, receive contributions from EMILY's List, the Women's Political Caucus, and, in Minnesota, from the Democratic-Farmer-Labor or Independent-Republican Women's caucuses, as well as from others interested in promoting representation of women in government (Gierzynski and Budreck 1995). The same is undoubtedly true for other demographic groups. It may also be true that certain social and demographic characteristics of candidates depress candidate revenues because of contributor prejudices, though there is little systematic evidence of this to date (Burrell 1985, Moncrief and Thompson 1991, Uhlaner and Scholzman 1986).

Constants of Campaign Finance Behavior

Having identified the classes of factors that lead to variation in campaign finance behavior from one setting to another, it is important to examine whether there are some principles of behavior that are constant across all campaign finance systems. Are there any general laws that campaign finance behavior follows regardless of context? If so, how do they operate? Two such possible principles are discussed below.

Money and Power

One aspect of campaign finance that will not change from system to system is the purpose of money in elections. Money in electoral systems is about power—power to influence the course governments follow and ultimately power to influence public policy. As a result, money flows to the sources of power within the system. This is true when a corporate PAC contributes to incumbent members of committees whose jurisdiction concerns the PAC's parent organization, when an ideological PAC

Figure 2-2   *Power and Contributions in Political Systems*

Power Resides in:	Power Over Policy Areas	
	Centralized	Fragmented
Elections	contributions to parties based on ideology	contributions to candidates based on stand on policy over which their office would have control
Incumbent Officials	contributions to party or leaders in power	contributions to individual incumbents with power over policy realm

attempts to unseat incumbents who are "public enemy number 1," when a political party contributes to challengers in order to increase their seats in the legislature, and when a candidate spends money trying to persuade voters to elect her so she can have a role in policymaking.

The financial route taken to influence the course of government depends on the interaction of two additional political factors concerned with the nature of power in a political system: (1) the effectiveness of elections as mechanisms for policy change and (2) the extent to which power over policy areas is centralized or fragmented (see Figure 2-2).

The effectiveness of elections as mechanisms for policy change says a lot about the location of power within a political system. In systems where elections are an effective means of instituting change, power will reside in those who can win elections. Consequently, those seeking change will follow an electoral strategy by supporting candidates favorable to that change. A majoritarian democratic republic is one such system. In systems where elections are ineffective, power will reside in the incumbent officials of the regime. Those seeking change in such a system will follow a legislative strategy that seeks to change policy by influencing legislators. This is characteristic of pluralistic democracy.

The relative importance of elections in combination with the relative fragmentation and centralization of power over separate policy areas helps to shape the flow of money in the system because money flows to the sources of power. In political systems where incumbent officials hold the balance of power and where control over policy areas is fragmented—such as in the U.S. House of Representatives—money will be directed to the incumbents who have influence over the policy area: committee and subcommittee chairs. In political systems in which elections are most important in determining policy and in which policy control is concentrated—such as in parliamentary systems—money will be directed to the party whose interests are most similar to that of the contributors. In systems where incumbents hold the balance of power and in which power is concentrated—such as state legislatures with strong speakers or strong parties—contributions will go to the leader or party in power. Finally, in campaigns in systems in which elections are most important in determining policy and in which power over policy areas is divided—such as a state agriculture commissioner or state treasurer—contributions would go to candidates who will have power over the policy area and are friendly to the contributors' interests.

The common thread in each of these systems is that money flows to those who have power over policy. This search for the sources of power will remain consistent across different campaign finance systems, though the ultimate route that it takes will be modified by the political, legal, structural, and electoral factors that characterize the campaign finance system.

Constrained Rational Actors

Underlying the argument that money flows to the sources of power is an assumption that actors in campaign finance systems act rationally, that is, they attempt to maximize their goals—one of which is power over policy. While this may be a questionable assumption for the average voter, it is a rather common assumption in studies of campaign finance. With a recognition of the constraints placed upon the actors by resource limitations and organizational factors, it is supported by a significant body of empirical research (Box-Steffensmeier and Dow 1992, Eismeier and Pollock 1985, Gierzynski 1992, Grier and Munger 1993).

That actors in campaign finance systems are rational is an aspect of campaign finance behavior that will remain constant across all campaign finance systems. Actors will attempt to attain their goals, navigating around the political, legal, structural, and electoral characteristics of the campaign finance system.

SUMMARY

To understand and explain campaign finance behavior in general, we must examine it in numerous settings, through comparative study. The key is to identify how campaign finance system factors affect that behavior and recognize the constants of campaign finance behavior, that is, those aspects that should operate in all campaign finance systems. This chapter identifies political, legal, structural, and electoral factors that make campaign finance behavior vary from one context to the next. It also identifies two aspects of campaign finance—the common purpose of money and the rational nature of participant decision making—that should remain constant. These factors and principles have guided the research presented in the chapters that follow.

REFERENCES

Abramowitz, Alan I. 1988. "Explaining Senate Election Outcomes." *American Political Science Review* 82: 385–404.

Alexander, Herbert E. 1991. *Reform and Reality: The Financing of State and Local Campaigns.* New York: Twentieth Century Fund Press.

Alexander, Herbert E. 1992. *Financing Politics: Money, Elections, and Political Reform,* 4th ed. Washington, D.C.: Congressional Quarterly Press.

Baker, Ross K. 1989. *The New Fat Cats: Members of Congress as Political Benefactors.* New York: Priority Press Publications.

Bibby, John F., Cornelius P. Cotter, James L. Gibson, and Robert Huckshorn. 1990. "Parties in State Politics." In *Politics in the American States: A Comparative Analysis,* 5th ed., edited by Virginia Gray, Herbert Jacob, and Robert Albritton. Glenview, Ill.: Scott, Foresman/Little, Brown Higher Education.

Box-Steffensmeier, Janet M., and Jay K. Dow. 1992. "Campaign Contributions in an Unregulated Setting: An Analysis of the 1984 and 1986 California Assembly Elections." *Western Political Quarterly* 45: 609–628.

Breaux, David. 1990. "Specifying the Impact of Incumbency on State Legislative Elections: A District-Level Analysis." *American Politics Quarterly* 18 (July): 270–285.

Breaux, David and Anthony Gierzynski. 1991. " 'It's Money that Matters': Campaign Expenditures and State Legislative Primaries." *Legislative Studies Quarterly* 16: 429–443.

Burrell, Barbara C. 1985. "Women's and Men's Campaigns for the U.S. House of Representatives, 1972–1982." *American Politics Quarterly* 13: 251–272

Cain, Bruce, John Ferejohn, and Morris Fiorina. 1987. *The Personal Vote: Constituency Service and Electoral Independence.* Cambridge: Harvard University Press.

Caldeira, Gregory A., and Samuel C. Patterson. 1982. "Bringing Home the Votes: Electoral Outcomes in State Legislative Races." *Political Behavior* 4: 33–67.

Clucas, Richard A. 1992. "Legislative Leadership and Campaign Support in California." *Legislative Studies Quarterly* 17: 265–284.

Eismeier, Theodore J., and Philip H. Pollock III. 1984. "Political Action Committees: Varieties of Organization and Strategy." In *Money and Politics in the United States: Financing Elections in the 1980s,* edited by Michael Malbin. Washington, D.C.: American Enterprise Institute for Public Policy Research and Chatham House.

Eismeier, Theodore J., and Philip H. Pollock III. 1985. "An Organizational Analysis of Political Action Committees." *Political Behavior* 7: 192–216.

Garand, James C. 1991. "Electoral Marginality in State Legislative Elections." *Legislative Studies Quarterly* 16: 7–28.

Gierzynski, Anthony. 1992. *Legislative Party Campaign Committees in the American States.* Lexington, Ky.: University Press of Kentucky.

Gierzynski, Anthony, and David Breaux. 1991. "Money and Votes in State Legislative Elections." *Legislative Studies Quarterly* 16: 203–217.

Gierzynski, Anthony, and David Breaux. 1993. "Money and the Party Vote in State House Elections." *Legislative Studies Quarterly* 18: 515–533.

Gierzynski, Anthony, and David Breaux. 1994. "The Role of Parties in Legislative Campaign Financing." *American Review of Politics* 15: 171–189.

Gierzynski, Anthony, and David Breaux. 1996. "Legislative Elections and the Importance of Money." *Legislative Studies Quarterly* 21: 337–358.

Gierzynski, Anthony, and Paulette Budreck. 1995. "Women Legislative Caucus and Leadership Campaign Committees." *Women & Politics* 15: 23–36.

Giles, Michael W., and Anita Pritchard. 1985. "Campaign Expenditures and Legislative Elections in Florida." *Legislative Studies Quarterly* 10 (February): 71–88.

Glantz, Stanton A., Alan I. Abramowitz, and Michael P. Burkart. 1976. "Election Outcomes: Whose Money Matters?" *Journal of Politics* 38: 1033–1041.

Green, Donald Philip, and Jonathan S. Krasno. 1988. "Salvation for the Spendthrift Incumbent: Reestimating the Effects of Campaign Spending in House Elections." *American Journal of Political Science* 32: 884–907.

Green, Donald Philip, and Jonathan S. Krasno. 1990. "Rebuttal to Jacobson's 'New Evidence for Old Arguments.' " *American Journal of Political Science* 34 (May): 363–372.

Grenzke, Janet. 1989. "PACs and the Congressional Supermarket: The Currency Is Complex." *American Journal of Political Science* 33 (February): 1–24.

Grier, Kevin B., and Michael C. Munger. 1993. "Comparing Interest Group PAC Contributions to House and Senate Incumbents." *Journal of Politics* 55: 615–643.

Herrnson, Paul S. 1986. "Do the Parties Make a Difference? The Role of Party Organizations in Congressional Elections." *Journal of Politics* 48: 589–615.

Herrnson, Paul S. 1988. *Party Campaigning in the 1980s.* Cambridge, Mass.: Harvard University Press.

Huckshorn, Robert J. 1985. "Who Gave It? Who Got It?: The Enforcement of Campaign Finance Laws in the States." *Journal of Politics* 47: 773–789.

Jacobson, Gary C. 1980. *Money in Congressional Elections.* New Haven: Yale University Press.

Jacobson, Gary C. 1985. "Money and Votes Reconsidered: Congressional Elections 1972–1982." *Public Choice* 47: 7–92.

Jacobson, Gary C. 1985. "Party Organization and Distribution of Campaign Resources: Republicans and Democrats in 1982." *Political Science Quarterly* 4: 603–625.

Jacobson, Gary C. 1990. "The Effects of Campaign Spending in House Elections: New Evidence for Old Arguments." *American Journal of Political Science* 34 (May): 334–362.

Jewell, Malcolm. 1984. *Parties and Primaries: Nominating State Governors.* New York: Praeger.

Jewell, Malcolm, and David Breaux. 1989. "The Effect of Incumbency on State Legislative Elections." *Legislative Studies Quarterly* 13: 495–514.

Jones, Ruth S. 1981. "State Public Campaign Finance: Implications for Partisan Politics." *American Journal of Political Science* 25 (May): 342–361.

Jones, Ruth S. 1984. "Financing State Elections." In *Money and Politics in the United States: Financing Elections in the 1980s,* edited by Michael Malbin. New Jersey: Chatham House.

Jones, Ruth S., and Thomas J. Borris. 1985. "Strategic Contributing in Legislative Campaigns: The Case of Minnesota." *Legislative Studies Quarterly* 10: 89–105.

Jones, Ruth S., and Anne H. Hopkins. "State Campaign Fund Raising: Targets and Response." *Journal of Politics* 47: 433–449.

Krasno, Jonathan S., and Donald Philip Green. 1988. "Preempting Quality Challengers in House Elections." *Journal of Politics* 50: 920–936.

Lott, W. F., and P. D. Warner. 1974. "The Relative Importance of Campaign Expenditures: An Application of Production Theory." *Quality and Quantity* 8: 99–106.

Moncrief, Gary F., and Joel A. Thompson. 1991. "Race, Gender, and State Legislative Campaign Contributions: A Comparative Analysis." Paper presented at the 1991 annual meeting of the Southwestern Political Science Association.

Morehouse, Sarah M. 1990. "Money Versus Party Effort: Nominating for Governor." *American Journal of Political Science* 34 (August): 706–724.

Owens, John R., and Edward C. Olson. 1977. "Campaign Spending and the Electoral Process in California." *Western Political Quarterly* 30: 493–512.

Page, Benjamin I., Robert Y. Shapiro, and Glenn R. Dempsey. 1987. "What Moves Public Opinion." *American Political Science Review* 81: 23–44.

Ragsdale, Lyn. 1985. "Legislative Elections and Electoral Responsiveness." In *Handbook of Legislative Research,* edited by Gehard Loewenberg, Samuel Patterson, and Malcolm Jewel. Cambridge, Mass.: Harvard University Press.

Rosenthal, Alan. 1990. *Governors & Legislatures: Contending Powers.* Washington, D.C.: CQ Press.

Sorauf, Frank J. 1988. *Money in American Elections.* Glenview, Ill.: Scott, Foresman and Co.

Sorauf, Frank J. 1992. *Inside Campaign Finance: Myths and Realities.* New Haven: Yale University Press.

Squire, Peverill, and John Wright. 1990. "Fundraising by Nonincumbent Candidates for the U.S. House of Representatives." *Legislative Studies Quarterly* 15: 89–98.

Stewert, Charles III, and Mark Reynolds. 1990. "Television Markets and U.S. Senate Elections." *Legislative Studies Quarterly* 15 (November): 495–524.

Stonecash, Jeffrey M. 1988. "Working at the Margins: Campaign Finance and Party Strategy in New York Assembly Elections." *Legislative Studies Quarterly* 13: 477–493.

Thomas, Scott J. 1989. "Do Incumbent Campaign Expenditures Matter?" *Journal of Politics* 51: 965–976.

Thompson, Joel A., and William Cassie. 1992. "Party and PAC Contributions to North Carolina Legislative Candidates." *Legislative Studies Quarterly* 17 (August): 409–426.

Thompson, Joel A., William Cassie, and Malcolm E. Jewell. 1994. "A Sacred Cow or Just a Lot of Bull? Party and PAC Money in State Legislative Elections." *Political Research Quarterly* 47: 223–237.

Tucker, Harvey J., and Ronald E. Weber. 1987. "State Legislative Election Outcomes: Contextual Effects and Legislative Performance Effects." *Legislative Studies Quarterly* 12: 537–553.

Uhlaner, Carole Jean, and Kay Lehman Shlozman. 1986. "Candidate Gender and Congressional Campaign Receipts." *Journal of Politics* 48: 30–50.

Welch, William P. 1976. "The Effectiveness of Expenditures in State Legislative Races." *American Politics Quarterly* 4: 336–356.

Welch, William P. 1981. "Money and Votes: A Simultaneous Equation Model." *Public Choice* 36: 209–234.

Part II

SPENDING PATTERNS

CHAPTER THREE

Candidate Spending in State Legislative Races

Gary F. Moncrief

There have been few basic changes in campaigns for the state legislature in the past twenty years. . . . The real change has been in money—the amount, where it comes from, where it goes.

—Tom Loftus, former Speaker of the Wisconsin Assembly

INTRODUCTION

In 1992 Frank Sorauf, one of the leading authorities on campaign financing in the United States, wrote a book entitled, *Inside Campaign Finance*. The subtitle was "Myths and Realities." Another leading authority, Herbert Alexander, had published in 1991 *Reform and Reality,* a book on financing state and local political campaigns. It is significant that the term *reality* appears in both titles. The issue of campaign financing is so complex, so illusory, and increasingly so emotive that we often talk above, below, or past each other on the subject. In part this is because we do not agree on what is the "reality" of campaign finance.

Reasonable discussion on the topic at the state level is further hampered by a lack of consistent, comparable, and relatively complete data from one state to another. As Sorauf (1992, 32) notes, "Beyond illustrations and scraps of data, however, campaign finance is just one more aspect of state politics on which even the ordinarily brave hesitate to make more than a rough estimate."

It is the aim of this chapter—indeed, of this book—to get beyond scraps and anecdotes and provide some "hard numbers" that are reasonably comparable from one state to another. It is the particular aim of this chapter to do so longitudinally—that is, to take a look at data over time. Surely one of the "realities" that most people have adopted is a belief that campaign spending for state legislative office is soaring to ever-higher levels with each new election. But is this in fact true in all states, all the time, or is this true for only some states? Is it true for all types of candidates? If so, under what conditions is it reality and under what conditions is it illusion?

WHAT IS KNOWN ABOUT THE RISE IN CAMPAIGN SPENDING?

The Political Science Literature

The public perception that state legislative campaign spending is rising dramatically is probably based in part on what is known about congressional campaign spending. There is ample evidence that congressional campaign costs have "increased at a much faster rate than inflation" (Keefe and Ogul 1997, 121). The average expenditure by a candidate running for the U.S. House of Representatives in 1976 was $73,316. By 1992 that figure had reached $409,836 (Rieselbach 1995, 51). Even after controlling for inflation, this is an increase of 130 percent!

Campaign spending has increased in many states, as well. For example, Alexander (1991, 125) reports that between 1978 and 1982 spending doubled on state legislative races in California. Between 1972 and 1980 the average amount spent on Florida house races tripled (Giles and Pritchard 1985, 75). Another study of five states found that between 1978 and 1986 the increase ranged from a *low* of 80 percent to a high of more than 300 percent (Gierzynski and Breaux, 1991, 207). A study in Wisconsin found that expenditures doubled in state senate races and tripled in state assembly contests over a twelve-year period, 1978–1990 (Mayer and Wood 1995, 79–80).

While many of the increases are indeed dramatic, they do not reflect controls for inflation. Since the 1970s and 1980s were decades of relatively high inflation, this can have a distorting effect. One study that controlled for inflation for the 1980–1988 period in four states found that while mean campaign spending increased in all four states, the increase was modest in some instances (Moncrief 1992, 552).

Beyond these studies, there is little comparative research on the increase in state legislative campaign costs. This is remarkable, given the widespread public perception that campaign costs have rapidly increased everywhere. It is far more likely that such increases are not universal. As Malcolm Jewell (1993, 2) points out, the increase in campaign costs is related to increased costs of running an effective campaign and to the increased number of competitive seats in some state legislatures. The increase in running an effective campaign stems from the growing "professionalization" of the campaign itself: the use of campaign man-

agers, sophisticated mail-targeting and polling techniques, and more reliance on media advertising. But these factors are highly variable by
state, and it is unlikely that they will drive up campaign costs across
states in anything approaching a uniform manner. For example, in many
states, candidates for the legislature still do not rely on television or
radio advertising; nor do they hire campaign specialists.

In short, not only is there great variation among state legislatures in
terms of the demands of the job, but there is tremendous variation in the
context of campaigning for that job. Legislators in full-time, professional state legislatures overwhelmingly perceive that campaigning has
changed in the past fifteen or so years—changes they believe require
them to spend more time and effort raising campaign funds. Legislators
in part-time, "citizen" state legislatures—which have relatively short sessions, small staffs, and low salaries for the legislators—are far less likely
to perceive such changes (Thompson, Kurtz, and Moncrief 1996, 359).

Issues of Measurement

Means and Medians

When the question is, "What do the numbers tell us?" the first answer should be, "It depends on which numbers are being looked at."
This is not a trite or flippant response. In some cases it matters very
much whether *mean* (average) expenditures or *median* expenditures are
being looked at. Means can be affected by large increases in spending in
just one or two races; since medians reflect the number at which half the
candidates spent more and half spent less, they are far less sensitive to
the effect of just one or a few races with hyperinflated spending. In
much of the analysis in this chapter, both means and medians are reported. As the data presentation becomes more complex (such as when
spending over time or between candidate types is looked at), median figures are used because they are less susceptible to distortion by one or
two races.

Lower Versus Upper Chambers

The data reported throughout this book are from campaigns for lower
chamber seats. Undoubtedly, more money is spent for the average state
senate seat than for the average house or assembly seat. The reasons are
obvious—fewer senate seats are up for election in any given time period;
senate districts are often considerably larger than house districts; fewer
senate seat swings are required to change the majority-minority status of
a party and therefore each senate seat may be more critical. Evidence

comparing state lower and upper chambers is limited, but one study of four northwestern states finds that the average money spent per candidate in 1988 for senate seats was at least 75 percent higher than the mean spent per house candidate.[1] In states where the senate districts encompass three or more house districts, the costs will be even greater.

Time Frame

It also matters which time frame is investigated. Sorauf (1992, 13) found that spending in congressional races flattened out (and actually declined in some years when controlled for inflation) in the decade of the 1980s. In the 1990s, however, there has been a definite rise in congressional candidate spending.

Most of the data analyzed in this book are from the 1986–1992 time frame, a period in which data for eighteen states was collected. In this chapter some 1994 data are also used, but the nature of the 1994 data is limited in two ways. First, data are available for only fourteen states instead of eighteen. Thus, most of the analysis in this chapter is based on the period 1986–1994, but limited to fourteen states.[2] Basically, the data set was extended for another electoral cycle, but at the cost of losing four states from the analysis. Because time trends are particularly interesting, this "tradeoff" between number of years and number of states was easily justified.

The second way in which the 1994 data are limited is that the full range of variables is not available in the 1986–1992, eighteen-state data set. For example, the 1994 files do not presently include information about the transfer of money between candidates; nor do they include information about candidate status. Thus, when issues of incumbency and transfers are discussed (toward the end of this chapter), the 1986–1992 data set is used, which permits a more detailed analysis.

All other things being equal, increased spending might be expected in years surrounding the redistricting cycle (Neal 1992, 21). Thus, in the "0" year of a decade (e.g., 1990) spending might be higher than usual, as both parties (and the interests and individuals associated with each party) seek to gain a majority in the chamber in order to control the process by which districts will be drawn. Moreover, the "2" year (e.g., 1992) will likely witness higher spending because the product of most redistricting plans is increased uncertainty and often an increase in the number of open seats.

In fact, any time control of the chamber is in doubt, spending is likely to increase (Moncrief and Patton 1993, Stonecash 1988, Stonecash 1990). This is especially true for contests in the more competitive (i.e., marginal) electoral districts, as well as for most open-seat contests, because the electoral outcome in each of these districts may determine which party will form the majority in the legislative chamber.

Contested Elections

It also makes a difference upon which candidates the analysis focuses. In some states 20 percent or more of the candidates may run unopposed in the general election. This phenomenon may be the result of natural areas of party strength in specific regions of the state, biased districting, or the popularity of a particular incumbent. If there is a substantial proportion of districts in which there is no contest, this will distort both the mean and median figures, since little or no money need be expended when a candidate runs unopposed.

For this reason, unopposed candidates were excluded from our analysis. The focus instead was on candidates in *contested* races (defined here as elections in which a candidate receives more than 10 percent but less than 90 percent of the total votes cast).

Competitive Elections

In his study of campaign financing in Illinois, Kent Redfield (1995, 6) observed that there are two different electoral worlds in state legislative politics:

> The first is the world of very expensive, strongly contested elections. . . . This is a relatively small world. . . . The larger world of Illinois legislative elections is one where the well-financed winning candidates, often incumbents, run unopposed or run against weak opponents who spend little or no money.

Because spending is often so much greater in competitive races than in those which are simply contested, sometimes the focus of the analysis will be narrowed to just the competitive races. The precise definition of *competitive* varies from analyst to analyst, but usually is limited to races in which the winning candidate receives less than 55 or 60 percent of the total vote. Throughout this chapter candidates in competitive races are defined as those receiving more than 40 percent but less than 60 percent of the total votes cast in the general election.

Total Expenditures

Further, it matters how expenditures are measured. Because of the nature of the reporting requirements and the timing of the deadlines for filing campaign finance reports, it is impossible in many states to determine how much was received and spent in the primary compared to the general election. All figures reported in this chapter are *total* figures, combining both primary and general election expenditures. In chapter 5 David Breaux and Anthony Gierzynski analyze a subset of states in which revenues and expenditures for the primary and general elections can be separated.

Candidate Expenditures Versus Independent and Party Expenditures

Finally, it is important to note that the data in this analysis capture *candidate-centered* contributions and spending. Any money spent outside the candidate's reporting system is not accounted for. Specifically, spending by outside organizations or individuals who choose to spend their own money in support of or in opposition to an individual's candidacy is not measured. These expenditures, which are known as *independent expenditures,* are not captured through the system of candidate-centered data collection used in this analysis. Fortunately, independent expenditures are not yet a significant factor in most state legislative elections—although there is evidence that independent expenditures are growing in some states (Murakami 1996, A1).

However, state party organizations (especially state legislative campaign committees) are significant factors in some states. One study finds that legislative parties in New York accounted for more than 40 percent of the total spending in assembly races in 1988 (Dwyre and Stonecash 1992, 336). Two comments about this phenomenon are in order. First, the New York situation is certainly unusual; in most states party spending as a proportion of total spending for or by candidates probably does not come close to the New York figure. Second, these expenditures are targeted for "general party promotion" activities such as fund raising, voter registration, and party advertising—activities increasingly associated in the federal campaign finance system with the term *soft money.* In other words, these monies do not *usually* go directly toward the election of a specific candidate, and are therefore not part of the candidate-centered data base.

Spending in State Legislative Races: A Look at 1994

Before analyzing the longitudinal trends, it is worth taking a look at the expenditures from state to state in a single year: 1994. These data appear in Tables 3-1, 3-2, and in Figure 3-1. The states are arranged by "legislative professionalism" type, since it is expected that generally the more professional legislatures will also have higher costs (as discussed in chapter 1). The expenditures in contested races are shown in Table 3-1 and Figure 3-1.

Table 3-1   *Total Expenditures Per Candidate in Contested House Races, 1994*

Legislative type	State	(N)	Mean	Median
C	California	(156)	$322,688	$ 219,320
I	Illinois	(162)	106,391	69,015
	Wisconsin	(117)	25,290	19,363
II	Oregon	(103)	54,814	49,913
	Washington	(162)	37,231	36,040
	North Carolina	(79)	30,632	21,182
	Minnesota	(246)	19,883	20,577
	Missouri	(210)	17,132	14,315
	Delaware	(42)	16,274	12,988
III	Idaho	(64)	8,593	6,656
	Utah	(127)	6,552	6,047
	Montana	(155)	5,633	4,629
	Wyoming	(56)	4,201	3,471
	Maine	(246)	3,947	3,243

Note: Contested races are those in which the candidate receives at least 10 percent, but less than 90 percent, of the general election vote. Total expenditures include expenditures in both the primary and general election cycle. C = California; I = professional legislature; II = hybrid legislature; III = citizen legislature.

By far, the largest average expenditures appear in California (mean = $322,688, median = $219,320). This amount is more than three times greater than the amount for the next most expensive state in our analysis (Illinois, with a mean of $106,391 and a median of $69,015). The magnitude of the California expenditure pattern is especially evident in Figure 3-1.

More than half the states in our sample have mean or median candidate expenditures under $20,000. In fact, four states (Utah, Montana, Wyoming, and Maine) exhibit means and medians under $7,000 in contested races! Contrary to public opinion, the cost of running for state legislature in many states is still quite low. With the exception of a few states such as California, "the much smaller district sizes and much larger numbers of districts ensure that state legislative candidates will never have available the large war chests that most members of Congress routinely possess" (Salmore and Salmore 1996, 66).

Explaining the Differences Between States

There are some interesting observations to make about the spending patterns both between and within categories of legislative types. Aside from the fact that California is clearly in a league of its own, there is a

Figure 3-1   *Median Spending by Candidates in Contested House Races, 1994*

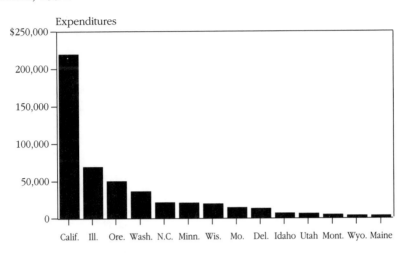

Note: Contested races are those in which the candidate receives at least 10 percent, but less than 90 percent, of the general election vote. Total expenditures include expenditures in both the primary and general election cycle. States are grouped by legislative professionalism: most professional to least professional.

substantial difference between Type II (hybrid) and Type III (citizen) states. The mean and median campaign spending in citizen legislatures is much less—generally less than half—what is found in the hybrid states.

Within the Type II category, there is a rather wide range, with some interesting differences. A good place to start is to compare Washington and Missouri. These two states are very similar in terms of state population (about 5 million in the 1990 census) and geographic size (between 65,000 and 70,000 square miles). Moreover, prior to the 1994 election, the Democrats held a substantial majority (greater than 60 percent) of the house seats in both states.

Given these similarities, how can the differences in candidate spending between Washington and Missouri be explained? Part of the explanation is district size. There are 163 seats in the Missouri house; each seat represented about 31,000 people in 1990. There are only 98 house seats in Washington. This, of course, means that the districts are larger in Washington; in 1990 each house seat represented about 50,000 people. The larger the population one tries to reach in a campaign, the greater the campaign costs (see chapter 4, on district spending, for an elaboration on this relationship).

Another difference is the proportion of marginal (competitive) seats. Recall that here "competitive" seats are defined as those in which the candidates receive between 40 and 60 percent of the general election vote. "Noncompetitive," or "safe" seats, on the other hand, are those in which the winning candidate receives more than 60 percent of the vote. In safe districts, the outcome is rarely in doubt, and therefore contestants in safe districts spend considerably less money than candidates running in competitive districts. This is quite evident if the figures in Table 3-1 are compared to those in Table 3-2, which presents the mean and median spending by candidates in competitive races only. The final column of Table 3-2 shows the percentage increase in median spending in competitive races versus contested races. As one would expect, the figures in Table 3-2 are higher—in some instances much higher—than those in Table 3-1.

In most years, including 1994, there are more safe seats in Missouri than in Washington. Usually only about 20–30 percent of the Missouri house seats are truly competitive. In Washington, on the other hand, the figure in most years is closer to 40–50 percent. With smaller districts and fewer truly competitive districts, it is no surprise that campaign expenditures for the state house are lower in Missouri than in Washington.

Table 3-2   *Total Expenditures Per Candidate in Competitive House Races, 1994*

Legislative Type	State	(N)	Mean	Median	Percent Increase Over Contested Median[a]
C	California	(51)	$430,994	$438,361	99.8
I	Illinois	(49)	190,528	189,266	174.2
	Wisconsin	(48)	38,153	35,495	83.3
II	Oregon	(53)	78,646	75,627	51.5
	Washington	(82)	45,695	44,072	22.3
	North Carolina	(54)	37,078	26,755	26.3
	Delaware	(10)	24,683	19,428	49.6
	Missouri	(77)	23,818	20,905	46.0
	Minnesota	(120)	22,008	22,204	7.9
III	Idaho	(36)	9,252	7,031	5.6
	Utah	(45)	9,040	7,679	27.0
	Montana	(71)	6,660	5,485	18.4
	Wyoming	(37)	4,450	4,159	19.8
	Maine	(150)	4,449	3,607	11.2

Note: Competitive races are those in which the candidate receives at least 40 percent, but less than 60 percent, of the general election vote. Total expenditures include expenditures in both the primary and general election cycle. C = California; I = professional legislature; II = hybrid legislature; III = citizen legislature.

[a] Median taken from Table 3-1.

These qualities also help explain why Oregon has the highest expenditures in the Type II category. There are only sixty seats in the Oregon house; each house district comprises almost 50,000 people. Moreover, the division of seats between Democrats and Republicans is usually very close in the Oregon house, so that a change in just a few seats will result in a change in which party controls the house of representatives. This was indeed the case in 1994. Prior to the election, the Republicans held thirty-two seats, the Democrats held twenty-eight. Under these circumstances, each seat becomes critical, and therefore more money is spent on campaigning for that seat. Moreover, almost half the districts in Oregon are usually competitive, so the battle to control the chamber is waged on numerous fronts, in many districts. The result is higher average campaign costs in Oregon.

Finally, Wisconsin appears to be an anomaly. It is a state that is usually categorized as "Type I"—a professional legislature, which would lead to the prediction of higher campaign expenditures. The district size is almost identical to Oregon's, and control of the chamber is often in doubt (again, similar to the case in Oregon). Why, then, are the mean and median campaign expenditures per candidate so much lower in Wisconsin than Oregon? One reason appears to be that there are fewer competitive districts in Wisconsin (generally about 20–25 percent of the districts are truly competitive). Thus, while control of the chamber may be in doubt, the battle for control is fought out in a smaller percentage of the districts in Wisconsin than in Oregon. This, of course, means fewer districts in which the campaign expenditures will be high.

Another reason that campaign expenditures are lower in Wisconsin almost certainly has to do with the campaign finance laws in that state. Wisconsin offers some public funding to candidates who agree to limit their campaign spending. Oregon had no such law in effect in 1994. Moreover, Wisconsin has relatively strict contribution limits. For example, political action committees (PACs) can only give $500 per year to a candidate for the Wisconsin House of Representatives, and corporations and labor unions are not permitted to contribute to candidates at all. In comparison, as of 1994 Oregon had no limits on how much a corporation, labor union, or PAC could contribute to a legislative candidate.

Competitive Races and Legislative Professionalization

As previously mentioned, and as expected, candidate spending is higher in competitive races than in ones that are simply contested. Of course, it is not always possible to say whether spending was higher in those races because the outcome was anticipated to be close, or whether the electoral outcome was close because spending was greater. Nonetheless, there is a clear relationship between spending and electoral margin.

A less obvious relationship appears in the last column of Table 3-2. The magnitude of the increase in spending in competitive races versus contested races is closely related to the professionalism of the state legislature. The increase in median spending in competitive (over contested) races is very high in California, Illinois, and Wisconsin. Median spending in competitive races in California and Wisconsin is virtually double the figure for contested races; in Illinois it is almost three times as large. In the hybrid state legislatures, the increase is substantial but not exorbitant (ranging between 7.9 percent and 51.5 percent). In the citizen (Type III) state legislatures, the increases are generally modest—the greatest being 27 percent in Utah.

Campaign Expenditures Over Time

In the subsequent analysis total expenditure data for state legislative races over time are presented. With one exception,[3] the data represent elections in five electoral cycles: 1986, 1988, 1990, 1992, and 1994.

Increased Spending Between 1986 and 1994

What are the trends over time? The data in Table 3-3 show the increase in spending in contested house campaigns between 1986 and 1994. The fourteen-state average during this period was about a 70 percent increase (a 67.3 percent rise in median spending and a 70.2 percent jump in mean expenditures). But there is wide variation from state to state. Some states (e.g., Illinois, Oregon, North Carolina, and Utah) witnessed dramatic increases in candidate spending between 1986 and 1994. The rise was much more modest in Wyoming, Minnesota, Delaware, and even California.

It is important to keep in mind that the figures expressed in Table 3-3 do not reflect the effect of inflation on the rise in campaign costs. At the bottom of the table the increase in the Consumer Price Index (CPI) over the corresponding period is shown. The increase in the CPI is often used as a measure of inflation. About half the total increase in campaign spending during the period 1986–1994 can be attributed simply to the effect of inflation. In several states (e.g., Minnesota) the increase in campaign expenditures is actually less than the increase in the CPI; in other words, if inflation is controlled for, campaign costs appear to have actually *dropped* between 1986 and 1994 in a few states. This is made clear in Figure 3-2, in which inflation was controlled for in median spending patterns.

Table 3-3   *Increase in Candidate Spending in Contested House Races, 1986–1994, in Percentages*

State	Increase in Median Spending	Increase in Mean Spending
California	26.4	19.5
Illinois	158.6	171.1
Wisconsin	60.5	101.9
Oregon	103.3	80.2
North Carolina [a]	92.4	135.9
Washington	81.6	64.2
Missouri	60.7	71.8
Delaware	23.2	51.9
Minnesota	33.1	22.6
Utah	101.9	79.4
Idaho	86.6	99.3
Montana	66.1	78.3
Maine	59.4	61.4
Wyoming	13.6	11.5
Average increase	67.3	70.2
CPI increase	34.5	34.5

Note: The Consumer Price Indices are based on the July figures for each year. States are grouped by legislative professionalism, from most professional to least professional.

[a] North Carolina data are from 1988–1994 only. The corresponding CPI increase was 24.4 percent. Because of the different time frame, North Carolina is not included in the average increase for all states.

There is no immediately discernible pattern in regard to the states in which there is a marked rise in spending compared to those where no such dramatic increase occurs. In the four states with the highest increase, there is a "professional" state legislature (Illinois), a "citizen" legislature (Utah,), and two legislatures (Oregon and North Carolina) that are in-between the professional and citizen poles.[4]

Spending Patterns Year-to-Year

The pattern of campaign spending shifts a bit from year to year and state to state. For example, the average increase between electoral cycles for the fourteen states is shown in Figure 3-3. Overall, the greatest jump was between 1986 and 1988 (a 26 percent average increase in spending in 1988 over the 1986 figure). The second largest jump is in 1992. Recall that a substantial increase in 1992 was hypothesized because of the uncertainty surrounding redistricting. The data certainly support this idea.

It was also anticipated that there might be a significant increase in 1990, since the legislature elected in 1990 would control the redistrict-

Figure 3-2   *Inflation-Adjusted Spending in Contested House Races,*
1986–1994

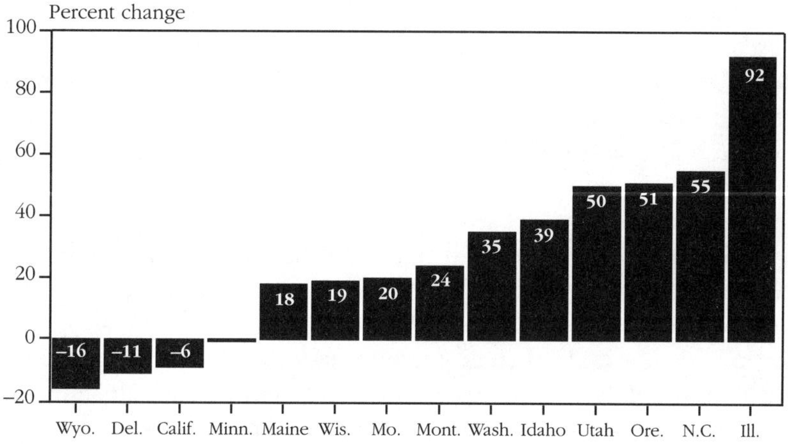

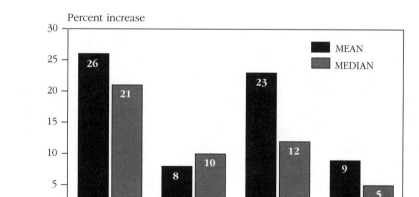

Note: Value increase is Consumer Price Index adjusted. Contested races are those in which the candidate receives at least 10 percent, but less than 90 percent, of the general election vote.

Figure 3-3   *Increase in Candidate Spending in Contested House*
Races, 1988–1994

Note: Contested races are those in which the candidate receives at least 10 percent, but less than 90 percent, of the general election vote.

ing process. As Figure 3-3 shows, such a jump did not occur in most states (the average increase was only 8 percent, which is close to the rate of inflation for that time period). In their chapter on campaign financing in primary elections, Breaux and Gierzynski suggest an alternative hypothesis about what might occur in the 1990 election cycle. They theorize that it might be more difficult to recruit "quality" candidates to run in the year just prior to the redistricting cycle because few serious candidates would want to win office for the first time only to have to run for reelection in a newly drawn district. Whatever the reason, the increase in spending from 1988 to 1990 is quite modest.

Figure 3-3 reveals the hint of a cyclical trend, where campaign costs jump up substantially in one election year, then fall back to about the rate of inflation in the subsequent election, then jump up again, then fall back. The possible cyclical nature of campaign spending will be addressed later, when the apparent effect of statewide races on state legislative spending patterns is discussed.

Even if such a cyclical trend were to be uncovered in the aggregate-level analysis, it is clear there is no trend common to *all* individual states. The three graphs in Figure 3-4 show the median expenditures by candidates in contested elections in the fourteen states being analyzed. One-third of the states show higher median expenditures in 1992 than in 1994. Again, this probably is related to the redistricting cycle. Nevertheless, it points out that campaign costs do not rise consistently in each new electoral cycle. In fact, there are only five states (Illinois, North Carolina, Missouri, Idaho, and Utah) in the sample that show an increase in median spending for each successive election.

Legislative Spending and the Gubernatorial Electoral Cycle

So far the potential effect of several contextual factors on the year-by-year increase in campaign spending has been discussed: the reapportionment cycle, the number of competitive races, and the fight for majority control of the chamber. It is also possible that the *pool of available money* for candidates is affected by cycles. In particular, it is anticipated that legislative candidates may find less donor money available to them during years in which the governor's office (and perhaps other statewide offices) is up for election. Most of the money contributed to campaigns for state offices comes from in-state contributors. The race for governor often absorbs huge amounts of financial resources, and therefore it is possible that there will be less money available for state legislative candidates. For example, in 1992 the total amount received by all house candidates in the state of Washington was $8.9 million; gubernatorial candidates received just over $7 million.

In 1994, Idaho gubernatorial candidates amassed (and spent) almost $3.5 million in campaign revenues. The total received by all state legislative candidates (house and senate combined) was $1.8 million. In other words, the governor's race attracted almost twice as much money

Figure 3-4   *Median Spending in Contested Races for State Legislatures,*
1986–1994

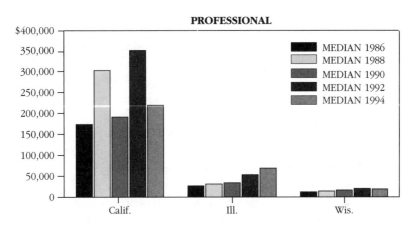

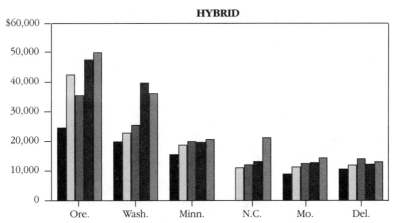

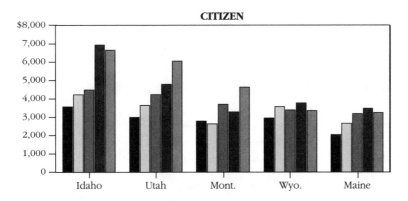

Note: Contested races are those in which the candidate receives at least 10 percent, but less than 90 percent, of the general election vote.

as the total for all the state legislative races. Moreover, other statewide races (for offices such as attorney general and lieutenant governor) attracted more than $1.5 million—money that might otherwise go to legislative candidates.

The data in Table 3-4 show the increase or decrease in spending—controlled for inflation—for each state and electoral cycle. It also shows the years in which gubernatorial elections occur. Half the states in our sample hold gubernatorial elections in presidential years (e.g., 1992, 1996); the other half hold gubernatorial elections in off-years (e.g., 1986, 1990, 1994). If, indeed, the governor's race has an effect on the pool of money available to state legislative candidates, then spending by contestants for legislative seats should be higher in the nongubernatorial years (which are shaded in Table 3-4). There appears to be a general relationship between spending and nongubernatorial years. For example, in eleven of the fourteen states the greatest increase in spending occurs during a nongubernatorial election year. Clearly, other factors—such as chamber marginality and redistricting—come into play, but it is quite possible that the presence or absence of the governor's election provides a basis for the relative increase in spending from year to year.

Table 3-4   *Gubernatorial Electoral Cycles and the Increase in Median Spending over Previous Election in Contested House Races, in Percentages*

| | Gubernatorial | Change in Median Spending | | | |
State	Election Year	1988	1990	1992	1994
California	1986, 1990, 1994	61.2	−42.4	**70.4**	−40.4
Oregon	1986, 1990, 1994	**60.2**	−24.0	24.7	−0.2
Maine	1986, 1990, 1994	**20.7**	9.1	1.4	−11.3
Wyoming	1986, 1990, 1994	**11.9**	−13.5	3.4	−15.5
Idaho	1986, 1990, 1994	9.6	−3.3	**34.6**	−2.6
Wisconsin	1986, 1990, 1994	7.9	6.7	**14.2**	−9.1
Illinois	1986, 1990, 1994	7.2	−0.4	**47.2**	22.5
Missouri	1988, 1992, 1996	**16.9**	0.2	−4.6	6.9
Utah	1988, 1992, 1996	12.6	5.6	5.3	**19.9**
Minnesota	1988, 1992, 1996	**12.1**	−3.2	−8.3	−0.4
Washington	1988, 1992, 1996	6.2	1.4	**45.3**	−13.7
Delaware	1988, 1992, 1996	4.3	**7.2**	−19.1	1.4
Montana	1988, 1992, 1996	−12.8	28.2	−17.4	**33.9**
North Carolina	1988, 1992, 1996	N/A	−0.7	1.5	**53.7**

Note: Figures indicate the change from the previous election cycle in median spending in contested races, controlled for inflation. Shaded cells indicate years in which there was no gubernatorial election and therefore are years in which we might expect larger increases in median spending. Bold figures indicate the year of the greatest increase in spending for each state. States are ordered by legislative professionalism: most professional and less professional. N/A = not available.

Spending Patterns Among Incumbents and Challengers

It has long been known that incumbents outspend challengers in congressional elections and in state legislative elections. Is the gap between incumbent and challenger spending increasing? Alexander (1992, 124) reports that in 1976 California assembly incumbents held a 3 to 1 spending ratio over challengers; by 1986 that ratio was 30 to 1. What do the data tell us about this trend?

Intercandidate Transfers and Net Expenditures

The data set for this part of the analysis is somewhat different than the data set used up to this point. First, data from 1986 through 1992 are used; comparable data for 1994 are not included. Second, since the 1986–1992 data set was used, eighteen states can be analyzed rather than the fourteen to which the study has been limited thus far. Third, *net* expenditures rather than *total* expenditures are used as the basis for the analysis. For most states the difference between total and net expenditures is very slight. But for a few of the states in the sample (e.g., California, Illinois, and Oregon), the difference can be quite meaningful. The difference centers around the issue of *intercandidate transfers,* whereby money moves from one candidate to another. Most of the transfers occur when legislative leaders accumulate large amounts of money through campaign contributions and then redistribute that money to candidates from their party. Transfers also occur when a candidate with little or no electoral competition sends money to a colleague who is in a close race.

For the candidate making such a transfer, these funds are not actually expenditures on behalf of his or her campaign; instead, these funds are being given to another candidate or to the party. Occasionally these funds may be transferred to the party or to a committee in order to purchase services (media time, polling, targeted mailings) at lower unit-cost rates on behalf of the original candidate,[5] but generally transfers are simply money passed from one candidate to another.

Since these funds are usually not spent on the campaign of the individual who originally received them, such funds are omitted from the analysis here. In other words, a measure best described as *net expenditures,* which is defined as total expenditures (primary and general election combined) minus transfers to other candidates and party organizations, is used. This is an important issue at this point of the analysis because most transfers are made by incumbents, and at this stage of the discussion spending patterns between incumbents and other candidates are being compared.

Challengers' Versus Incumbents' Expenditures

The data in Table 3-5 show challengers' median expenditures as a percentage of incumbents' median spending in contested elections. Median figures are used here because the number of cases is relatively small in some instances, and means are therefore subject to distortion.

There is a definite inverse relationship between legislative professionalization and the challenger-incumbent ratio. The Pearson's product moment correlation between these two variables is r=−.66 (p <.005). In other words, the higher the state legislature scores on the professionalization index,[6] the less likely it is that challengers can attract enough money to be competitive. For example, by looking at the 1992 column, it can be seen that in California challengers in contested races spent, on average, only 6 percent as much money as incumbents. In New Jersey, challengers spent only 27.2 percent as much and in Pennsylvania they spent 18.7 percent as much as incumbents. On the other hand, in states such as Montana (75.5 percent), Utah (76.1 percent), and Wyoming

Table 3-5   *Median Net Expenditures by Challengers, as a Percentage of Median Expenditures by Incumbents in Contested House Races*

| | | Year | | | |
Type	State	1986	1988	1990	1992
C	California	3.2	4.0	3.0	6.0
I	Illinois	17.4	8.6	22.3	20.7
	New Jersey	32.4	10.8	21.0	27.2
	Pennsylvania		22.4	20.8	18.7
	Wisconsin	84.6	60.5	62.1	51.6
II	Oregon	42.2	37.0	26.6	25.2
	Washington	26.4	24.2	16.2	19.4
	Delaware	51.1	49.9	43.9	92.7
	North Carolina		45.6	41.4	54.7
	Missouri	37.4	52.5	50.6	38.8
	Minnesota	54.8	48.2	52.1	44.3
	Kansas	43.6	40.2	40.7	41.1
III	Utah	97.0	64.9	65.5	76.1
	Idaho	58.1	46.7	90.5	44.2
	Wyoming	64.6	70.0	77.3	74.7
	Mississippi		38.6		31.5
	Maine	60.4	58.7	59.3	42.8
	Montana	86.3	95.2	82.4	75.5

Note: Contested races are those in which the candidate receives at least 10 percent, but less than 90 percent, of the general election vote. C = California; I = professional legislature; II = hybrid legislature; III = citizen legislature. Mississippi data are from 1987 and 1991; New Jersey data are from 1978, 1989, 1991, and 1993.

(74.7 percent), challenger spending was much closer to the level of incumbent spending.

The reason is simple enough: "citizen" legislatures tend to be found in less populous states, and it costs much less to reach 7,000 people (the approximate size of a house district in Montana) than it does to reach 375,000 (the approximate size of an assembly district in California). Challengers almost always have more trouble raising money than incumbents, but even a challenger can find $3,000 or $4,000 to run a credible race in Wyoming. In California it costs several hundred thousand dollars to be competitive, and most challengers cannot raise that kind of money.

Among the more professional state legislatures, only in Wisconsin are challengers able to spend even half as much as incumbents. This is directly related to the public funding aspect of the Wisconsin campaign finance laws. Even there, however, a decline is seen in the challenger's ability to spend vis-à-vis incumbents.[7]

The longitudinal trends in the challenger-incumbent ratios can also be assessed. There are three basic trends represented by the data in Table 3-5. First, there are the states wherein the ratio does not change much from year to year. Kansas is the best example of this; median challenger expenditures are between 40 and 44 percent of median incumbent spending in each electoral cycle. Other states (California, Minnesota, Mississippi, Pennsylvania, and Washington) exhibit roughly the same pattern, although with a little more variation from one year to the next.

Second, a few states show a steady and relatively consistent decline in challenger spending relative to incumbent spending. The clearest example of this is Oregon (42.2 percent, 37.0 percent, 26.6 percent, 25.2 percent), but Wisconsin and Maine also generally fit the pattern.

Finally, a handful of states do not appear to fit either of the previously mentioned patterns (e.g., Delaware, Idaho, Utah, and New Jersey). In these states there is often one year in which the ratio is at considerable variance with the ratios in that state in the other years. This is likely the product of idiosyncratic factors—a single issue that affected members of one party, for example.

One thing that is clear from the data in Table 3-5 is that the relative position of challengers is not improving in most states. If the 1992 figures are compared with the 1986 figures, for example, the challengers' position is significantly improved in only one state, Delaware (and even this case may be an aberration in a single year; available figures for 1994 show that challengers' spending was only 26.4 percent of incumbents' expenditures). On the other hand, median challenger spending is significantly less by 1992 in at least four states: Maine, Oregon, Utah, and Wisconsin.

As might be expected, challengers do much better in competitive races, where their median spending is usually between 50 and 90 percent of incumbents' median spending, depending on the state and circumstances surrounding the particular election.[8] Because the number of cases is so small in some instances (e.g., the number of competitive races per year in Delaware ranges between seven and nine; in California it ranges between seven and fourteen), longitudinal analysis is risky.

CONCLUSION

There are five main conclusions to draw from this chapter. First, the amount spent on state legislative races is remarkably different from one state to another. There are still some states where the average amount of money spent per candidate is quite low. One can easily spend more on a home computer than what the average candidate spends to run for the house in Wyoming, Montana, or Maine. For substantially less than the cost of a standard automobile today, one can run a competitive campaign in more than half the states studied. On the other hand, the average spent in Illinois and Oregon in 1994 was more than $100,000 and $50,000, respectively. In California the *average* spent in 1994 was more than $320,000! Students of state politics often speak of variation between the states, and there is no more descriptive word than *variation* when state campaign finances are discussed.

Second, the rate of spending growth is highly variable. There are some states in which average or median spending was increasing at a rate below the inflation rate. Then again, half the states in the sample experienced significant growth (more than 25 percent above the inflation rate, for example) in candidate spending for state legislative races.

Third, the rate of spending growth appears to be tied to both the gubernatorial electoral cycle and the redistricting cycle. Spending increases in state legislative races are generally higher in years in which there is no campaign for the governor's office. Spending jumped up in many states in 1992, which was the election immediately after district lines had been redrawn in most states. It is likely that other factors, such as the size of the majority party in the chamber, also have an effect.

Fourth, spending patterns are quite different in competitive contests compared to noncompetitive races. Both mean and median spending are considerably higher for competitive elections than contested races in most states, and there is a definite correlation between legislative professionalization and increased spending in competitive versus contested races.

Finally, the challenger-to-incumbent spending ratio is different in the highly professionalized legislatures compared to the other legislatures. Because it costs so much to be competitive in the "bigger" (and, consequently, more professionalized) states, challengers are severely disadvantaged in their ability to spend on their campaign. In many states the relative position of challengers vis-à-vis incumbents in terms of campaign spending is worsening. This is probably tied, in part, to the role of PACs. As William Cassie and Joel Thompson demonstrate in chapter 9, PAC money goes overwhelmingly to incumbents.

NOTES

1. Calculated by author from data appearing in Table 1, p. 553, of Moncrief (1992).
2. The 1986–1992 data were collected specifically for this project. Most of the 1994 data reported in this chapter were collected by Robert Hogan while he was a graduate student at Rice University. I wish to acknowledge his generosity in allowing the use of his data in this chapter.
3. The exception is North Carolina, for which 1986 data were not available. The observant reader will note that later in this chapter—and indeed throughout most of the book—eighteen states are used in the analysis. We are limited to fourteen in this part of our discussion because we only have 1994 data for those fourteen states. In essence, by expanding the analysis to include 1994 data, the "cost" was losing four states for this portion of the chapter.
4. This categorization is based on National Conference of State Legislatures' designations, as in Figure 5-2, p. 176, of Patterson (1996).
5. Redfield (1995) refers to this as "buy-backs" in his discussion of campaign financing in Illinois.
6. The index is Peverill Squire's Index of Professionalization. See Table 1, p. 72 of Squire (1992).
7. For a more detailed discussion of the Wisconsin law and recent trends, see Mayer and Wood (1995, 69–87). An interesting comparison between the Wisconsin and Minnesota situations can be obtained by reading Donnay and Ramsden (1995, 351–364).
8. Because of the small n's, the data for competitive elections are not presented in the text. Data are available from the author.

REFERENCES

Alexander, Herbert. 1991. *Reform and Reality: The Financing of State and Local Campaigns.* New York: Twentieth Century Fund.

Alexander, Herbert. 1992. *Financing Politics: Money, Elections, and Political Reform,* 4th ed. Washington, D.C.: CQ Press.

Donnay, Patrick, and Graham Ramsden. 1995. "Public Financing of Legislative Elections: Lessons From Minnesota." *Legislative Studies Quarterly* 20: 351–364.

Dwyre, Diana, and Jeffrey Stonecash. 1992. "Where's the Party? Changing State Party Organizations." *American Politics Quarterly* 20: 326–344.

Gierzynski, Anthony, and David Breaux. 1991. "Money and Votes in State Legislative Elections." *Legislative Studies Quarterly* 16: 203–217.

Giles, Michael, and Anita Pritchard. 1985. "Campaign Spending and Legislative Elections in Florida." *Legislative Studies Quarterly* 10: 71–88.

Jewell, Malcolm. 1993. "What Does Research on Legislative Campaign Finance Tell Us About Reform Proposals?" Paper presented at the annual meeting of the Southern Political Science Association, Savannah, Ga., November 3–6, 1993.

Keefe, William, and Morris Ogul. 1997. *The American Legislative Process*, 9th ed. Upper Saddle River, N.J.: Prentice Hall.

Mayer, Kenneth, and John M. Wood. 1995. "The Impact of Public Financing on Electoral Competitiveness: Evidence From Wisconsin, 1964–1990." *Legislative Studies Quarterly* 20: 69–87.

Moncrief, Gary. 1992. "The Increase in Campaign Expenditures in State Legislative Elections." *Western Political Quarterly* 45: 549–558.

Moncrief, Gary, and W. David Patton. 1993. "Upping the Campaign Ante as Parties Compete to Control the Legislature." *State and Local Government Review* 25: 39–44.

Murakami, Kerry. 1996. "State Campaign Reform Merely Rerouted PAC Cash." *Seattle Times* April 4, 1996, A1.

Neal, Tommy. 1992. "The Sky-High Cost of Campaigns." *State Legislatures* (May): 21.

Patterson, Samuel. 1996. "Legislative Politics in the States," in *Politics in the American States,* 6th ed., edited by Virginia Gray and Herbert Jacob. Washington, D.C.: CQ Press.

Redfield, Kent. 1995. *Cash Clout.* Springfield: University of Illinois, Springfield Press.

Rieselbach, Leroy. 1995. *Congressional Politics: The Evolving Legislative System,* 2nd ed. Boulder: Westview Press.

Salmore, Stephen, and Barbara Salmore. 1996. "The Transformation of State Electoral Politics," in *The State of the States,* 3rd ed., edited by Carl Van Horn. Washington, D.C.: Congressional Quarterly Press.

Sorauf, Frank. 1992. *Inside Campaign Finance: Myths and Realities.* New Haven: Yale University Press.

Squire, Peverill. 1992. "Legislative Professionalization and Membership Diversity in State Legislatures." *Legislative Studies Quarterly* 17: 69–79.

Stonecash, Jeffrey. 1988. "Working at the Margins: Campaign Finance and Party Strategy in New York Assembly Elections." *Legislative Studies Quarterly* 13: 477–493.

Stonecash, Jeffrey. 1990. "Campaign Finance in New York Senate Elections." *Legislative Studies Quarterly* 15: 247–262.

Thompson, Joel, Karl Kurtz, and Gary Moncrief. 1996. "We've Lost That Family Feeling: The Changing Norms of the New Breed of State Legislators." *Social Science Quarterly* 77: 344–362.

CHAPTER FOUR

Variations in District-Level Campaign Spending in State Legislatures

Robert E. Hogan and Keith E. Hamm

INTRODUCTION

In 1960 Alexander Heard wrote a book entitled *The Costs of Democracy,* in which he examined the sources and sums of spending in American political campaigns. The implication of the study's title is that it costs money to elect representatives in a democratic society. Like Heard's study and others that have followed, this chapter focuses on the "costs" associated with electing representatives to office by examining spending in state legislative races in the 1990s. Unlike similar studies, however, we view the costs of electing a candidate not just as the amount of money spent by one candidate's campaign, but instead as the amount spent by all candidates running in a given electoral district. By using a measure of spending aggregated to the district level, we can better estimate the costs of the entire campaign effort for a given seat in the state legislature.

If the spending by all candidates in a given district were totaled for both the primary and general election periods, how much would it cost to elect a state legislator? Given the amount of attention focused on the rising costs of campaigns in recent years (Alexander 1991; Moncrief 1992; Neal 1992; Singer 1988; Moncrief this book, chapter 3), many people would probably estimate a fairly high dollar amount. In many cases such an estimate would be accurate. For instance, candidates running in the Third Assembly District of California spent a total of more than $1.5 million in 1992. However, in that same year in Wyoming, candidates running in the Twelfth District spent a total of only $1,813. Some might be shocked to learn that it costs so little to elect a state legislator. Some earlier studies have noted wide variations in campaign spending across legislative districts (Gierzynski and Breaux 1991, Jones 1984, Moncrief 1992). This chapter will show that the cost of running for office varies dramatically across districts within states, as well as across states. In some districts the sums spent to elect a candidate are enormous, while in many others the costs are surprisingly low.

In addition to documenting the different levels of district spending, this chapter will also examine those factors responsible for variations in spending. For example, what might be the cause of the spending disparities between the districts just mentioned in California and Wyoming? One structural factor may simply have to do with the relative size of their voting populations. The average voting-age population of an assembly district in California is nearly fifty times greater than that of the average Wyoming house district. It simply costs more money to campaign when there are more voters to contact. However, there are other explanations for these spending disparities that should also be considered. One electoral explanation has to do with the level of competition in the districts. In the Wyoming district there were only five candidates running, while in California there were nine. In addition, both major parties' primaries were contested in California, but in Wyoming there was only one contested primary. The nature of the legislative institutions in the two states might also lead to spending differences at the state level. Because the California assembly is a much more professional institution than the Wyoming house, we might expect that spending would be greater there. Seats in professional legislatures are generally more highly prized due to their larger salaries and other amenities afforded members. Competition for seats in these legislatures is, therefore, probably greater with candidates raising large sums to either win or retain their positions.

These are just some of the differences among districts and states that result in spending disparities. The relative importance of each of these factors along with the structural features of the district, electoral characteristics, and state-level conditions will be explored in an analysis of spending by lower house candidates running in nineteen states in the early 1990s.[1]

A DISTRICT-LEVEL PERSPECTIVE

This research departs from previous research in two important ways. First, spending is used as a dependent variable—variation in spending is what is to be explained. Unlike other studies that examine expenditures as an independent variable (e.g., Gierzynski and Breaux 1991, Giles and

Pritchard 1985, Tucker and Weber 1987), this analysis will look beyond the characteristics of the candidate to determine variation in spending across districts and investigate how the characteristics of the district and state influence spending levels.

The second way this study departs from previous research is in its conceptualization of spending. The focus in this chapter is on all spending directed at winning a legislative seat in a given election cycle. For the purposes of measurement, spending by all state legislative candidates in both party primaries as well as in the general election campaign is aggregated for each district. *The result is a figure that represents the total spending by all the candidates vying for each seat in the legislature.* Most other studies focus on the differences between candidates, but this study focuses on the differences between *districts*. This type of investigation therefore calls for an analysis in which the district is the unit of analysis.[2]

DATA

The data for this analysis were compiled from reports filed by legislative candidates running for the lower house of state legislatures in nineteen states. Total expenditures in the district were calculated as the aggregated spending by all candidates running in both the primary and general election campaigns.[3] The data for sixteen of the states are from the 1992 election cycle. Data from Mississippi and New Jersey are from 1991 (when they held their regularly scheduled elections), while the data from Texas are from the 1988 election period.[4] The states in the sample vary on a number of important dimensions, including professionalism of the legislature, chamber party competitiveness,[5] region, and average population of the states' legislative districts. There is also variation in terms of district type. One state, New Jersey, has multimember districts (two candidates elected per district); North Carolina, has a combination of single-member and multimember districts.[6]

In the analysis that follows the focus is only on those districts where elections are contested by major party candidates. While incumbent candidates often spend money when there is only a minor party or independent candidate running, seldom are these races competitive. This analysis includes only those districts where there is some competition; therefore, to be included in the analysis a district must have more than one major party candidate running in either one of the two major party primaries or in the general election.

VARIATIONS IN DISTRICT-LEVEL SPENDING

Across State Variations

How much do all the candidates competing in a given district spend trying to get elected to the state legislature? The data in Table 4-1 display both the mean and median levels of district spending across each of the nineteen states in the sample. As the table clearly shows, spending in some states is fairly high while in others it is quite low.

To get some sense of the typical amount of money spent in a given district, we have averaged the spending from all 1,564 districts. The average, or mean, spending for all districts is slightly more than $80,000. However, this value might be skewed if there are a few districts with very high or very low levels of spending. To control for this, the median level of spending, which represents the middle value of a distribution (where half the values are above and half are below), is also provided. For the entire set of districts in the sample, the median level of district spending

Table 4-1   *Average District-Level Spending by Candidates Running for the State Legislature*

State	Mean Spending	Median Spending	Number of Districts
California	$643,018	$493,074	76
New Jersey	239,386	185,301	40
Illinois	160,362	123,077	109
Oregon	102,843	93,398	50
Texas	98,708	78,340	83
Washington	89,605	76,777	91
Pennsylvania	57,450	52,076	180
Wisconsin	46,952	41,470	71
North Carolina	43,839	30,392	73
Minnesota	42,128	40,857	124
Missouri	31,779	28,430	110
Delaware	27,480	25,758	29
Kansas	23,324	23,423	100
Idaho	16,314	16,240	50
Utah	11,146	10,833	59
Wyoming	$9,586	8,901	51
Mississippi	$8,951	5,609	68
Montana	$7,940	7,211	75
Maine	$7,868	7,018	125
AVERAGE	83,303	32,213	1,564

Note: Only districts where there was competition in either the primary or general election are included. Figures are from 1992, except for Mississippi and New Jersey (1991) and Texas (1988).

is only slightly more than $30,000. This total is not nearly as high as some might expect, considering that this includes spending by all candidates running in both primary and general election contests.

Probably the most striking feature from Table 4-1 is the dramatic variation in spending across the sample of states. In about one-fifth of the states the average level of spending exceeds $100,000. States in this category include California, New Jersey, Illinois, and Oregon. However, in about another one-fifth of the states, spending is rather low—on average less than $10,000. States in this low category include Wyoming, Mississippi, Montana, and Maine. The large differences in spending across states are most apparent in the difference between the state with the highest level of spending, California ($643,018), and the state with the lowest level of spending, Maine ($7,868). Spending in the average California assembly district race is more than eighty times greater than spending in the average Maine house district contest.[7]

A large amount of variation across states has been shown. Before moving to a discussion of variation within states, it is probably prudent to consider a factor that is most important in affecting the variation observed so far: population of the district.

Across State Variation When Controlling for Population

A major factor that affects total spending is the number of eligible voters in each state legislative district. District populations often vary dramatically between states. We expect that the costs of contacting voters will be higher in states where districts have tens or hundreds of thousands of potential voters, while the costs will be dramatically lower in states where the voting population is only one or two thousand. Numerous observers recognize that district population will affect expenditures and often control for population when conducting their analysis. Rosenthal, for instance, says that "[c]osts are higher in larger districts than in smaller ones" (1981, 33). However, variation in the total population is not the only explanation. For example, Sorauf (1992, 36) examined average spending by legislative candidates across five states while controlling for the average number of residents per district and concluded that "the differences are considerable," ranging from $0.64 in Missouri to a high of about $1.37 per resident in California.

The average number of potential voters per district varies a great deal across states in our sample. Potential voters are defined here as the number of residents in a district who are eighteen years old or older.[8] In Wyoming (5,301) and Montana (5,770) the district average is quite low, but in others states, such as New Jersey (148,268) and California (275,116), the average is quite high. To control for the effects of population on spending, we have calculated the spending costs per eligible voter in each district and displayed the results in Figure 4-1.

There is considerable variation in spending per eligible voter across the states. District-level spending is highest in Oregon, with nearly $3.00 spent per eligible voter in 1992. Districts in California, Delaware, and Illinois are not far behind, with average spending of less than $2.50 per eligible voter. Spending is lowest in Idaho, Minnesota, Mississippi, North Carolina, and Utah, where less than $1.00 is spent per eligible voter. These results indicate that population may be driving some of the variations in spending among the states, but certainly not all. Sorauf (1992, 36) notes that these remaining differences in spending among states are "not easy to explain."

In comparing the rankings of states from Table 4-1 with the rankings in Figure 4-1 a good bit of consistency can be seen across most states. States such as California, Illinois, and Oregon, which ranked high in district-level spending, also ranked high in spending per eligible voter. Similarly, states such as Idaho, Mississippi, and Utah, which ranked low in average total spending, continued to rank low when spending was calculated per eligible voter. However, others states are not as consistent. While average spending appears to be rather low in Delaware and Kansas, once we control for the number of eligible voters per district, we find that spending in these states is rather high. In fact, Delaware ranks extraordinarily high, falling behind only California and Oregon in terms of per eligible voter spending. Such an inconsistency (though in the opposite direction) can also be observed in North Carolina. While this state ranked near the middle of the sample in terms of average spending, it ranks close to the bottom of the sample in spending per eligible voter.

Within-State Variation

Large differences have been shown in district-level spending across states. We now want to consider the extent of within-state variation. One way to examine within-state variations is to focus on the standard deviations in per eligible voter spending within each of the states in the study. The standard deviation is a measure of dispersion representing the typical amount by which a value deviates from the mean, or in this case the average spending per eligible voter.

Figure 4-2 displays the range of the standard deviation of per eligible voter spending for each of the sample states. The line represents the range of spending values that fall within one standard deviation of the mean. Overall, there appear to be wide variations in spending across districts in each state. In California, Illinois, and Oregon there is a very high degree of variation across districts, while in Idaho, Minnesota, and

Figure 4-1   *District-Level Spending Per Eligible Voter by Candidates for the Lower House*

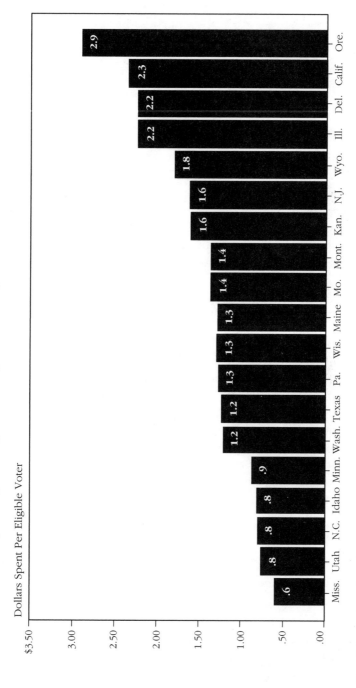

Dollars Spent Per Eligible Voter

Note: Only districts where there was competition in either the primary or general election are included. Figures are from 1992, except for Mississippi and New Jersey (1991) and Texas (1988)

Figure 4-2   *Range of the Standard Deviations of District-Level Spending Per Eligible Voter*

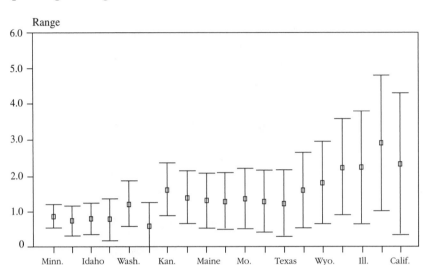

Note: Only districts where there was competition in either the primary or general election are included. Figures are from 1992, except for Mississippi and New Jersey (1991) and Texas (1988). The standard deviation is a measure of dispersion representing the typical amount by which a value deviates from the mean (the average spending per eligible voter).

Utah there is much less. However, it is important to point out that even within the state with the lowest standard deviation (Minnesota, 0.321), there is still a wide range in levels of spending across the districts. In this state, the values within one standard deviation range from a high of $1.20 to a low of $0.56 per eligible voter.

Having established that there are significant variations in spending both across and within states, we will now examine the factors that are responsible for these variations: electoral and structural features on the district level, state-level factors associated with features of the legislature (professionalism and chamber competition), and campaign finance regulations.

ELECTORAL AND STRUCTURAL INFLUENCES ON SPENDING

Electoral Factors

There are several variables related to the electoral conditions of the district that may have an influence on the amount of money allocated per eligible voter. Three factors will be examined: number of candidates, extent of electoral competition, and the presence of an incumbent candidate.

Number of Candidates

A seemingly obvious factor that influences total campaign spending is the number of candidates in the race. As the number of candidates increases, we expect that the aggregate level of spending in a given district will also increase. This variable is calculated as the total number of candidates in the primary plus the total number of candidates in the general election. In this way the winners of the primary contests are actually counted twice—once in the primary election and again in the general election. The reasoning behind this is simple: the primary and general elections are two separate races—when both elections are contested, the amount of money spent by the candidates is likely to be higher.[9] (See chapter 5 for information on candidate activity during primary elections.)

Electoral Competition

General election competition is expected to be highly correlated with district-level spending patterns. When a race is hard fought and the outcome is in doubt, we expect candidate spending to be much higher. Candidates in close races will probably exert more energy raising funds and contributors will probably be more likely to donate when they believe their money can make a difference. General election competition in this analysis is calculated as the winner's percent of the two-party vote. We anticipate that spending will be higher when the winning candidate receives a lower percentage of the final vote share.

Competition in the primary election is also likely to increase the amount of spending in a given legislative district. A contested primary means that candidates must first expend energy in securing their party's nomination—something that costs money. Spending is likely to be higher in districts where one or both of the primaries are contested.

Presence of an Incumbent

Incumbent candidates in state legislative races have a high rate of success in general elections (Holbrook and Tidmarch 1991, Jewell and Breaux 1989) as well as in primary contests (Jewell and Breaux 1991). While many studies have tried to link incumbents' success to their advantages in name recognition, perquisites of office, and levels of campaign funding, a more basic explanation for why incumbents win elections is simply because quality candidates do not run against them. A large number of incumbents often go unchallenged in state legislative contests. While little research on the state level has focused on questions of candidate quality, evidence from the congressional level shows that candidates who have the ability to raise large sums of money often wait to run until a seat is vacated by an incumbent (Jacobson and Kernell 1981). Indirect evidence is provided for this in studies of state legislative contests that show that average spending by open-seat candidates is often as high or higher than spending by incumbents (Giles and Pritchard 1985).

For these reasons we predict that the presence of an incumbent will have a dampening effect on district-level spending. When a seat is open, however, more candidates will decide to run, especially the candidates who can raise and subsequently spend a larger amount of money. In addition, open seats probably invite greater competition in primary contests, which also increases spending levels.

Structural Factors

The urban or rural character of the district is a structural factor that we expect to have an influence on the level of spending. A different style of campaigning may be utilized in urban versus rural districts. In rural districts a much more personalized form of voter contact is generally undertaken. People in rural areas are more likely to know one another and the dissemination of campaign messages by word of mouth is probably viewed by campaigners as more effective than a "packaged" media campaign. Paid advertising is more likely to be used in the more urban settings where campaigners are faced with a larger constituency and higher advertising costs. For these reasons, spending in urban districts will probably be greater than spending in rural districts.

Each district in this analysis is coded as either urban or rural. A district is considered urban if any part of it overlaps a metropolitan statistical area as defined by the U.S. Census Bureau.

Findings

How important are these electoral and structural features to levels of district spending? Table 4-2 displays the average spending per eligible voter across each category of factors.

In the first category, number of candidates running, district spending increases substantially for each additional candidate who runs. When there are only two candidates, spending is about $1.11 per eligible voter. The addition of a third and fourth candidate increases spending to $1.38 and $1.60, respectively. When five or more candidates are running, spending is slightly more than $2.02 per eligible voter.

Does the presence of an incumbent have an effect? Table 4-2 indicates that spending is much higher when there is no incumbent present ($1.68) than when there is one in either the district's primary or general election ($1.30). As expected, it appears that the presence of an incumbent has a dampening effect on district-level spending.

Table 4-2   *Effects of Electoral and Structural Factors on District-Level Spending Per Eligible Voter*

Factor	Spending	Number of districts
Number of candidates[a]		
2	$1.11	863
3	1.38	42
4	1.60	359
5 or more	2.02	300
Incumbent in race		
Yes	1.30	1,145
No	1.68	419
Primary competition[b]		
0	1.19	794
1	1.51	645
2	2.23	125
General election competition[c]		
> 80%	0.83	200
71–80%	1.01	137
61–70%	1.26	486
55–60%	1.62	393
< 55%	1.85	348
Character of the district		
Rural	1.24	473
Urban	1.47	1,091

[a] Total number of candidates running in primary and general campaigns.

[b] Number of primaries. Democratic and Republican primaries are considered two separate contests for purposes of this analysis.

[c] Winner's percent of the two-party vote.

Is electoral competition as measured by primary contestation and general election competitiveness important for influencing levels of spending? It seems that both variables play a role. Average spending when there is no primary contest is about $1.19. When there is a primary contest in at least one of the parties the cost rises to $1.51 and jumps again to $2.23 when both parties' primaries are contested. A similar trend is observed with regard to general election competition. When competition is relatively low (the winner's percentage of the two-party vote is greater than 80 percent), average spending per eligible voter in a district is also relatively low ($0.83). However, when competition is high (the winner's percentage of the two-party vote is less than 55 percent), then spending is also high, with about $1.85 spent per eligible voter. Competition in both primary and general election contests appears to be an important determinant of spending.

Whether a district is urban or rural also has an impact on spending. As expected, average spending in urban districts is somewhat higher ($1.47) than spending in rural districts ($1.24).

STATE-LEVEL EXPLANATIONS FOR VARIATIONS IN SPENDING

While the preceding analysis tells us a great deal about variations across districts, what about the large variations across states as noted in both Table 4-1 and Figure 4-1? We now examine three system-level factors to account for these differences. Two are political factors: legislative professionalism and competitiveness of the parties in the chamber; the third is a legal factor: the strictness of campaign finance laws.

Legislative Professionalism

Mooney (1995, 48–49) describes legislative professionalism as a legislature's ability to provide its members with "adequate resources to do their jobs in a manner comparable to that of other full-time political actors, and set up organizations and procedures that facilitate lawmaking." Legislatures that rank high on this measure of professionalism are called "professional," those ranking near the bottom are considered "citizen," and those ranking near the middle are considered "hybrid," as they contain elements of both professional and citizen legislatures. We hypothesize that spending will be much higher in states with professional legislatures than in states with less professional or "citizen" legislatures, for two reasons. First, professional legislatures are usually in session for a longer period of time each year and are generally more capable of affecting policy than less professional legislatures. This means that the stakes are higher for interest groups in states with more professional legislatures, where policy is continually being created and updated. Interest groups in such states, therefore, will be inclined to contribute more money to candidates running for office. The effect of these contributions will be to drive up the costs of campaigns in states with more professional legislatures.

The second reason that district spending will probably be higher in states with professional legislatures is that a seat in such a chamber is probably more prized by candidates. Legislators in more professional institutions are usually adequately paid, receive office allowances, and are more likely to consider their jobs as a career. Legislators serving in citizen legislatures, on the other hand, are usually paid little, have few perks, and are more likely to consider their service to be a part-time vocation. Because of these differences, we expect that candidates in states with more professional legislatures should be willing to fight harder to get elected by spending more of their own money as well as engaging in aggressive fund-raising efforts. Moncrief (1992) finds support for this, but considers only a sample of western states.

To categorize the state legislatures, we utilize the modified Kurtz classification discussed in chapter 1, with one change.[10] For purposes of simplifying the figures, we group California with the other professional states—Illinois, New Jersey, Pennsylvania, and Wisconsin. Seven states have citizen legislatures: Idaho, Maine, Mississippi, Montana, North Carolina, Utah, and Wyoming. All the other states in the sample fall into the middle range of professionalism.

Chamber Competitiveness

Another system-level variable worthy of consideration is the competition for control of the legislative chamber. Both Stonecash (1990) and Moncrief (1992) note the importance of this variable; if control of the chamber is in doubt, the political consequences of each legislative race take on heightened importance, and the amount of money spent in quest of each seat is likely to escalate. The chamber competitiveness measure is calculated as the percentage of seats held by the minority party prior to the election.

To determine the effects of chamber competitiveness, we have categorized states into low, medium, or high levels of chamber competition. Four states have rather high levels of competition, where the minority party holds more than 45 percent of the seats in the chamber: Kansas, New Jersey, Oregon, and Pennsylvania. Five states have relatively low levels of chamber competition where the minority party holds 36 percent or fewer of the seats: Idaho, Maine, Mississippi, North Carolina, and Wyoming. The other states are placed into the moderate category (the minority party holds more than 36 percent of the seats but fewer than 46 percent).

Campaign Finance Laws

Campaign finance laws adopted by a state may have a significant impact on the amount of money available for candidates to spend. Herbert Alexander has documented the extensive variations in campaign finance laws (1991). He finds that some states have many restrictions on funding while other states have few, if any, restrictions or prohibitions concerning the sources of campaign funding. We anticipate that the stricter campaign finance laws will result in lower levels of district spending.

To test this proposition, we divided the states based on their campaign finance laws into three categories: low, medium, and high. States with low levels of restrictions set no limitations on direct contributions from corporations or labor unions, nor any limits on the amount of money

that political action committees (PACs) can contribute. States in this category include Idaho, Illinois, Missouri, Oregon, and Utah. Other states
have much more strict regulations on where candidates can receive campaign dollars. Two states in the sample (Minnesota and Wisconsin) prohibit corporate and labor funding and place limits on PAC contributions. In addition, these provide public funding to those candidates who
agree to adhere to spending limits. We categorize these states as having
the most strict campaign finance regulations (high category). The
remaining states in the sample are considered to be in the middle category and generally have prohibitions on corporate and union contributions in addition to some limits on the amount of PAC contributions.

Findings

Because general election competition is such an important factor
influencing district-level spending, we decided to include it in this analysis of the system-level factors. Districts are divided into those with high
competition (winner received 55 percent or less of the two-party vote)
and low competition (winner received greater than 55 percent of the
two-party vote).

How important are these state-level variables to levels of spending in
legislative districts? Figure 4-3 displays the average spending per eligible
voter across the three categories of professionalism (high, medium, and
low). As expected, the level of spending appears to increase with the
level of professionalism. This is true for districts with both high and low
levels of general election competition. Among highly competitive districts, average district spending is about $2.50 in professional legisla-
tures, but less than $1.50 in citizen legislatures. Similar differences can
be seen among districts with lower levels of general election competition.

The effects of state legislative professionalism on district-level spending should not be underestimated. An examination of average spending
differences between high and low competition districts across levels of
legislative professionalism makes this point clear. Figure 4-3 shows
that district spending in *low-competition* districts in states with highly
professional legislatures is actually higher than spending in *high-
competition* districts in citizen legislatures. Such findings highlight the
importance of legislative professionalism.

What about the effects of chamber competitiveness on district-level
spending? Figure 4-4 displays the average spending per eligible voter in
those districts where chamber competition is low, moderate, or high. A
positive relationship exists between chamber competition and level of
spending. Among high-competition districts in states with high levels of
chamber competition, average spending per eligible voter is approxi-

Figure 4-3   *District-Level Spending Per Eligible Voter by Legislative Professionalism and General Election Competition*

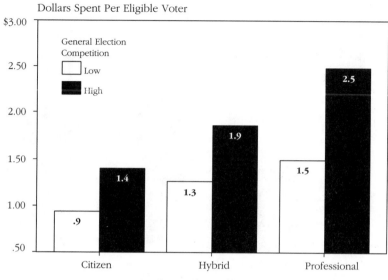

Note: Only districts where there was competition in either the primary or general election are included. High competition = winner received 55 percent or less of the two-party vote; low competition = winner received greater than 55 percent of the two-party vote.

mately $2.30, but among states with low chamber competition the amount spent is less than $1.50 per eligible voter.

Finally, what impact do campaign finance laws have on district-level spending? In Figure 4-5 states are grouped into those with low, moderate, or high restrictions on how candidates can receive their campaign funds, divided by levels of general election competition. As with the other system level variables, it is apparent that campaign finance laws have an influence on levels of spending. States with fewer restrictions seem to have higher rates of spending per eligible voter. Among highly competitive districts in states with low restrictions, slightly more than $2.00 per eligible voter is allocated, while similar districts in states with high restrictions have spending levels of about $1.30 per eligible voter.

ADDITIVE EFFECTS OF SELECTED FACTORS ON DISTRICT-LEVEL SPENDING

While we have examined independent effects of variables on levels of spending, we have not given much attention to the additive effects of

Figure 4-4   *District-Level Spending Per Eligible Voter by Level of Chamber Competition and General Election Competition*

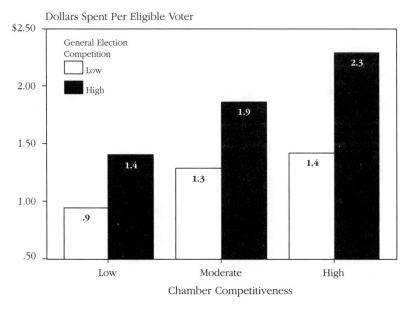

Note: Only districts where there was competition in either the primary or general election are included. High competition = winner received 55 percent or less of the two-party vote; low competition = winner received greater than 55 percent of the two-party vote. Chamber competitiveness is the percentage of seats held by the minority party prior to the election; low = 36 percent or fewer of the seats, moderate = more than 36 percent but fewer than 46 percent, high = more than 45 percent of the seats.

these variables. How does spending vary across districts when several of these factors are working in combination?

To examine these combined effects, a linear regression model has been used to determine which of the variables already discussed are the most important. Through this process it was found that three factors are both strong and consistent predictors of district spending. These variables include a legal factor (strictness of campaign finance laws), an electoral factor (district-level competition), and a state political factor (legislative professionalism).

The combined effects of these factors on levels of per eligible voter spending are displayed in Table 4-3. Each cell represents a different combination of these variables. The professionalism and district competition variables are measured in the same manner as they were in previous parts of this chapter. For the sake of simplicity, we have chosen to use a dichotomous measure for campaign finance laws (more restrictive or less restrictive) instead of the trichotomous measure previously

Figure 4-5   *District-Level Spending Per Eligible Voter by Strictness of Campaign Finance Laws and General Election Competition*

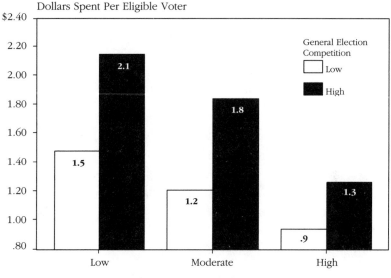

Campaign Finance Law Restrictions

Note: Only districts where there was competition in either the primary or general election are included. High competition = winner received 55 percent or less of the two-party vote; low competition = winner received greater than 55 percent of the two-party vote. Low restrictions = no limitations on direct contributions from corporations or labor unions, no limits on PAC contributions; moderate = prohibitions on corporate and union contributions in addition to some limits on the amount of PAC contributions; high = prohibits corporate and labor funding and places limits on PAC contributions, provides public funding to those candidates who agree to adhere to spending limits.

employed. States are divided into those with less restrictive campaign finance laws (at a maximum there are limits on contributions) and those with more restrictive laws (in addition to contribution limits there are prohibitions on corporate and union contributions and in some states public financing attached to spending limits).

The data in Table 4-3 show that spending varies dramatically across the different possible combinations. Spending is very low where we expect it to be low—in districts with low levels of district competition in states with more restrictive finance laws and less professional legislatures. Spending in such districts on average is about $1.09. Spending is nearly three times greater ($2.96) in districts where we would expect it to be higher—in districts with high levels of district competition in states with less restrictive finance laws and more professional legislatures. In combination, these factors appear to play a large role in influencing levels of spending in state legislative districts.

Table 4-3   *System- and District-Level Factors Affecting Average Spending Per Eligible Voter*

Campaign Finance Laws	District Competition	Legislative Professionalism		
		Low	Medium	High
More Restrictive	Low	$1.09 (N=127)	$0.91 (N=154)	$1.18 (N=211)
More Restrictive	High	$1.61 (N=72)	$1.34 (N=53)	$1.85 (N=40)
Less Restrictive	Low	$0.86 (N=233)	$1.47 (N=265)	$1.90 (N=170)
Less Restrictive	High	$1.22 (N=79)	$2.12 (N=115)	$2.96 (N=55)

Note: Only districts where there was competition in either the primary or general election are included.

CONCLUSION

This analysis shows clearly that campaign spending varies dramatically across state legislative districts. In some districts spending is rather low, while in others it is quite high. This variation exists both between and within individual states.

What seems to be driving the costs of state legislative elections? The biggest factor is the population of eligible voters in the district. Because it costs more money to contact a larger number of voters, spending is much higher in more heavily populated districts. A large part of the variance in spending across states is explained by this one variable.

However, population of the district cannot explain all the observed variation. Even when we controlled for district population by calculating a measure of spending per eligible voter, large differences across states remain. In addition, there are large variations in spending within states. Further investigation shows that electoral and structural features of districts are important determinants of spending. The number of candidates running, competition in the primary and general election campaigns, open seat contests, and the nature of the district (urban or rural) all contribute to higher levels of campaign spending per district. System-level features are also important with professionalism of the chamber, chamber competition, and less restrictive campaign finance laws all positively correlated with high rates of campaign spending. While each by itself can have an impact, in combination they contribute to large variations in spending across districts.

These findings have implications for those attempting to reform the campaign finance system. These results suggest that attempts to limit spending or reduce the size of contributions probably need to consider the characteristics of the legislative districts. Because a large portion of the variation in costs is determined by the number of eligible voters, what might be considered a reasonable spending limit or contribution limit in one state might be unreasonable in another. Where there are more potential voters in a district, the costs of campaigning are higher. Limits on spending that are set too low might prevent voters in heavily populated districts from hearing about some candidates, especially those who are new to the political scene. Limits on contributions and spending may have the unintended consequence of providing added advantages to candidates who are already well-known, especially incumbents.

Another finding that may have some bearing on reform efforts has to do with the correlation between competition and spending. While high spending is often perceived to inhibit competition, the present analysis appears to indicate the opposite. Spending is higher in districts when there are more candidates contesting elections and where both primary and general elections have slates of candidates running. From the perspective of this analysis, the high costs of some campaigns reflect a healthy degree of competition. The linkage between these variables needs to be explored in future studies, however, the findings from this chapter would seem to indicate that care be taken to ensure that reforms aimed at reducing spending do not also reduce levels of electoral competition.

Finally, these results point to the importance of system-level conditions such as the professionalism of the legislature and the strictness of campaign finance laws. While there is little to be done about professionalism, the importance of campaign finance laws provides some hope for reform efforts aimed at controlling spending. The findings from this chapter show that campaign finance laws can have an impact on levels of candidate spending. For example, district-level spending in Minnesota and Wisconsin is much lower than spending in states that have less stringent campaign finance guidelines. Thus, reforms aimed at regulating the flow of money into candidate campaigns can be effective. Whether or not these laws actually remove money from the political process, or whether they simply shift money from the hands of candidates into the hands of parties or interest groups making independent expenditures, remains to be determined.

NOTES

1. Please see Data section for an explanation concerning the choice of states used in the analysis.

2. The words *seat* and *district* are used almost interchangeably throughout this chapter, however, they are not the same thing. Two states in the analysis (Idaho and Washington) have districts that have more than one candidate assigned to each. These are considered multimember districts, but unlike "free-for-all districts" (districts where each candidate runs against the others) they have posts or seat assignments for which candidates run. In such districts, no candidate is running against all the others; they compete only against those running for the same seat or post within the district. The district boundaries and characteristics are the same for all the posts or seats within that particular district. For this analysis, the seat is the unit of analysis for those districts that have multimember districts with posts or seats.

3. Three states have some irregularities. District-level spending figures for Maine and Utah do not include spending by candidates who lost in the primary election. Because there were so few primary election candidates in 1992 in these states, this omission does not seem large. Also, the figures for Illinois include expenditures made only in 1992 and not for the entire election period (which for other states includes 1991 expenditures). Therefore, spending in Illinois is underestimated, but because little is usually spent during this period, the figures are probably close to the actual figure.

4. The data from Texas are from 1988 because this is the only year data are available in the form needed for this analysis. Texas campaign finance laws allow legislators to use their campaign funds to supplement their district office expenditures and living expenses during the legislative session. In order to use the Texas data, the expenditures were first "cleaned" of expenditures unrelated to the campaign. To accomplish this, each itemized line of expenditures was examined, with noncampaign spending excluded. This is a time-consuming task that has only been completed for the 1988 election period.

5. A high percentage of seats held by the minority party would indicate a high degree of chamber competitiveness.

6. The aggregated measure of spending is calculated the same for both single-member districts and free-for-all multimember districts, even though more than one candidate is elected in the multimember districts. Because more than one candidate is elected, we clearly expect spending to be higher in these districts.

7. While the median level of spending in most states is generally lower than the mean level of spending, the rank ordering of states on both measures is similar

8. District-level measures were created by dividing the number of each state's eligible voters by the total number of legislators elected in a given state The resulting figure represents the average voting age population of each state legislative district. Adjustments were made for states with multimember districts.

9. Only candidates who had competition in a primary or general election contest were considered to have been in an election. While unopposed primary and general election candidates in many states are often listed on the ballot and receive votes, they have no actual competition. For purposes of calculating this measure, only races where the candidate faced another major party candidate are counted (independent and third-party candidates are excluded).

10. This categorization is based on National Conference of State Legislatures' designations, as it appears in Patterson (1996, 176).

REFERENCES

Alexander, Herbert. 1991. *Reform and Reality: The Financing of State and Local Campaign.* New York: Twentieth Century Fund.

Gierzynski, Anthony, and David Breaux. 1991. "Money and Votes in State Legislative Elections." *Legislative Studies Quarterly* 16: 203–217.

Giles, Michael W., and Anita Pritchard. 1985. "Campaign Expenditures and Legislative Elections in Florida." *Legislative Studies Quarterly* 10: 71–88.

Heard, Alexander. 1960. *The Costs of Democracy.* Chapel Hill: University of North Carolina Press.

Holbrook, Thomas, and Charles Tidmarch. 1991. "Sophomore Surge in State Legislative Elections, 1968–1986." *Legislative Studies Quarterly* 16: 49–63.

Jacobson, Gary C., and Samuel Kernell. 1981. *Strategy and Choice in Congressional Elections,* 2nd ed. New Haven, Ct.: Yale University Press.

Jewell, Malcolm, and David Breaux. 1989. "The Effect of Incumbency on State Legislative Elections." *Legislative Studies Quarterly* 13: 495–514.

Jewell, Malcolm, and David Breaux. 1991. "Southern Primary and Electoral Competition and Incumbent Success." *Legislative Studies Quarterly* 16: 129–143.

Jones, Ruth. 1984. "Financing State Elections," in *Money and Politics in the United States,* edited by Michael J. Malbin, pp. 172–213. New Jersey: Chatham House.

Moncrief, Gary F. 1992. "The Increase in Campaign Expenditures in State Legislative Elections: A Comparison of Four Northwestern States." *Western Political Quarterly* 45: 549–558.

Mooney, Christopher Z. 1995. "Citizens, Structures, and Sister States: Influences on State Legislative Professionalism." *Legislative Studies Quarterly* XX (February): 47–67.

Neal, Tommy. 1992. "The Sky-High Cost of Campaigns." *State Legislatures* (May): 16–22.

Patterson, Samuel. 1996. "Legislative Politics in the States," in *Politics in the American States,* 6th ed., edited by Virginia Gray and Herbert Jacob. Washington, D.C.: CQ Press.

Rosenthal, Alan. 1981. *Legislative Life.* New York: Harper & Row.

Singer, Sandra. 1988. "The Arms Race of Campaign Financing." *State Legislatures* (July): 24–28.

Sorauf, Frank. 1992. *Inside Campaign Finance.* New Haven, Ct.: Yale University Press.

Stonecash, Jeffrey. 1990. "Campaign Finance in New York Senate Elections." *Legislative Studies Quarterly* 15: 247–262.

Tucker, Harvey J., and Ronald E. Weber. 1987. "State Legislative Election Outcomes: Contextual Effects and Legislative Performance Effects." *Legislative Studies Quarterly* 12: 537–553.

CHAPTER FIVE

Candidate Revenues and Expenditures in State Legislative Primaries

David A. Breaux and Anthony Gierzynski

The research on campaign finance has focused almost exclusively on campaign finance behavior in general elections, leaving us virtually in the dark regarding what goes on in the primaries (the exceptions being Welch 1976, Breaux and Gierzynski 1991). One of the main reasons that we are so uninformed about the financing of primaries is because researchers have been unable to obtain separate data on primary elections. This inability to obtain information on primary financing is due to the reporting practices utilized by the agencies that report on campaign finance practices. Many states simply do not report campaign finance data separately for primary and general elections. The lack of information has, consequently, prevented numerous questions concerning the role of money in primaries from being investigated, including:

- How much money is raised by candidates running in primary elections?
- Is the amount of money raised in the primaries more or less than the amount raised in general elections?
- Is the incumbency advantage in fund raising the same in primary and general elections?
- Does the incumbency advantage come from early fund raising or from fund raising during the primary or general election?
- How much money is spent by candidates running in legislative primaries?
- How does the amount of money spent in legislative primaries compare to the amount spent in general elections?
- What is the effect of campaign spending on the primary vote?

- Is the translation of money into votes conditioned by the cost of elections or the level of partisan competition for the office?
- What effect do campaign finance laws have on this process?

In this chapter we will search for answers to some of the above questions by examining the financing of state legislative primaries in several states. Unfortunately, the number of states included in our analysis is limited by the previously stated fact that many states simply do not report campaign finance data separately for primary and general elections. Given this limitation, this chapter will necessarily be more exploratory than other chapters in this volume. We will be analyzing data from various subsets of the states used in the rest of this book. This is due to different state practices in recording candidate finances.

PRIMARY ELECTIONS

Before turning to the financing of primary elections, a brief discussion of primary elections is in order. Primary elections are the means by which candidates in most states win their party's nomination for the general election. There are some things common to all primaries, and there are unique practices in some of the states with regard to the primaries.

Primaries tend to have lower turnout than general elections. Competition in primaries is greater when the chance of winning the general election is greater (Key 1949). Fewer primaries are contested than general elections (Jewell and Breaux 1991), and primaries differ from general elections in that in primaries one of the most important decision-making cues for voters—party affiliation—is absent. Without this information, voters must rely more heavily upon other information upon which to base their decision, information that may come from knowing the incumbent or from contact with the candidates. With all these factors complicating the primary election process, money often takes on an important role.

There are differences in the procedures that states set for primary elections. These legal factors can have an effect on campaign finance behavior. The date on which the primary is held varies from state to state (see Table 5-1 for the primary dates of some of the states we use). Some states have early primary dates (such as Illinois, which holds its primary in early March). Other states hold their primaries later in the year (such as Missouri, which holds its primary in early August). In a few states, the political party organizations play a role in either endorsing a candidate before the primary (Minnesota parties follow such a practice) or controlling who can run on the primary ballot (as in Colorado and

Delaware). In most of the states (and all the states studied here) the nominating decision is left completely up to the voters in the primary election. States also differ with regard to how "open" their primaries are. Some states allow only voters registered with that party to vote in the primary (such as Kentucky), while others allow voters to choose the party whose primary they want to participate in when they arrive to vote. One state, Alaska, allows voters to participate in different party's primaries for different offices.

Primary elections differ from general elections in some important ways, taking place under different legal and electoral conditions. These differences lead us to suspect that what goes on with regard to the financing of these contests is important: important for determining the nature of those contests and important because knowledge of that behavior can enhance our understanding of the overall picture of campaign finance behavior. The rest of this chapter will focus on the revenues raised and expenditures made in state legislative primary elections.

PRIMARY REVENUES

Raising campaign finance money during primary election seasons is important not just for those facing competition for their party's nomination, but also for raising money for the general election. This is especially true for those states in which the general election season is made short by a late primary. This section will examine revenue raising in the primaries, comparing it to revenue raising in the general elections and examining the advantage incumbents have in fund raising in primary versus general elections.

How Much?

One of the most basic questions with regard to campaign revenue in primary elections is: How much? How much money is raised by state legislative candidates during the primary election, and how does that amount compare to the amount raised during the general elections? The total and average revenue raised in primary and general elections by candidates in a number of states is presented in Table 5-1.

Not surprisingly, there is a great deal of variation in the total amount raised during primary elections. Candidates in California, the state in our analysis with the most professional legislature (i.e., a legislature with high pay, long sessions, and large staff), clearly tops the list, followed by candidates in Missouri, New Jersey, North Carolina, and Oregon. Candidates in Mississippi, the state in our analysis with one of the least professional legislatures, raised the least amount of money. The

Table 5-1 *Primary and General Election Revenues, All Candidates*

	Primary Date	Total Primary Revenue	Average Primary Revenue per Candidate	General Revenue	Average General Revenue	% Revenue Raised During Primary
California						
1986	6/3	$24,543,550	$139,452	$20,479,678	$132,127	54.5
1988	6/7	32,622,114	169,907	26,503,536	167,744	55.2
1990	6/5	26,883,759	144,536	13,067,795	96,087	67.3
1992	6/2	22,267,310	67,682	28,713,425	187,669	43.7
1994	6/7	31,309,633	121,355	25,893,218	165,982	54.7
New Jersey						
1989	6/10	1,851,369	10,702	11,125,962	64,312	14.3
1991	6/10	2,172,108	24,406	9,531,846	61,102	18.6
North Carolina						
1990	5/8	1,440,282	5,354	2,208,802	8,211	39.5
1992	5/5	1,124,209	4,291	2,140,636	8,265	34.4
Missouri						
1986	8/5	2,121,372	6,448	1,957,714	5,950	52.0
1988	8/2	2,691,894	7,917	2,353,104	6,921	53.4
1990	8/7	3,111,511	10,135	2,778,360	9,050	52.8
1992	8/4	3,217,597	8,603	2,962,003	7,920	52.1
Oregon						
1986	5/20	1,286,760	9,532	2,360,587	20,005	35.3
1990	5/15	1,848,212	12,488	3,891,999	29,385	32.2
1992	5/3	2,783,993	18,811	5,310,454	45,780	34.4
Mississippi						
1987	3/8	454,466	1,910	239,048	1,004	65.5
1991	6/5	204,512	1,028	356,278	1,790	36.5

average amount of money raised ranged from $1,028 by Mississippi candidates in 1991 to $169,907 by California candidates in 1988.

Missouri provides some evidence of the impact of the timing of the primary on the amount of money raised during the primary season. Although it is ranked fourth according to the classification scheme presented in chapter 1 (Table 1-2), candidates in Missouri raised the second highest amount during the primaries. This is most likely due, in part, to the fact that Missouri had the latest primary among all the states in the table. Such a late primary forces candidates to raise money (and sometimes spend money) for the general election during the primary season.

Perhaps more interesting is the comparison of primary and general election revenues. Primary revenue as a percent of the total revenue raised by candidates is presented in the last column of Table 5-1. With the exception of a few cases, the percentage of total revenue raised during primary elections is consistently between 30 and 60 percent of the total revenues raised. The exceptions are California in 1990 and Mississippi in 1987, where about 67 and 66 percent, respectively, of total revenues were raised during the primary, and New Jersey in both 1989 and 1991, where less than 20 percent of the revenues were raised during the primary.

In Mississippi a higher percentage of revenues raised in primaries is to be expected. Legislative elections are still dominated by one party, the Democrats. Consequently, primary elections in Mississippi should be where most of the competition happens. In 1991 Mississippi is more in line with the rest of the states in terms of the percentage of revenues raised in the primary. This may be due to the increase in Republican strength that has been a trend across the South (indeed, Mississippi had a Republican governor by 1991). The results for California are due to an overall drop in campaign revenues during that year. This is likely due in large part to the fact that 1990 is the election prior to redistricting, which may have suppressed competition; few serious candidates would want to win office for the first time only to have to run for reelection in a newly drawn district in 1992. This drop is also undoubtedly due, in part, to Proposition 73, which took effect for the first time that year. Proposition 73 banned two major sources of revenues for California assembly candidates: transfers from one candidate to another and legislative caucus campaign committees. The proposition was overturned by California courts before the 1992 elections.

Given the relatively late date of the New Jersey primaries, it is rather surprising that primary revenues make up so small a percentage of total revenues. The best possible explanation is the opposite of the explanation for the Mississippi results. Party competition at both the state and district level in New Jersey is very high. New Jersey rates a .910 out of 1.00 on the Ranney state competition index[1] according to Bibby and Holbrook (1996), and ranks eighth among the states with regard to district-level competition (Holbrook and Van Dunk 1993). The fierce competition in the general elections between the parties probably increases the amount of money poured late into the campaigns to try to tip the balance in the closest races. The parties are likely to give late contributions as a part of their strategy to target close races and New Jersey parties contribute a significant amount of money to legislative campaigns (see chapter 10).

Raising Money for Primaries or General Elections

Given the fact that many states hold primaries relatively close to their general elections, one has to wonder how much of the money raised during the primary season is being raised because there is a primary contest and how much is being raised with an eye toward the general elections. To answer this question, the amount of money raised in contested and uncontested primaries is presented in Table 5-2. While separating

Table 5-2   *Primary Revenues Raised by Candidates in Contested Versus Uncontested Primaries*

	Contested[a]	Uncontested	% of Total, Contested Primaries	Number of Candidates Contested	Number of Candidates Uncontested
California					
1986	$ 8,434,260	$16,109,290	34.4	123	106
1988	10,092,760	22,529,354	30.9	68	131
1990	11,705,919	15,180,840	43.5	114	103
1992	18,280,167	3,987,143	82.1	261	72
1994	13,738,241	17,571,392	43.9	167	103
Missouri					
1986	958,605	1,162,767	45.2	138	191
1988	1,227,246	1,464,648	45.6	172	168
1990	1,203,570	1,907,941	38.7	136	189
1992	1,568,488	1,649,109	48.7	190	184
Oregon					
1986	468,209	818,551	36.4	48	83
1990	648,353	1,199,859	54.0	60	87
1992	1,275,982	1,508,011	45.8	78	70
Mississippi					
1987	416,283	37,318	91.8	161	178
1991	116,452	88,060	56.9	64	135

[a]More than one candidate.

money raised by candidates in contested and uncontested primaries is far from a perfect indicator of how much money is raised for the primary and how much is raised for the general election (since some candidates may face minimal primary opposition, allowing them to save a large portion of the money raised during the primary season for the general election), it does provide a cursory look at this question.

In most states, it appears that much of the fund raising done by candidates during the primary election season is done with an eye toward the general election. Two obvious exceptions are the 1987 election in Mississippi, where more than 90 percent of the total money raised was by candidates with primary competition, and the 1992 election in California, where 82 percent of the funds came from candidates in contested races. We can think of two reasons why such a high percentage of the money raised in the primary in Mississippi was for contested races. One is the same as used above to explain the results in Table 5-1: in 1987 in Mississippi the real competition in this one-party Democratic state occurred in the primaries, not the general election. The last column of Table 5-2 bears this out: in 1987 there were 161 candidates in contested races and in 1991 there were only 64. A second explanation is that Mississippi had a very early primary in 1987 (March 8). An early primary gives candidates more time during the general election to raise money and thus reduces the need to raise money in the primary for the general election. When the state moved its primary to early June in 1991, the percent of revenues raised in contested elections fell to 57 percent, making it more like the rest of the states.

The high percentage of revenues raised by candidates in contested races in California in 1992 is undoubtedly due to increased primary competition generated by the state's redistricting. California's legislative districts had been drawn by the Democrats (to their advantage) following the 1980 census and the Republicans redrew the maps following the 1990 census, to their advantage. This change meant a great deal of uncertainty with regard to the general election. The uncertainty encouraged greater retirement of incumbents. Greater uncertainty and fewer incumbents means greater competition in the primaries because they both translate into a better chance of winning the general election. This reasoning is supported by the fact that there were 261 candidates in contested primaries in California that year, over 100 more than in previous years.

The Incumbency Advantage

The advantage incumbents have in raising money in general elections is well documented at both the state and congressional level. The question is: Does this advantage hold for primary elections as well? Also,

Table 5-3   *The Incumbency Advantage: Average Revenue in Contested Races*

	Primary Election			General Election		
	Challenger	Incumbent	Ratio	Challenger	Incumbent	Ratio
California						
1986	$ 7,791	$217,619	27.93	$ 44,085	$151,217	3.43
1988	65,507	566,950	8.65	113,793	231,843	2.04
1990	47,836	327,458	6.85	43,498	137,580	3.16
1992	22,895	201,565	8.80	101,515	282,278	2.78
1994	46,899	175,552	3.74	66,316	253,677	3.83
Illinois						
1986	10,150	36,211	3.57	20,267	76,430	3.77
1988	8,658	47,635	5.50	23,121	102,036	4.41
Missouri						
1986	4,416	14,676	3.32	4,847	14,448	2.98
1988	3,794	13,548	3.57	5,102	14,153	2.77
1990	5,684	20,554	3.62	8,323	18,364	2.21
1992	4,993	19,212	3.85	7,055	18,672	2.65
Oregon						
1986	4,780	14,678	3.07	15,814	23,681	1.50
1990	6,761	31,221	4.62	27,060	43,354	1.60
1992	7,224	42,118	5.83	27,430	54,913	2.00
Kansas						
1986	2,428	11,839	4.88	5,424	13,005	2.40
1988	2,146	6,968	3.25	5,742	13,555	2.36
1990	2,014	8,989	4.46	7,651	15,934	2.08
1992	2,387	6,696	2.81	6,127	16,365	2.67
Mississippi						
1987	1,154	3,953	3.43	3,431	3,799	1.11
1991	1,000	2,780	2.78	2,336	3,475	1.49

Note: The ratio is the incumbents' revenues compared to challengers' revenues.

how does the incumbency advantage compare to the advantage incumbents hold in general elections. To help answer these questions, the average revenue raised by incumbents and challengers in contested races during primary and general elections is presented in Table 5-3.[2]

It is clear that as in general elections, incumbents hold a substantial advantage over challengers in raising money for primaries. In fact, the ratio of incumbent revenues to challenger revenues is greater in eighteen of twenty cases. As in the case of the total amount of money raised (Table 5-1), the advantage in raising money enjoyed by incumbents appears to be conditioned by a state's level of legislative professionalism. The greatest advantage occurred in California, the state with the most professional legislature, where in 1986 incumbents out-raised challengers by an overwhelming ratio of almost 28 to 1. The lowest ratio of incumbent to challenger fund raising occurred in Mississippi, where in 1991 incumbents were still able to out-raise challengers by a ratio of almost 3 to 1.

Having revenue data broken down by primary and general election cycles also allows us to take a preliminary look at when the incumbency advantage in raising money occurs. Do incumbents hold an advantage over challengers because they are able to raise money early, or is the incumbency advantage in fund raising one that occurs throughout the year? Table 5-4 presents data on fund raising for *general election candidates* tracked over the electoral cycle. More specifically, the table includes general election candidates' beginning balances, primary election revenues, and general election revenues.

It appears that in most states the advantage in raising money held by incumbents comes from the early start they get. Beginning balances for incumbents are simply overwhelming relative to that of challengers. This is particularly true in California, where in both 1990 and 1992 the ratios indicate that incumbents began their campaigns with more than 100 times as much money as did challengers. Incumbents continue that advantage in early fund raising in the primaries, where the ratio of incumbent revenues to challenger revenues is uniformly greater than the incumbent to challenger ratio in the general election. The general election period seems to be where challengers reduce the gap in fund raising, though, in most cases, they remain at a distinct disadvantage.

In sum, the amount of money raised during primary elections varies in ways that seem to be associated with a state's level of legislative professionalism, as well as political and legal factors. Generally, 30 to 60 percent of all revenues raised in an election year is raised during the primary season. A lot of the money raised by candidates during the primaries is raised by those who face no primary opposition (the two exceptions being cases where there was a great deal of competition in the primary and an early primary date). As in general elections, incumbents enjoy an advantage over challengers in raising money. The incumbency advantage in general elections seems to result from early activity. As a result of carrying over surplus money from their previous election and their significantly greater ability to raise money during the primaries, incumbents are able to enter the general election with rather hefty campaign war chests, creating an advantage in fund raising that most challengers simply cannot overcome.

PRIMARY EXPENDITURES

Candidate spending in primary elections is of interest for a number of reasons. The obvious reason candidates spend money in the primaries is

Table 5-4 Charting the Incumbency Advantage, General Election Candidates

	Average Beginning Balance			Average Primary Revenue			Average General Revenue		
	Challenger	Incumbent	Ratio	Challenger	Incumbent	Ratio	Challenger	Incumbent	Ratio
California									
1986	$ 0	$38,510		$15,329	$247,419	16.14	$ 44,085	$149,562	3.39
1988	850	34,310	40.36	25,075	351,105	14.00	109,342	228,263	2.09
1990	230	34,088	148.21	48,619	275,205	5.66	43,498	132,892	3.06
1992	480	54,697	113.95	20,833	144,299	6.93	109,503	274,099	2.50
1994	1,010	27,119	26.85	22,316	313,795	14.06	66,316	250,249	3.77
Missouri									
1986	789	5,028	6.37	2,717	9,717	3.58	4,847	9,683	2.00
1988	683	6,305	9.23	2,721	12,486	4.59	5,044	11,586	2.30
1990	216	5,905	27.34	5,132	14,712	2.87	8,323	12,998	1.56
1992	1,099	7,319	6.66	3,411	15,323	4.49	6,955	14,643	2.11
Oregon									
1986	63	2,619	41.57	6,416	13,463	2.10	16,828	22,572	1.34
1990	0	4,867		7,916	21,435	2.71	26,530	41,416	1.56
1992	531	8,136	15.32	11,331	33,113	2.92	31,737	52,454	1.65
Mississippi									
1987	0	6		947	2,351	2.48	2,478	980	0.40
1991	0	0		43	1,584	36.84	1,691	1,737	1.03

Note: The ratio is the incumbents' revenues compared to challengers' revenues.

to win the primary. As with fund raising, the impact of candidate financial activity during the primary election season is not limited to the primaries. Unopposed candidates (as well as candidates in contested primaries) gain by spending during the primary season. Nonincumbents can use the time to build name recognition and incumbents can spend preemptively to inoculate themselves against attacks from the opposition.

How Much?

Just as with candidate revenue, the most basic question regarding candidate expenditures during primary elections is: How much? How much money do candidates spend in primaries, and how does this compare with the amount they spend in general elections? The total and average expenditure for all candidates in primary and general elections is presented in Table 5-5.

Table 5-5   *Expenditures During Primary and General Elections*

	Primary Expen- diture	Average Primary Expen- diture	General Election Expen- diture	Average General Election Expen- diture	% Expen- diture in Primary
California					
1986	$21,921,676	$109,063	$23,048,287	$148,699	48.7
1988	26,846,972	140,560	32,104,020	212,609	45.5
1990	23,860,528	128,282	17,264,999	126,949	58.0
1992	19,735,333	59,986	30,558,377	205,090	39.2
1994	28,457,378	108,616	29,494,644	189,068	49.1
New Jersey					
1989	1,275,723	7,374	9,043,146	52,273	12.4
1991	1,385,982	8,011	8,244,028	52,510	14.4
North Carolina					
1990	1,199,409	4,459	2,258,353	8,395	34.7
1992	900,880	3,753	1,968,013	8,375	31.4
Missouri					
1986	1,245,321	3,785	1,168,265	3,551	51.6
1988	1,535,458	4,516	1,445,783	4,252	51.5
1990	1,679,631	5,471	1,628,605	5,305	50.8
1992	2,001,245	5,351	1,839,372	4,918	52.1
Oregon					
1986	917,905	6,039	2,289,323	16,352	28.6
1990	1,388,896	9,448	3,296,225	25,752	29.6
1992	1,702,922	11,585	3,650,039	31,197	31.8
Mississippi					
1987	604,045	2,538	309,339	1,230	66.1
1991	226,393	1,143	484,148	2,433	31.9

The conclusions that can be drawn from the data in Table 5-5 are similar to those drawn from the revenue data in Table 5-1. As with candidate revenue, there is great variation in the total amount of money spent by candidates running in primaries. Moreover, the variation in candidate expenditures appears to be correlated with a state's level of legislative professionalism. Primary spending totals range from more than $26 million by candidates running in California in 1988 to approximately $226,000 by candidates running in Mississippi in 1991. The average amount of money spent by candidates running in primaries ranged from $140,560 in California in 1988 to $1,143 in Mississippi in 1991.

In terms of the proportion of election year spending that occurs during the primary, about 30 to 60 percent of all expenditures made during an election year are made during the primary (with the exception of Mississippi). Candidates clearly spend less than they raise during the primaries. To see this, primary revenues, average primary revenues, and the percent of revenues raised during the primary from Table 5-1 are compared to the corresponding expenditure figures in Table 5-5. This comparison adds further evidence to the notion that a great deal of fund raising during the primaries is for use in the general election.

Expenditures by Party and Incumbency

How does spending differ by party and by incumbency? The data in Table 5-6 address this issue. The totals were obtained by calculating the average expenditure for Democratic and Republican incumbents, challengers, and open-seat candidates.

As in the case of fund raising, incumbents appear to enjoy an advantage in spending over challengers. The average amount of money spent by both Democratic and Republican incumbents is higher in every election cycle in every state. Open-seat candidates also spend, on average, much more than challengers in every single case. In fact they spent, on average, more than incumbents in seven cases (see the bold entries in Table 5-6). The high level of spending in open-seat races is due to the very reason they are called "open" seats: there is no incumbent. The lack of an incumbent means the odds of winning both the primary and the general election are greater because no candidate has the advantages that come with incumbency (i.e., greater name recognition, the perquisites of office, and, as demonstrated above, superior fund raising). This encourages candidates with strong credentials to run, which increases competition, which increases the amount of money spent.

When comparing candidates across party some differences in spending appear in the two states with the lowest level of competition be-

Table 5-6   *Mean Primary Expenditures, by Party and Incumbency*

	Democrats			Republicans		
	Challenger	Incum-bents	Open	Challenger	Incum-bents	Open
California						
1986	$ 8,400	$233,541	$160,981	$ 7,503	$154,682	$103,796
1988	44,581	289,361	233,490	29,213	252,798	114,636
1990	34,421	230,458	80,896	49,398	234,518	108,258
1992	12,316	135,493	48,173	18,942	154,029	63,068
1994	29,480	312,714	87,559	22,836	222,002	74,735
Missouri						
1986	3,974	5,037	4,200	2,211	3,278	2,526
1988	2,889	5,716	**6,860**	2,733	3,362	**5,196**
1990	4,364	6,469	**8,851**	3,998	5,562	4,463
1992	4,241	9,936	5,383	2,407	3,783	**4,750**
Oregon						
1986	2,975	7,792	7,581	3,940	7,759	**13,456**
1990	5,249	15,634	11,197	6,973	13,172	9,084
1992	7,077	14,821	10,838	10,130	13,532	**15,077**
Mississippi						
1987	2,174	2,681	**4,334**	247	1,312	2,442
1991	969	1,868	1,095	0	0	44

Note: Bold entries indicate races where open-seat candidates outspent incumbents.

tween Democrats and Republicans. In Missouri, Democratic incumbents spent more money in their primaries than did Republican incumbents. In Mississippi, all Democratic candidates spent more than their Republican counterparts. The Democratic party dominance in these states leaves many district constituencies lopsided in favor of the Democratic party.[3] Thus, entrance to the legislature has to come through the Democratic primaries in these districts. Republicans are not only competitive in fewer districts, but as a minority party, they probably conserve their resources for competitive general election races.

Money and the Vote

One of the more interesting but difficult questions to answer is to what extent candidate spending in primary elections influences performance at the polls? In more blunt terms, does money buy party nominations in the primary? Table 5-7 presents the average amount of money spent by primary winners, losers, and unopposed candidates.

The numbers provide some initial evidence of the importance of spending in primary elections: in every election cycle in every state, the average amount of money spent by winners is greater than the average

Table 5-7   *Average Expenditures in Primary Elections, by Outcome*

	Losers	Winners	Ratio	Unopposed
California				
1986	$70,138	$108,874	1.55	$126,206
1988	78,067	248,508	3.18	134,465
1990	62,450	202,241	3.24	135,634
1992	42,553	110,705	2.60	46,487
1994	67,312	117,770	1.75	146,412
Illinois				
1986	9,652	19,942	2.07	N/A
1988	10,942	27,204	2.49	N/A
Missouri				
1986	4,753	6,675	1.40	2,512
1988	4,763	7,564	1.59	3,071
1990	5,741	11,984	2.09	3,684
1992	4,529	10,268	2.27	3,705
Oregon				
1986	4,587	10,040	2.19	5,580
1990	4,325	16,693	3.86	9,300
1992	9,264	15,048	1.62	11,163
Kansas				
1986	3,303	4,354	1.32	N/A
1988	2,324	3,333	1.43	N/A
1990	2,316	4,001	1.73	N/A
1992	2,141	3,475	1.62	N/A
Mississippi				
1987	2,937	4,455	1.52	247
1991	2,074	2,750	1.33	534

Note: The ratio is the winners' expenditures compared to the challengers'. N/A = not available.

amount spent by losers. The average amount of money spent by candidates who were unopposed in their primaries provides us with more evidence that much of the money spent in the primary is spent with an eye toward the general election. This is most obvious in California, where from 1986 to 1994 the average amount of money spent by candidates without primary opposition is greater than the average amount spent by losing candidates.

Comparing the average expenditures of winners and losers, while suggestive, does not give us sound evidence that candidate spending affects candidate performance at the polls. The average expenditures for winners may be higher than the average for losers for a number of reasons that have nothing to do with the outcome of the primary race. The difference, for example, could be due to the incumbency factor: incumbents are more likely to win the primary and incumbents (as we have seen earlier in this chapter) are also better fund-raisers. In order to more rigorously assess the impact of candidate spending in primaries, other aspects of the race that could affect the outcome, like the presence of an incumbent, must be controlled for. This is done using a statistical technique known as multiple regression. Multiple regression allows us to isolate the effect of candidate spending on their primary vote share regardless of the incumbency status of the candidate, the amount the candidate's opponents spend, the number of candidates in the primary, and the expected competitiveness of the race. When such an analysis was conducted, a statistically significant positive relationship between candidate spending and their vote share was found in seventeen of the twenty cases in the study. Furthermore, candidates' opponents' expenditures had a statistically negative impact on a candidate's share of the vote in eighteen of twenty cases. For the full results of the regression analysis see the Appendix Table 5A-1. The rest of the discussion will focus on what was found with regard to the impact of candidate spending.

The results of the regression analysis in Appendix Table 5A-1 were used to calculate how much candidates have to increase their campaign spending to increase their share of the primary vote by one percentage point (note that many of these races are multicandidate affairs, so one point can make a great difference). The data in Table 5-8 present the average amount of additional expenditures required to increase a candidate's primary vote by that one percentage point.

As expected, there is considerable interstate variation in the amount needed to increase a candidate's share of the vote. In states where the cost of primary campaigns is relatively high, candidates must spend more to increase their share of the vote than do candidates in states where the cost of primary campaigns is relatively low. For example, candidates running in California in 1988 needed to spend an additional $33,333 in order to increase their share of the primary vote by one percent. Candidates running in Kansas in 1988 needed to increase their spending by only $625 to purchase an additional one percent of the vote.

In sum, expenditures in the primary, like revenues, vary dramatically from state to state, with greater primary spending occurring in the more professional states and the states with less party competition. Expenditures in the primary constitute 30 to 60 percent of the expenditures made during the entire election year. Candidates do not spend all of what they raise during this period in the primary election. This fact, plus the high levels of spending by unopposed candidates, demonstrates that a lot of the financial activity that goes on in the primary is not necessarily for the primary but is also conducted for the general election con-

Table 5-8   *Expenditures by Candidate and Opponents Needed to Change Candidates' Vote by One Percentage Point*

	Candidate	Opponents
California		
1986	$16,667	($250,000)
1988	33,333	(25,000)
1990	20,000	(33,333)
1992	20,000	(33,333)
1994	14,286	(50,000)
Illinois		
1986	3,333	(5,000)
1988	5,000	(5,000)
Missouri		
1986	2,000	(2,000)
1988	1,000	(1,667)
1990	1,429	(3,333)
1992	2,500	(2,500)
Oregon		
1986	1,111	(1,111)
1990	2,000	(2,500)
1992	2,500	(3,333)
Kansas		
1986	1,429	(909)
1988	625	(1,000)
1990	909	(1,111)
1992	909	(769)
Mississippi		
1987	10,000	(10,000)
1991	10,000	(10,000)

Note: For an explanation of how numbers were calculated, see Table 5A-1 in chapter appendix. Opponents' entries are the amount needed to decrease a candidate's vote by one percentage point.

tests. Incumbents tend to spend the most in the primary, though there are a number of instances where the average spending by open-seat candidates is greater than that of incumbents. Finally, it is clear that the money candidates spend in the primary is important for their performance in the primaries, a finding that supports a previous study of ours (Breaux and Gierzynski 1991).

CONCLUSION

The purpose of this chapter was to begin to shed some light on candidate financial activity during the primary election. Even with the limited number of states available, some consistent patterns in that financial activity were found, patterns that have implications for candidates for state legislative office and for those who wish to reform the financing of elections. One of the biggest problems with campaign finance is the skewed distribution of money. This study makes it clear that the incumbent advantage in campaign money has its roots early on, not only in what they start with but also in what they raise during the primaries (which is not necessarily spent to win a primary). The implication of this finding is that challengers may need to begin their campaigns earlier in order to be competitive. Reformers who wish to reduce the inequality among candidates need to be aware that this head start might make reforms such as strict limits on contributions an even greater handicap for challengers.

In order to determine whether what was found in this study extends to most states, more data are needed for analysis. Hopefully, as more states computerize their campaign finance records in more sophisticated ways, researchers will be able to extend our knowledge about primaries beyond the states examined here.

Appendix

To assess the impact of candidate spending on the vote, the candidates' vote share is regressed on the candidates' spending, the spending of the candidates' opponents, a variable indicating whether the candidate was an incumbent, a variable indicating whether the candidate was an open seat candidate, the average vote for the candidate's party in the district (not available in the election following redistricting), a variable indicating whether the race involved three candidates, and a variable indicating whether the race involved four or more candidates. The results are shown in Table 5A-1.

The numbers indicate the change in the candidate's share of the vote for each one unit increase in the factor while holding all other factors constant. For example, the variable for incumbent equals either 1 or 0— 1 if the candidate was an incumbent and 0 if not. When the variable goes from 0 to 1, meaning the candidate is an incumbent, the candidate's vote increases 42.92 percent in the case of the 1986 election in California (regardless of the other factors that can affect the vote). The numbers for the spending variables are small because the unit is a dollar: one dollar increase in spending will not increase a candidate's vote much (.0003 of a percentage point in the case of the 1986 election in Illinois), so one should view it in terms of thousands of dollars (an increase in spending of $1,000 in 1986 in Illinois increases the candidate's vote percent by .3 of a percentage point).

Table 5A-1 Regression Analysis Results

	Candidate Spending	Opponents' Spending	Incumbent	Open Seat	Average Vote	3 Candidate Race	4 or More Candidate Race	Constant	Adjusted R2	Number
California										
1986	0.00006	-0.000004	42.92	-1.65	-0.51	-11.80	-26.06	68.68	0.64	78
1988	0.00003	-0.00004	21.05	3.84	-0.10	-13.22	-7.79	52.58	0.67	66
1990	0.00005	-0.00003	10.71	0.52	-0.05	-11.08	-14.41	48.80	0.69	87
1992	0.00005	-0.00003	15.59	2.88	n/a	-14.87	-23.13	46.23	0.65	253
1994	0.00007	-0.00002	15.57	-0.96	n/a	-13.06	-24.16	44.95	0.68	156
Illinois										
1986	0.0003	-0.0002	25.79	8.10	-0.21	-11.33	-14.45	54.60	0.57	106
1988	0.0002	-0.0002	23.72	7.25	-0.17	-10.52	-18.92	53.97	0.66	101
Missouri										
1986	0.0005	-0.0005	-0.32	3.43	0.38	-13.26	-15.71	38.60	0.65	138
1988	0.0010	-0.0006	19.11	9.14	0.04	-8.60	-12.43	37.91	0.43	172
1990	0.0007	-0.0003	28.60	10.20	-0.15	-14.20	-21.88	46.94	0.60	94
1992	0.0004	-0.0004	17.42	6.64	n/a	-14.89	-20.67	44.27	0.51	190
Oregon										
1986	0.0009	-0.0009	16.92	7.56	n/a	-10.80	-8.84	45.25	0.55	60
1990	0.0005	-0.0004	11.69	0.10	-.07	-13.58	-18.08	51.41	0.54	58
1992	0.0004	-0.0003	22.59	2.68	n/a	-12.91	n/a	45.78	0.54	77
Kansas										
1986	0.0007	-0.0011	10.95	10.46	-0.02	-13.05	n/a	49.61	0.26	68
1988	0.0016	-0.0010	14.60	4.16	-0.08	-12.08	-19.96	49.59	0.38	76
1990	0.0011	-0.0009	15.71	3.46	n/a	-12.48	-19.62	45.17	0.52	162
1992	0.0011	-0.0013	11.83	2.42	n/a	-12.36	-23.34	47.61	0.46	141
Mississippi										
1987	0.0001	-0.0001	19.83	8.57	-0.05	-13.65	n/a	45.38	0.34	157
1991	0.0001	-0.0001	11.35	5.67	-3.52	n/a	n/a	44.32	0.12	62

The bold numbers are those that pass a test of statistical significance—that is, we can be 95 percent confident that the factors have a real impact on the vote.

NOTES

1. The Ranney Index is a measure of party competition at the state level that is computed from gubernatorial election results and party control of the state legislature.
2. We define incumbency by whether any candidate in the district was running for reelection in either primary. All nonincumbent candidates in both primaries were considered challengers if an incumbent was running in either primary.
3. In terms of district-level competitiveness, as measured by Holbrook and Van Dunk (1993), Missouri and Mississippi rank forty-third and forty-seventh, respectively.

REFERENCES

Bibby, John F., and Thomas M. Holbrook. 1996. "Parties and Elections." In *Politics in the American States: A Comparative Analysis,* edited by Virginia Gray and Herbert Jacob. Washington, D.C.: CQ Press.

Breaux, David, and Anthony Gierzynski. 1991. " 'It's Money That Matters': Campaign Expenditures and State Legislative Primaries." *Legislative Studies Quarterly* 16: 429–443.

Holbrook, Thomas M., and Emily Van Dunk. 1993. "Electoral Competition in the American States." *American Political Science Review* 87: 955–962.

Jewell, Malcolm E., and David Breaux. 1991. "Southern Primary and Electoral Competition and Incumbent Success." *Legislative Studies Quarterly* 16: 129–143.

Key, V. O. 1949. *Southern Politics in State and Nation.* New York: Alfred A. Knopf.

Welch, William P. 1976. "The Effectiveness of Expenditures in State Legislative Races." *American Politics Quarterly* 4: 336–356.

CHAPTER SIX

Expenditures and Election Results

William E. Cassie and David A. Breaux

The amount of money being spent on elections is often perceived by the American public as a significant problem. While the cost of an election may be considered by some as simply too high, the more troubling issues arise when money is perceived to actually influence the election results. If campaign expenditures substantially affect election outcomes, then the system is open to the charge that elections in the United States can be bought and sold. Moreover, if money is extremely important in elections, then those who contribute the money—especially large contributors—may be able to buy favoritism with elected officials. The states provide an interesting arena in which to investigate the relationship between money and elections because of the great variations in political and financial environments.

The role that money plays in shaping election outcomes has received a great deal of attention. Recent research has brought us to a basic understanding of the empirical relationship between money and votes. It is widely accepted that there is a positive relationship between candidate expenditures and votes in congressional elections (Green and Krasno 1990, Jacobson 1980, Thomas 1989), state legislative primaries and general elections (Breaux and Gierzynski 1991, Caldeira and Patterson 1982, Gierzynski and Breaux 1991, Gierzynski and Breaux 1993, Giles and Pritchard 1985, Tucker and Weber 1987, Welch 1976), and gubernatorial elections (Jewell 1984, Morehouse 1990). It is also recognized that the relationship between candidate spending and votes is conditioned by whether the candidate is an incumbent or challenger, with challengers' expenditures having a larger impact than incumbents' expenditures. Furthermore, the impact of candidate spending tends to follow the principle of diminishing returns, with initial expenditures having a larger impact on the vote than spending at higher levels. This is especially true for relatively unknown candidates.

Understanding the relationship between expenditures and election results requires that we look not only at winners and losers, but also at the level of competition. David Mayhew (1974) first introduced the concept of "vanishing marginals" in congressional elections, but the same phenomenon has been observed in state legislative elections (Garand 1991; Weber, Tucker, and Brace 1991; Jewell and Breaux 1988). The term *vanishing marginals* refers to the decline in the number of districts in which elections are competitive. Competitive districts are sometimes referred to as "marginal" districts. The decline in the overall number of these marginal districts is often attributed to an increase in the electoral advantage held by incumbents. The disparity between incumbents and challengers in campaign funding has been identified as one possible component of this advantage.

The large sample of states used in this study allows us to examine the linkage between expenditures, incumbency advantage, and vanishing marginals. One important question addressed in this chapter is: Does money buy elections? More specifically, do the candidates who spend the most money usually win? If so, under what conditions does money seem to be particularly important in shaping the outcome of an election? There are many factors that affect the outcome of an election and it is simplistic to suggest that money alone can dictate the results. Elections are often viewed in terms of who wins and who loses, but the level of competition is also important. If money is critical to being competitive in an election, then the *lack* of money may in fact have a major impact on the outcome. Therefore, in this chapter attention will be focused on the relationship between money and electoral competition.

It is important to understand that the potential relationship between money and elections is veiled in a "chicken and egg" controversy that cannot be answered but must be addressed. The controversy is whether money actually *causes* election results, or whether money simply goes to those candidates who are already most popular with the voters and would win the election anyway. It is, in other words, a question of causation. Similarly, are incumbents advantaged by having more money available, or do incumbents get more money because they have served their district well, are popular, and thus are virtually guaranteed reelection regardless of the money received and spent? These questions cannot be answered definitively with the data available. This controversy will be addressed at the end of this chapter.

How do various factors condition the relationship between money and votes? For example, does the impact of money on votes vary with the cost of elections? As seen in Table 3-1, there is a considerable amount of variation in the cost of elections across states. For example, elections are very expensive in California; moderately expensive in Illinois, New Jersey, Oregon, and Washington; and quite inexpensive in Montana, Maine, and Wyoming. It is plausible that as costs increase, many candidates will find it more difficult to compete financially.

Is the impact of money on votes conditioned by legislative professionalism? States with more professional legislatures are characterized by higher salaries and greater institutional resources, making legislative service more attractive. This may in turn increase competition for seats and drive up election costs. This would suggest fewer, but better financed, candidates. It is also possible that professionalism provides incentives for incumbents to use their resources to gain an even greater financial advantage over would-be opponents.

How does party competition affect the relationship between expenditures and results? Greater statewide competition may lead to an increased number of well-financed candidates because seats are viable for either party. Similarly, because of the higher degree of competition, it is possible that challengers can be competitive with less funding because the voters may be focused on the parties as much as on the individuals.

Is the relationship between money and votes responsive to variation in campaign finance laws? Some states prohibit direct contributions from unions and corporations, others impose relatively low limits on individual and PAC contributions, and still others provide for public financing of legislative races. These are the types of issues that underlie the analysis presented in this chapter. The data discussed are based upon campaigns in eighteen states; the 1992 election campaign results are used for fifteen of the states, while data for Mississippi and New Jersey are from 1991 and Illinois are from 1988.

Winning and Spending

Does the candidate who spends the most money usually win? The answer to this question is definitively "yes." Figure 6-1 displays the percentage of contested races in which the winner outspent the loser. A clear (and often substantial) majority of races in every state is won by the candidate spending the most money. In eleven of the states the percentage exceeds 80 percent; in only three states (New Jersey, Utah, and Wyoming) does the winner outspend the loser less than 70 percent of the time.

It appears that some of the factors identified as possibly affecting variations in campaign finance across states are at work here. Of the seven states where the percentage falls below 80 percent, five (Maine, Mississippi, Montana, Utah, and Wyoming) are states with relatively in-

Figure 6-1 *Winners Outspending Losers in Contested Races, in Percentages*

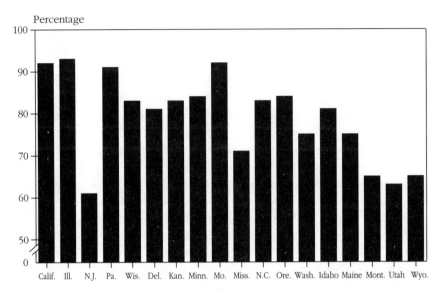

Note: Figures are from 1992, except for Mississippi and New Jersey (1991) and Illinois (1988). States are grouped by legislative professionalism: California, most professional to least professional. Contested races are those in which the candidate receives at least 10 percent, but less than 90 percent, of the general election vote.

expensive elections. As the level of spending decreases, it becomes easier for candidates to compete financially and therefore it becomes more likely that a losing candidate might outspend his or her opponent. The remaining two states with relatively lower percentages of winners outspending losers are New Jersey and Washington. In both of these states legislative elections are relatively expensive, yet the percentage of winners who outspend losers is comparatively low. In fact, New Jersey is the lowest among the eighteen states. These two states have one important characteristic in common—they are two of the most competitive states (in terms of party competition) in the sample (Holbrook and Van Dunk 1993). State party competition creates a situation whereby challengers, as well as candidates for open seats, are often well funded.

Despite the variation among the states, it is obvious that the candidate with the most money usually wins the election. Does this mean that money buys elections? This question cannot be answered yet, but at this point it seems apparent that there is a strong relationship between winning and spending. This is true, even in those states where the costs of elections are comparatively low.

The Incumbency Advantage

To examine the relationship between money and elections more closely, we turn our focus to only those races involving incumbents. The success of incumbents in state legislative elections is well documented, and campaign financing has been identified as one component of the "incumbency advantage."

Table 6-1 displays the percentage of incumbents in contested elections who win their elections. Table 6-1 also shows the percentage of incumbents who outspend their opponents. The results confirm conventional wisdom: incumbents usually win and generally outspend their challengers. The reelection rate for incumbents is more than 75 percent in all the states. In ten of the states the reelection rate exceeds 90 percent (and these figures *exclude* incumbents who ran unopposed; if they were included the reelection rate for all incumbents would be even higher).

A large majority of incumbents in all the states outspend their challengers. This ranges from a low of 66 percent in Utah to 100 percent in California. It appears that the states with less professional legislatures

Table 6-1   *Incumbency Advantage in Election Victories and Spending in Contested Elections, in Percentages*

State	Incumbents Defeating Challengers	Incumbents Outspending Challengers
California	94	100
Illinois	98	95
New Jersey	78	90
Pennsylvania	98	92
Wisconsin	93	79
Delaware	96	81
Kansas	88	83
Minnesota	91	95
Missouri	90	93
Mississippi	82	86
North Carolina	83	79
Oregon	90	93
Washington	93	91
Idaho	89	75
Maine	91	71
Montana	77	68
Utah	79	66
Wyoming	78	67

Note: Figures are from 1992, except for Mississippi and New Jersey (1991) and Illinois (1988). States are grouped by legislative professionalism: California, most professional to least professional. Contested races are those in which the candidate receives at least 10 percent, but less than 90 percent, of the general election vote.

are those in which incumbents are sometimes outspent by challengers. This is due, most likely, to lower costs of campaigning in these states. It is also worth noting that the incumbents in these states win far more often than they outspend their opponents. New Jersey stands out as the state where the percentage of incumbents outspending challengers is considerably higher than the percentage of incumbents winning. These findings help explain the low percentage of winners who outspent losers in New Jersey.

There is some evidence that public financing may have an impact on the relationship between money and votes. Wisconsin incumbents outspend their challengers only 79 percent of the time (still a vast majority of the time, but low compared to other states), even though incumbents were successful in 93 percent of their elections. It is possible that this is due to the public financing available to candidates. Wisconsin is the only state with a professional legislature in which the proportion of incumbents outspending challengers is less than 90 percent. The evidence is mixed, however, since a similar result is not found in Minnesota—the other state that had significant public financing of state legislative elections in 1992. It is possible that the manner in which the public financing is allocated (which is different in Wisconsin and Minnesota) creates these differences.

These findings support the notion that incumbents have an advantage and that money may be part of that advantage. It is still unclear if money simply flows to projected winners or if money helps to *produce* winners. If money actually affects the electoral outcome, then we can expect that as challenger spending increases, their electoral results will improve. To further address this question we take a more detailed look at the funding advantage enjoyed by incumbents and focus on the relationship between money and competitive elections.

Vanishing Marginals

Most incumbents spend more on their campaigns than their opponents, but how much more? In chapter 3, Gary Moncrief describes the differences in median incumbent and challenger spending for 1994 elections. These differences are often extreme. This relationship will be examined in more detail, using the full data set for the 1992 elections. This is accomplished by focusing on the proportion of challengers in each state who are able to reach specific levels of funding, relative to the incumbent. A ratio of challenger-to-incumbent spending is calculated for each contested race and then these ratios are placed into four quartiles: (1) challenger spends 25 percent or less than the incumbent, (2) chal-

Table 6-2   *Ratio of Challenger to Incumbent Spending in Contested Race, in Percentages*

State	Challenger Spending as Percentage of Incumbent Spending			
	0–25	26–50	51–75	76–100
California	74	10	6	10
Illinois	63	18	8	11
New Jersey	62	22	4	12
Pennsylvania	60	18	10	12
Wisconsin	17	21	26	36
Delaware	31	23	12	35
Kansas	35	26	14	25
Minnesota	18	41	22	20
Missouri	41	26	19	14
Mississippi	43	18	18	21
North Carolina	32	15	15	38
Oregon	48	21	14	17
Washington	47	25	9	19
Idaho	25	19	28	28
Maine	35	18	10	36
Montana	13	21	13	54
Utah	18	11	21	50
Wyoming	22	11	17	50

Note: Figures are from 1992, except for Mississippi and New Jersey (1991) and Illinois (1988). States are grouped by legislative professionalism: California, most professional to least professional. Contested races are those in which the candidate receives at least 10 percent, but less than 90 percent, of the general election vote.

lenger spends between 26 and 50 percent as much as the incumbent, (3) challenger spends between 51 and 75 percent of what the incumbents spends, and (4) challenger spends more than 75 percent of the incumbent's spending total. The results appear in Table 6-2.

The findings indicate that incumbents not only outspend their opponents but often this difference is dramatic. This is evident by examining the column representing the percentage of challengers whose total spending is 25 percent or less of the total spent by the incumbent in the race. In twelve of the states, at least 30 percent of the challengers fall into this category. The findings show a clear relationship between legislative professionalism and challenger disadvantage. For example, in California 74 percent of challengers in 1992 spent less than one-quarter as much as their incumbent opponent. In Illinois, New Jersey, and Pennsylvania (all professional state legislatures) more than 60 percent of the challengers spent less than one-quarter as much as incumbents.

The proportion of cases in which this extreme disparity between haves (incumbents) and have nots (challengers) exists drops as we go down the scale of professionalism: from professional to hybrid, and then to citizen legislatures. The major exceptions to this trend are Wisconsin and Minnesota, wherein the percentage is much lower than would be expected, given the level of legislative professionalism. The most reasonable explanation for these exceptions is the impact of public financing in these two states. The availability of these funds appears to help challengers compete financially with the incumbents.

The final column in Table 6-2 represents the proportion of cases in which relative parity exists—if relative parity is defined as cases in which the challenger is able to spend at least 75 percent as much as the incumbent. In only seven states do as many as 30 percent of the challengers reach this parity level. In only three of the states are more than half of the challengers able to spend at this level, and these are all states with citizen legislatures. As costs increase, the gap between incumbent and challenger spending increases as well. In the more expensive and professional legislatures, the percentage of challengers reaching parity is usually less than 20 percent.

Public financing seems to help challengers somewhat, but only in Wisconsin does it appear to help challengers significantly. Sixty-two percent of challengers were able to spend more than half of what incumbents spent in Wisconsin. This is a much higher percentage of relative parity than is found in any other professional or hybrid state legislature in this analysis. Wisconsin's challengers seem to be more financially competitive than might be expected, given similar characteristics.

We now have a fairly clear picture as to the extent of incumbents' financial advantage over challengers. Certainly incumbents have a big spending advantage overall. Does this make any difference in the election results? This question is addressed in Table 6-3, which shows the proportion of challengers who are involved in competitive elections (i.e., they receive at least 40 percent of the vote), for each of the spending ratio categories. The results indicate what would be expected: the ability of challengers to compete electorally is generally related to their ability to compete financially with the incumbent.

Earlier it was noted that many challengers find themselves financially overmatched—spending 25 percent or less of the amount spent by the incumbent. It is apparent from Table 6-3 that these challengers are generally unable to compete in the election. In only one state (Wyoming) were 50 percent or more of the challengers in this category able to run competitive races. In most of the states the percentage is low, indicating the dismal odds for the challenger who cannot compete financially. The number of states in which 50 percent or more of the challengers are competitive increases dramatically as we move up the ratio categories:

Table 6-3   *Competitive Challengers Categorized by Ratio of Challenger to Incumbent Spending, in Percentages*

| State | Competitive Challengers | | | |
	0–25	26–50	51–75	76–100
California	8	80	33	60
Illinois	2	13	100	56
New Jersey	39	55	50	50
Pennsylvania	4	23	46	53
Wisconsin	0	44	27	67
Delaware	0	33	33	67
Kansas	12	42	80	89
Minnesota	6	26	67	58
Missouri	10	39	85	90
Mississippi	25	60	40	100
North Carolina	47	71	70	70
Oregon	14	67	100	80
Washington	26	64	100	46
Idaho	11	71	70	70
Maine	15	64	88	57
Montana	14	33	43	73
Utah	29	25	75	79
Wyoming	50	100	100	78

Note: Figures are from 1992, except for Mississippi and New Jersey (1991) and Illinois (1988). States are grouped by legislative professionalism: California, most professional to least professional. The figures shown represent the percentage of challengers, in each category of incumbent spending, that were in competitive elections. Competitive races are those in which the winner received 60 percent of the vote or less.

nine in the second quartile, twelve in the third group, and seventeen in the final category (the one exception is Washington).

Overall it would appear that challengers have a good opportunity to be competitive if they can spend at least 50 percent as much as the incumbents' total. In some states, candidates are competitive even if they spend only 26–50 percent; this is particularly true in states with a high degree of party competition, such as New Jersey, North Carolina (in recent years), Oregon, and Washington. This is also true in some of the states in which legislative elections are least expensive. Challengers who fall below this level of spending are rarely competitive.

Challengers who can compete financially are generally able to compete electorally as well, while those who are greatly outspent have little chance of competing. We suggest that an incumbent whose opponent does not exceed 25 percent of his or her spending level is "financially unopposed," and the election result is generally a foregone conclusion.

The relationship between money and competitive elections seems quite strong, but we cannot confirm that it is a causal relationship. We have no way of knowing if the noncompetitive challengers would have been more successful if they had more money. The best conclusion is that money may be *necessary* but not *sufficient* to produce a competitive election. Money appears necessary because candidates without money are rarely competitive, but money alone does not guarantee a competitive race. Other factors enter into the equation, such as the candidate's attributes, the quality of the campaign, and the political nature of the legislative district.

THE COST OF COMPETITION

Thus far, challenger spending relative to incumbent expenditures has been our focus. There are, however, other ways to consider the question of spending and competing. For example, if challenger A spends $5,000 and incumbent A spends $10,000, is this dramatically different from the case in which challenger B spends $5,000 while incumbent B spends $6,000? It may be possible to identify an amount of money for each state that provides challengers with a relatively good probability of competing, regardless of how much their opponent spends. In other words, is there a "threshold" or "spending floor" for each state that represents the minimum expenditure necessary in order for the challenger to be competitive?

Several guidelines were followed to identify the cost of competition for challengers. We wanted to find for each state the smallest amount of money (in thousand dollar units) spent by challengers that would permit more than 50 percent of them to be competitive. Once that amount was determined, we focused on three questions: (1) what percentage of challengers reached this amount? (2) what percentage of these were competitive? and (3) what percentage of those candidates who failed to reach this "threshold" level of spending were competitive? The final question is critical in determining if the amount of money spent is truly related to the ability of challengers to compete. If a large proportion of challengers are competitive despite spending less than this threshold amount, then it would be difficult to argue that the particular spending level was really important. If, on the other hand, the challengers spending less than this amount were generally not competitive, then we indeed would have identified an important threshold in spending. The results are presented in Table 6-4.

The amount of money a challenger needs in order to have a reasonable chance of being competitive (i.e., of getting at least 40 percent of the general election vote) does not vary as much as one might expect, given the large variations in average and median costs of these elections

Table 6-4   *The Cost of Competing as a Challenger*

State	Threshold to Be Competitive	Percent Reaching Threshold	Percent Reaching Threshold and Competitive	Percent Competitive with Less Than Threshold
California	$100,000	29%	57%	9%
Illinois	15,000	35	52	0
New Jersey	3,000	64	56	22
Pennsylvania	15,000	25	53	5
Wisconsin	11,000	60	60	12
Delaware	6,000	54	64	0
Kansas	3,000	74	60	16
Minnesota	10,000	59	53	17
Missouri	3,000	69	57	9
Mississippi	1,000	52	77	13
North Carolina	1,000	89	77	20
Oregon	5,000	69	70	0
Washington	3,000	75	58	7
Idaho	3,000	69	64	36
Maine	1,000	70	57	22
Montana	1,000	89	58	17
Utah	1,000	88	69	20
Wyoming	1,000	78	86	50

Note: Figures are from 1992, except for Mississippi and New Jersey (1991) and Illinois (1988). States are grouped by legislative professionalism: California, most professional to least professional. Threshold is the minimum expenditure required for a challenger to be competitive. Competitive races are those in which the winner received 60 percent of the vote or less.

(Moncrief, chapter 3). Of course, the mean and median expenditures are affected by the level of incumbent spending, which is generally quite high. But, in fact, the amount of money necessary for a challenger to be competitive is often surprisingly low, as shown in Table 6-4. In one-third of the states the amount necessary to have a reasonable chance of being competitive is only $1,000 (Maine, Mississippi, Montana, North Carolina, Utah, and Wyoming), and in another five states it is just $3,000 (Idaho, Kansas, Missouri, New Jersey, and Washington). These are amounts of money that candidates for state legislature should be able to raise, even if they have to use personal funds.

The threshold appears to be a function of professionalism and costs, coupled with party competition. The cost of competing is by far the greatest in California, the state categorized in this study as being most like the congressional model. This is followed by the other professional states, with the exception of New Jersey. The "competitive threshold" in New Jersey is strikingly lower, probably due to the high level of party competition in the state. Challengers simply do not need as much money to be competitive because of the partisan competition within the districts. The other states with low costs of competitive elections are generally those states with lower overall costs and citizen legislatures.

The percentage of challengers able to reach the spending threshold in each state is worth noting. A majority of challengers are able to reach this level in all but three states (California, Illinois, and Pennsylvania). Not surprisingly, these are the three states with the highest cost of competing. Despite the fact that the threshold is also comparatively high in Wisconsin and Minnesota, approximately 60 percent of challengers reached the necessary level of spending in those states. Again, this is most likely due to the public financing available in these states. This additional source of funds assists challengers in their ability to compete financially with incumbents.

The percentage of competitive challengers at these levels of spending is, by our definition, in excess of 50 percent. The percentage of challengers who were competitive while spending less than the threshold amount indicates that we have accurately identified an amount of money necessary to have a reasonable chance of being competitive. The vast majority of challengers spending less than the threshold simply were not competitive, with the exception of those in Wyoming. A challenger there had a 50 percent chance of being competitive even if he or she spent less than $1,000. In three of the states (Delaware, Illinois, and Oregon) no challenger was competitive when spending less than the amount identified.

These findings have several important implications. Rising costs are a potential problem with respect to the outcome of elections. As the costs of competing rise, the number of challengers able to fund a competitive campaign declines. Public financing appears to be a viable method for countering this effect.

The costs of competing are not always simply a function of overall increased spending in elections. They may also be affected by high degrees of party competition. The costs of competing in New Jersey, Oregon, Washington, and to a certain degree North Carolina, are much less than might be expected given the higher levels of spending in these states. Each of these states has a high degree of party competition. Voters in highly contested partisan elections may not need as much information about a candidate in order to vote for the person. They may only need to be aware that their party has someone on the ballot.

IMPLICATIONS AND CONCLUSIONS

The initial question posed in this chapter was, "Does money buy elections?" We have seen that winners usually outspend losers. A closer examination reveals that incumbents usually win and generally outspend their challengers. The relationship between incumbent and challenger spending goes much deeper than simply incumbents having more money. Incumbents generally have a great deal more money. In most of the states considered, most challengers were unable to spend at least half the total spent by the incumbent they opposed. In fact, challengers often spend 25 percent or less of the incumbent's total. We also find that the ability to keep up with incumbent spending is related to the ability to compete in the election. Similarly, challengers who are unable to reach a certain level of spending in each state (regardless of the incumbent's expenditures) are rarely competitive. Taken collectively, this suggests that the answer to the question "Does money buy elections?" is a tentative "Yes."

This answer requires some qualification. Our findings indicate quite strongly that a lack of money, whether it is in comparison to one's opponent or simply a certain dollar amount, virtually guarantees that a challenger cannot be competitive. (The exceptions to this are in the least expensive states, where little money is spent on campaigns in general.) However, the opposite is not true. Having money does not guarantee that a candidate will be competitive and have a chance to win. Furthermore, it is evident that winners do not always outspend losers. We therefore conclude that what money "buys" is an opportunity to compete and that money only "buys" elections when one's opponent does not have sufficient funds.

These findings have several implications for what many observers and reformers might identify as other problems associated with contemporary elections—namely the vanishing marginals and the incumbency advantage. Our findings indicate that expenditures are related to competitiveness and that incumbents enjoy a clear advantage in terms of finances. The declining number of competitive elections (i.e., the vanishing marginals) seems to be linked to the inability of challengers to compete financially. This problem is exacerbated by rising costs. As costs rise, fewer challengers are able to compete financially, and the linkage between competing financially and electorally is stronger. This serves as evidence that there is reason to be concerned about the rising costs of campaigns.

The categorization of states used throughout this book proves to be a useful way of explaining differences among the states. California is certainly different from other states, with results that may be more similar to Congress than other state legislatures. California and the other professional states are more expensive generally, but it does not appear that this is due to enhanced competition. In fact, in these states the challengers were generally less competitive. While professional legislative seats may appear more attractive to potential candidates, they are also more attractive to those who already hold them. Also, incumbents in professional legislatures may be in a better position to exercise advantages, such as the ability to provide greater constituency service, because they have greater resources. In the least professional states we find lower costs and greater competitiveness.

Party competition appears to play a role in explaining the variations among states. Challengers in competitive states are able to compete in elections with less money than might be expected, given the overall level of spending in those states (e.g., New Jersey, Oregon, and Washington). These findings may suggest something even more profound about money and elections with respect to party competition. Candidate-centered campaigns may simply require more money than partisan campaigns. In New Jersey the candidates most often raise and spend money as a ticket, with the party and district as the focus, rather than the individuals. It is logical that if voters are focusing on the party, then this method would be sufficient to attract their attention and support. It is also plausible that it is much easier (i.e., less expensive) to find out about the issues and concerns of a political party than it is to find out about many different individuals.

The final factor that could explain variation among the states is the campaign finance laws. For this particular chapter, the laws with regard to the amounts of contributions and who may contribute are not directly relevant. These things may relate to differences in costs but there is no reason to suspect that they affect outcomes. The one aspect of campaign finance legislation that is relevant is public financing. Wisconsin and Minnesota were the only two states that allowed for significant public financing of state legislative elections at the time of this study. Public financing appears to have an impact on the issues considered here. In both states we find that challengers are less likely to be severely disadvantaged in terms of money, relative to incumbents. Also, despite the higher costs of competitive elections in both states, a high percentage of challengers are able to reach these levels. Public financing may be one answer to combating the problems of rising costs and declining electoral competitiveness.

We have noted on several occasions that the relationship between money and votes may not be a causal relationship. Money may simply go to those candidates who are politically stronger and therefore will be strongest in the election results. Incumbents obtain money because they are popular and likely to be reelected. Challengers who are perceived to be strong and competitive receive more money than those challengers who do not have any chance in the election. This argument may well be true but it does not diminish the significance of campaign finance. We must remember that campaign expenditures are just that—money spent on a campaign. Without a campaign the election results would likely change. It is illogical to think that any candidate facing an opponent would win if he or she did not run a viable campaign. Campaigns cost money, so money is important.

The findings here indicate quite strongly that the inability of some candidates to raise money makes it virtually impossible for them to compete, let alone win. Providing these candidates with enough money to run a viable campaign may not change who wins the election, but it may change the nature of the campaigns. Any incumbent or candidate whose opponent cannot fund a campaign does not have to face the voters and answer tough questions raised by their adversary. A competition of ideas does not take place and, arguably, this lessens the democratic process. We must not minimize the importance of money by simply concluding that it goes along with public perceptions. Perceptions could change, but only when exposed to a viable campaign.

Reformers should review these findings carefully. Rising costs pose a problem by creating an environment in which money becomes more important and often more difficult for some candidates to obtain. This leads to elections that are less competitive, which in turn is (arguably) less democratic. However, simply finding ways to hold down costs (if this is possible) will not necessarily alleviate the problem. We would still have the problem of incumbents having money while challengers often do not. The solution lies in finding ways to help challengers compete financially so that they at least have an opportunity to compete electorally.

REFERENCES

Breaux, David A., and Anthony Gierzynski. 1991. "It's Money That Matters: Campaign Expenditures in State Legislative Primaries." *Legislative Studies Quarterly* 16: 429–443.

Caldeira, Gregory A., and Samuel C. Patterson. 1982. "Bringing Home the Votes: Electoral Outcomes in State Legislative Races." *Political Behavior* 4: 33–67.

Garand, James. 1991. "Electoral Marginality in State Legislative Elections." *Legislative Studies Quarterly* 16: 7–28.

Gierzynski, Anthony, and David Breaux. 1991. "Money and Votes in State Legislative Elections." *Legislative Studies Quarterly* 16: 203–217.

Gierzynski, Anthony, and David Breaux. 1993. "Money and the Party Vote in State House Elections." *Legislative Studies Quarterly* 18: 515–533.

Giles, Michael W., and Anita Pritchard. 1985. "Campaign Expenditures and Legislative Elections in Florida." *Legislative Studies Quarterly* 10: 71–88.

Green, Donald Philip, and Jonathan S. Krasno. 1990. "Rebuttal to Jacobson's 'New Evidence for Old Arguments.' " *American Journal of Political Science* 34: 363–372.

Holbrook, Thomas M., and Emily Van Dunk. 1993. "Electoral Competition in the American States." *American Political Science Review* 87: 955–962.

Jacobson, Gary C. 1980. *Money in Congressional Elections*. New Haven: Yale University Press.

Jewell, Malcolm. 1984. *Parties and Primaries: Nominating State Governors*. New York: Praeger.

Jewell, Malcolm E., and David Breaux. 1988. "The Effect of Incumbency on State Legislative Elections." *Legislative Studies Quarterly* 13: 495–514.

Mayhew, David. 1974. "Congressional Elections: The Case of the Vanishing Marginals." *Polity* 6: 295–317.

Morehouse, Sarah M. 1990. "Money Versus Party Effort: Nominating for Governor." *American Journal of Political Science* 34: 706–724.

Thomas, Scott J. 1989. "Do Incumbent Campaign Expenditures Matter?" *Journal of Politics* 51: 956–976.

Tucker, Harvey J., and Ronald E. Weber. 1987. "State Legislative Outcomes: Contextual Effects and Legislative Performance Effects." *Legislative Studies Quarterly* 12: 537–553.

Weber, Ronald E., Harvey Tucker, and Paul Brace. 1991. "Vanishing Marginals in State Legislative Elections." *Legislative Studies Quarterly* 16: 29–48.

Welch, William P. 1976. "The Effectiveness of Expenditures in State Legislative Races." *American Politics Quarterly* 4: 336–356.

Part III

CONTRIBUTION PATTERNS

CHAPTER SEVEN

Gender, Candidate Attributes, and Campaign Contributions

Joel A. Thompson, Gary F. Moncrief, and Keith E. Hamm

A study by the Center for American Women and Politics concluded that more women legislators could mean a higher priority will be given to issues such as abortion, child care and child support, domestic violence, education, the environment, equal pay, guaranteed health care, housing and sexual harassment.

—Rita Thaemert, *State Legislatures*

The quotation above is a broad statement about the potential impact of women in the legislative chambers. If it is even partially true, then the increasing number of women elected to the state legislature can mean important changes in public policy. But in order to serve in the legislature, one must first get elected. William Cassie and David Breaux demonstrate in their analysis in chapter 6 on expenditures and election results that there is a definite link between the ability to get elected and the capacity to raise campaign funds.

It is a matter of conventional wisdom that women candidates have more trouble than their male counterparts in obtaining campaign resources (Carroll 1985, 84–86; McGlen and O'Connor 1995). But conventional wisdom does not always square with reality. Given the rise of women in state legislative politics, and renewed interest in campaign financing procedures, it is surprising that so little has been written about the issue of gender and campaign funding. Are women, in fact, disadvantaged in the "money chase"?

One good reason to assume they are underfunded is the fact that until recently relatively few women held state legislative office. While the number of female state legislators is far greater today than twenty or thirty years ago, women are still substantially underrepresented relative to their proportions in society. Women comprise slightly more than 50 percent of the U.S. population, yet they constitute only about 20 percent of all state legislators. There are numerous theories explaining this discrepancy between population and representation. These include factors associated with differences in political socialization, career patterns, electoral structure, voter discrimination, and the financing of political campaigns (see, e.g., Darcy, Brewer, and Clark 1994, 51–73; Uhlander and Schlozman 1986, fn. 1–3).

This chapter will focus on the political finance issue to determine if indeed there are differences among men and women in their ability to raise campaign funds. This is an important issue; we know there is a linkage in American elections between money and vote share. If we find that female candidates are unable to attract contributions in competitive amounts relative to their male counterparts, then we may have discovered one factor that contributes to the underrepresentation of women in elected bodies in the United States. Specifically, we will try to determine whether (1) differences exist on the basis of gender in the amount of money raised and spent and (2) if such differences exist, whether these differences are due to the unwillingness of contributors to give to women (often called *donor bias*) or to some attributes (other than gender) particular to the candidates.

THE GENDER ISSUE

There is a small body of research on women candidates and campaign money in congressional elections (Berch 1996; Burrell 1985; Gaddie and Bullock 1996; Green 1996; Herrick 1995, 1996; Roberts 1991; Root 1994; Uhlander and Schlozman 1986; Wilhite and Theilmann 1986). These studies are remarkably consistent in their findings (although not necessarily in their interpretation of the findings). Each of these studies concludes that, indeed, female candidates usually have fewer campaign resources than male candidates. However, the disparity in funding is largely a product of differences in candidate attributes other than gender. Candidate attributes refer to factors such as whether or not the candidate is an incumbent or challenger, whether she has held previous political office (and hence has name recognition and a funding network), or whether she is in a position of institutional leadership (e.g., speaker of the house, chair of an important legislative committee, etc.). For example, numerous studies document that political action committees (PACs) give disproportionately to incumbents. Since fewer women are incumbents, they generally receive fewer PAC dollars. Moreover, PACs and other "big money" contributors favor incumbents who hold influential leadership and committee posts. Again, female candidates historically have not often held such posts.

However, when women are incumbents the situation is quite different. Analyzing elections from the 1972–1982 period, Barbara Burrell (1985) concluded that women were not disadvantaged financially when compared to men within each status group (e.g., male incumbents to female incumbents, male challengers to female challengers, male open-seat contestants to female open-seat contestants). In another study, Carole Uhlander and Kay Schlozman (1986, 43) found similar results, leading them to conclude: "Donors behaved like book makers—what mattered was which horse would cross the finish line first, not whether it was a filly or colt." In other words, contributors (especially PACs) are likely to contribute to the incumbent regardless of whether the incumbent is a man or a woman. One implication is that as women gain legislative office and eventually obtain leadership positions, they will increasingly benefit from the contribution patterns of PACs and other donors.

When comparing women to men within the same status, or attribute, categories (such as female incumbents to male incumbents), research on congressional campaigns consistently finds that women are able to raise about the same amount of money. Saying that women are competitive with men of the same candidate status in procuring funds is not, however, the same thing as saying they are electorally competitive. Rebekah Herrick (1996) argues, for example, that female challengers need more money than male challengers to affect the same vote percentage, because female candidates have to overcome a level of voter bias against female candidates. She provides evidence in support of this argument in congressional elections, although such results may be election-specific.

A recent study by Joanne Connor Green (1996) analyzes male-versus-female contests in open-seat races. She finds that women were indeed disadvantaged because "they did not receive similar returns for their campaign expenditures as the male candidates they faced," but that the disadvantage had disappeared by the 1992–1994 congressional elections.

There are few studies of the relationship between gender and campaign resources at the state level. In single-state studies, no systematic gender bias in campaign funding was found in Oklahoma (Darcy, Brewer, and Clark 1984), Pennsylvania (O'Connor 1984), or Massachusetts (Burrell 1990). Instead, these studies concluded that disparities in campaign funding were largely a product of candidate attributes (especially incumbency status). On the other hand, few studies have delved deeply into the issue, going beyond simple comparisons of the average contributions and expenditures of men and women, controlling for candidate status (incumbent, challenger, open-seat contestant). Almost all the previous studies have examined the gender issue relative to only one institution (congress or a single state legislature).[1]

One of the advantages of this project is that it allows us to extend the analysis across state legislative institutions—to examine systemic variables as well as candidate attributes. For example, we know that more women serve in "citizen" and "hybrid" legislatures than in "professional" ones. Is this because the campaign finance environment is different in professional legislatures, or is it due to other factors, such as differences in recruitment patterns or political culture?

DATA

Variables relevant to this particular chapter include individual candidate variables (e.g., gender, incumbency status), electoral data (e.g., electoral outcome, closeness of the vote), and campaign finance variables (e.g., total revenues received, donor sources). We use data primarily from the 1992 electoral cycle, because it is the most recent year for which we have a relatively complete set of variables. Candidates for election in 1992 to the lower chambers of fifteen states are represented; in addition, the results from two states holding elections in 1991 (Mississippi and New Jersey) and one holding elections in 1988 (Illinois) are included.

The states in the sample represent all three of Kurtz's categories of legislative professionalization (Kurtz 1992). Five of our states (California, Illinois, New Jersey, Pennsylvania, and Wisconsin) are generally considered to have professional state legislatures, which are distinguished by the full-time nature of the institution—long sessions, relatively high salary levels, and substantial staffing and other resources. Seven (Idaho, Maine, Mississippi, Montana, North Carolina, Utah, and Wyoming) represent citizen, or amateur state legislatures, characterized by small staff, low pay, and shorter legislative sessions. The remaining six states (Delaware, Kansas, Minnesota, Missouri, Oregon, and Washington) have hybrid state legislatures—in between full- and part-time. Our analysis will make use of these categories as well as a scheme based upon the costs of elections. These variables are important in defining the "nature of the legislative job" and the general institutional milieu (Thompson, Kurtz, and Moncrief 1996).

There are two features of the data that need to be noted at the outset. First, this particular sample of states is biased toward western states (n = 7) and underrepresents southern states (n = 2). As it happens, western state legislatures tend to have some of the highest proportion of female state legislators in the nation, while southern state legislatures have relatively low percentages of women serving. It is possible, then, that our sample overrepresents states in which the political culture or system is generally more receptive to female candidates.

The second point to keep in mind is that the particular electoral cycle analyzed here is 1992: the widely perceived "Year of the Woman." It may be that 1992 was a particularly good year for female candidates in regards to campaign financing. There is some evidence that this is true at the congressional level (Berch 1996, 187; Gaddie and Bullock 1995, 755–757). However, at the state level the gains by women were more incremental, probably because women were already making significant inroads at the state level. For example, the number of women in congress increased by about 70 percent—from 28 to 47—as a result of the 1992 election. In state legislatures the increase was only about 11 percent—from 1,368 to 1,524 (Center for the American Woman and Politics 1997, 1). To put this another way, the proportion of women in state legislatures before and after the 1992 elections went from 18.3 to 20.5 percent—a modest increase indeed.

Is There a Gender Gap in Campaign Financing?

The limited number of previous studies at the state level find no systematic funding bias against female candidates. Underfunding of female candidates is instead attributed to the fact that fewer women are incumbents or in positions of legislative leadership. Thus, any discrepancy in their funding levels is a function of their status as nonincumbents (that is, an attribute of their candidacy), not their gender specifically. But these conclusions are based on a few cases. Does this pattern hold true across a range of states, regardless of the type of legislative institution?

In Figure 7-1 we show the median total revenue for all major party (i.e., Democrat and Republican) female and male candidates. For ease of viewing, the figure is broken into three panels, depending on the median amount of revenue raised by all candidates. The top panel presents the low revenue states, for which the median total revenue did not exceed $9,000. The middle panel has moderate revenue states, ranging between a median of $10,000 to $35,000. The lower panel contains the high revenue states, where the median is greater than $35,000. It is important to keep these different scales in mind when comparing across the three panels. Otherwise, it would be easy to conclude, for example, that Idaho and California had similar revenue patterns, when in fact the states are separated by a magnitude of almost ten.

How do we evaluate whether males or females are advantaged in terms of the amount of campaign funds raised? Throughout the chapter, we will define those instances in which the median receipts for men and women are within 10 percent of each other as cases of relative *parity* in funding. In Figure 7-1 only two states (Delaware and Pennsylva-

Figure 7-1   *Median Total Revenue by Gender, All Candidates*

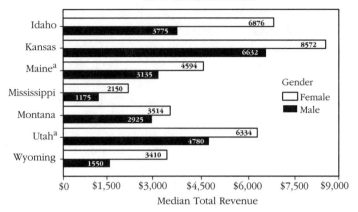

LOW REVENUE STATES

	Female	Male
Idaho	6876	3775
Kansas	8572	6632
Maine[a]	4594	3135
Mississippi	2150	1175
Montana	3514	2925
Utah[a]	6334	4780
Wyoming	3410	1550

Gender
□ Female
■ Male

Median Total Revenue

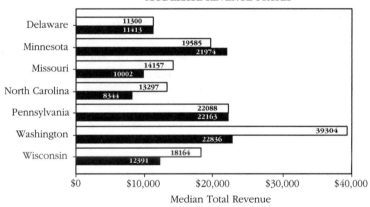

MODERATE REVENUE STATES

	Female	Male
Delaware	11300	11413
Minnesota	19585	21974
Missouri	14157	10002
North Carolina	13297	8344
Pennsylvania	22088	22163
Washington	39304	22836
Wisconsin	18164	12391

Median Total Revenue

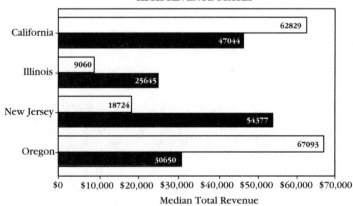

HIGH REVENUE STATES

	Female	Male
California	62829	47044
Illinois	9060	25645
New Jersey	18724	54377
Oregon	67093	30650

Median Total Revenue

[a]Primary losers not included.

122

nia) showed relative parity in funding between the sexes. Surprisingly, female candidates held the funding advantage over their male counterparts in thirteen of eighteen states; men held the advantage in only three states (Illinois, Minnesota, and New Jersey).

It is worth noting, however, that two of those states (Illinois and New Jersey) are considered professional, full-time state legislatures. In fact, in the five professional state legislatures, female candidates held a clear revenue advantage in only two states (California and Wisconsin). In one other (Pennsylvania), relative parity was achieved. If the analysis is restricted to just those fifteen states with data for 1992 elections (thus excluding Illinois, Mississippi, and New Jersey), 1992 was a good year for female candidates generally, and a very good year for female candidates running in the hybrid and citizen state legislatures. In those thirteen states, women candidates held a clear advantage (in terms of median receipts) in eleven. Relative parity existed in one (Delaware) and men had the advantage in only one (Minnesota).

This is a rather stunning finding. As a group, women candidates did extremely well in attracting money in 1992. They fared much better than they did in 1988 (the only other year for which a large cross-state study exists), when women held a clear advantage in only one state of eleven studied.[2]

Figure 7-1 provides information for all candidates, regardless of their status as incumbents, challengers, or open-seat contestants. But the ability to attract revenue and to be electorally competitive depends in part on incumbency status. So, how did women fare compared to men as challengers, in open-seat contests, and as incumbents? Once again, we must look at all candidates who ran in the primary or general election. Figure 7-2 indicates that female challengers attracted more money than male challengers in a majority of states. In thirteen of eighteen states, the median revenue generated by female challengers was greater than for male challengers. In some cases (e.g., California, Mississippi, Oregon, and Washington) the disparity is substantial. In Washington, for example, the median figure for female challengers is almost five times greater than the median for male challengers ($29,121 to $6,115). In only two states (Idaho and Illinois) did male challengers clearly attract more money than female challengers. Relative parity existed in the three remaining states (New Jersey, North Carolina, and Minnesota). These figures for state legislatures are consistent with Berch's findings for congress: women challengers (especially Democrats) outspent male challengers in 1992 congressional races (Berch 1996).

The same trend generally holds for open-seat contests (Figure 7-3). Women running for open seats received more money than men running

Figure 7-2   *Median Total Revenue by Gender, Challengers*

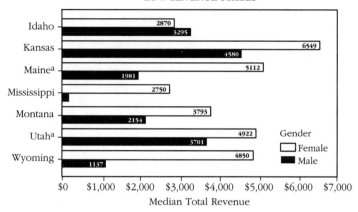

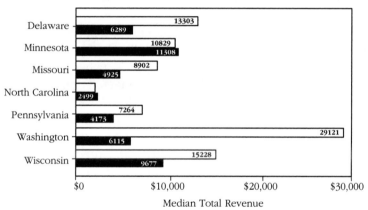

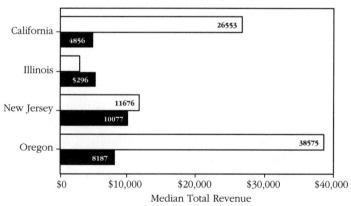

[a]Primary losers not included.

Figure 7-3   *Median Total Revenue by Gender, Open-Seat Candidates*

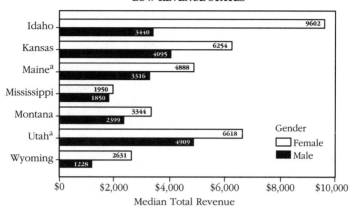

LOW REVENUE STATES

Idaho: Female 9602, Male 3440
Kansas: Female 6254, Male 4095
Maine[a]: Female 4888, Male 3316
Mississippi: Female 1950, Male 1850
Montana: Female 3344, Male 2399
Utah[a]: Female 6618, Male 4909
Wyoming: Female 2631, Male 1228

Gender
☐ Female
■ Male

Median Total Revenue

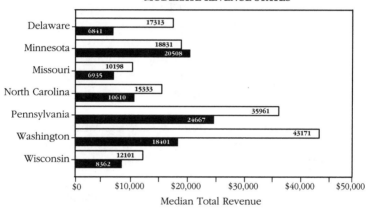

MODERATE REVENUE STATES

Delaware: Female 17313, Male 6841
Minnesota: Female 18831, Male 20508
Missouri: Female 10198, Male 6935
North Carolina: Female 15333, Male 10610
Pennsylvania: Female 35961, Male 24667
Washington: Female 43171, Male 18401
Wisconsin: Female 12101, Male 8362

Median Total Revenue

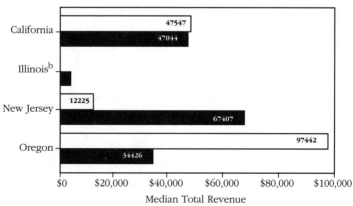

HIGH REVENUE STATES

California: Female 47547, Male 47044
Illinois[b]
New Jersey: Female 12225, Male 67407
Oregon: Female 97442, Male 34426

Median Total Revenue

[a]Primary losers not included.
[b]Female candidates received $0 revenue.

125

for open seats in thirteen states, men received more in three states (Minnesota, New Jersey, and Illinois), and relative parity existed in the remaining two states (California and Mississippi). Again, female candidates did particularly well in the states with the least professional state legislatures.

The picture is somewhat different when we look at incumbents (Figure 7-4). While women incumbents attracted more revenue than their male counterparts in six of seven amateur legislatures, men fared slightly better than women in four of six hybrid legislatures and in three of five professional legislatures (California, Illinois, and New Jersey).

We found an even more pronounced trend among incumbents in 1988: women did well attracting funds as challengers and open seat-contestants when compared with their male counterparts, but less well as incumbents (Thompson, Moncrief, and Hamm 1993). Why would this be the case? It is likely a product of leadership status. Obviously, only incumbents hold leadership positions (presiding officers, floor leaders, and chairs of important committees). More men than women are in leadership positions, and leadership positions tend to attract the most revenue. Moreover, historically it has been more difficult for "newcomers" to move into leadership positions in the more professional legislatures because turnover has tended to be much lower in such institutions. As the number of women in state legislatures increases over time, the gap between female and male incumbents' ability to attract campaign revenue should narrow. In fact, it diminished considerably between the 1988 and 1992 electoral cycles.

All the previous figures compare data from various categories of candidate status by gender: male incumbents are compared to female incumbents, male challengers are compared to female challengers, and so on. None of these comparisons control for the gender of the opponent. In other words, there are instances when a male incumbent faces a male challenger, a male incumbent faces a female challenger, a female incumbent faces a male challenger, etc. The most precise examination of the gender gap question should come from head-to-head contests—those cases where a male candidate meets a female candidate (Green 1996; Thompson, Moncrief, and Hamm 1993). These "gender-paired" elections are examined in Figure 7-5.

The data presentation in Figure 7-5 is different from the previous figures in two ways. First, all the candidates (male and female) who lost in the primaries have been eliminated. In many cases these are self-recruited, low-visibility candidates who spent little money and had virtually no chance of winning the election. By eliminating them from the analysis at this point we are able to concentrate more on what might be

Figure 7-4 *Median Total Revenue by Gender, Incumbents*

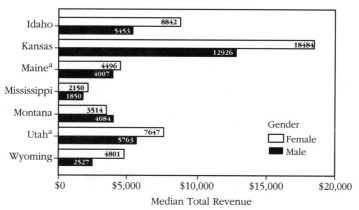

LOW REVENUE STATES

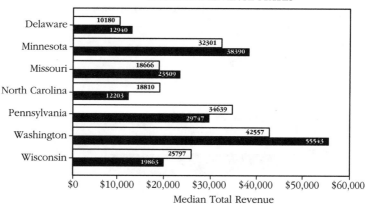

MODERATE REVENUE STATES

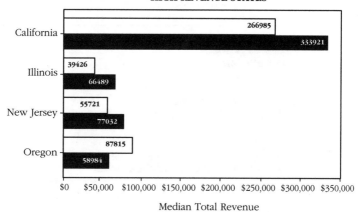

HIGH REVENUE STATES

[a]Primary losers not included.

Figure 7-5   *Median Revenue by Gender, Female Versus Male Contestants in General Elections*

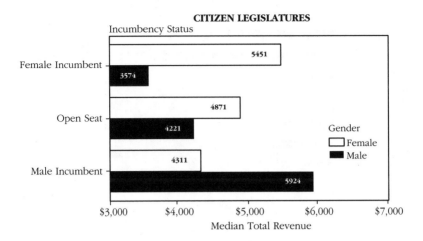

CITIZEN LEGISLATURES

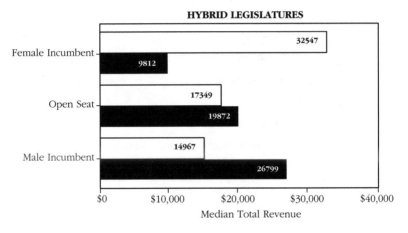

HYBRID LEGISLATURES

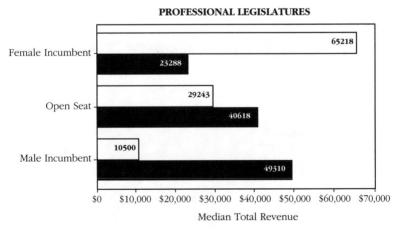

PROFESSIONAL LEGISLATURES

Note: All primary losers have been excluded.

called the "pool of legitimate contestants." Second, instead of presenting data from each state by each revenue level, all candidates from amateur legislatures are aggregated into one pool, those from professional legislatures into a second pool, and those from hybrid legislatures into a third.

Figure 7-5 presents clear evidence that female candidates were not disadvantaged in campaign funding. In the citizen (least professional) legislatures, female incumbents received more money than male challengers (median of $5,451 and $3,574, respectively). By the same token, male incumbents ($5,924) did better than female challengers ($4,311). Interestingly, female challengers did a bit better than male challengers in raising money. In open-seat contests where one candidate was a woman and the other a man, the female candidates held an advantage in funding (median receipts of $4,871 compared to $4,221 for men).

For hybrid (moderately professional) legislatures, female incumbents and male incumbents both overwhelmed their opposite-sex challengers. Female incumbents outspent their male opponents by a ratio of 3.3 to 1 while for male incumbents and female opponents the ratio is 1.8 to 1. In open-seat races, the results are reversed from that of amateur legislatures. Here, the males outspent females by more than 15 percent. Finally, in gender-paired contests in the most professional state legislatures, male and female incumbents maintain a wide the gap between themselves and their opposite-sex challengers. In open-seat contests in professional legislatures male contestants attract more funds than their female counterparts.

Another way to view the data is to ask how well candidates of each sex do across the three types of races. Remember that only those races in which a male faces off against a female in the general election are being looked at. An incumbent male challenged by a female, relative to a male who challenges a female incumbent, experiences a 166 percent increase in revenue in citizen legislatures, a 273 percent increase in hybrid legislatures, and a 212 percent increase in professional legislatures. Among females, the differences are more significant across the different types of legislatures. Female incumbents who are challenged by males outraise females who challenge male incumbents by 126 percent in citizen legislatures. In hybrid legislatures, this ratio rises to 217 percent and escalates to 652 percent in the most professional legislatures. In other words, in the professional legislatures studied, a female challenging a male incumbent raises a median of $10,500, while a female incumbent challenged by a male raises $65,218. Those females who are able to win initially in professional legislatures—most likely in open-seat races— have a significant advantage over the typical male challenger. Of course, females who challenge male incumbents in these states (California, Illinois, New Jersey, Pennsylvania, and Wisconsin) are woefully underfunded relative to their opponent.

REGRESSION ANALYSIS

As a final step in this analysis, the total revenue variable was regressed on a series of independent variables, including gender (see Table 7A-1 in the appendix to this chapter). All of the independent variables except gender are statistically significant. We interpret this to mean there are no significant differences between male and female challengers in their ability to attract campaign resources, no significant differences between male and female open-seat contestants in their ability to attract campaign resources, and no significant differences between male and female incumbents in their ability to attract campaign resources.

GENDER AND DONOR TYPES

A common perception is that PACs and organized interests collectively give more money to legislative candidates who are men than to those who are women. Numerous reasons are posited for this difference, including incumbency, donor bias, and general societal norms. The data in Figure 7-6 address this question.

In Figure 7-6, as well as Figures 7-7 and 7-8, all candidates (male and female) who lost in the primaries have been eliminated. Figure 7-6 provides median total contributions from PACs and organized interests for all major party candidates (i.e., Democrats and Republicans) in general election contests. In several states (e.g., Illinois, New Jersey, Idaho), corporations and unions may contribute to candidates' campaigns without forming a PAC. In other states, this practice is barred and contributions may only come from official PAC organizations. To capture the complete range of organized interest behavior, the non-PAC contributions from corporations and unions, where they are permitted, have been included in the study. In other words, the term *PAC,* as used here, includes direct corporate and labor contributions as well as those from PACs.

It should also be noted that not all PACs are the same. PACs represent a wide range of interests in American society. There are some PACs, for example, that give money exclusively to women candidates. These groups, such as Emily's List, have an important role to play in providing financial support for women candidates. But in most states contributions from such groups are actually relatively small and do not represent a particularly large share of the overall revenue received by women.

Figure 7-6   *Median PAC Contributions by Gender, All Candidates in Contested General Elections*

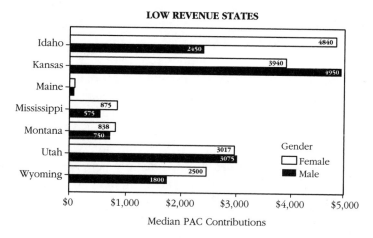

LOW REVENUE STATES

Idaho — Female 4840, Male 2450
Kansas — Female 3940, Male 4950
Maine —
Mississippi — Female 875, Male 575
Montana — Female 838, Male 750
Utah — Female 3017, Male 3075
Wyoming — Female 2500, Male 1800

Gender
☐ Female
■ Male

Median PAC Contributions

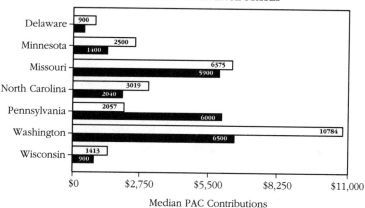

MODERATE REVENUE STATES

Delaware — Female 900
Minnesota — Female 2500, Male 1400
Missouri — Female 6375, Male 5900
North Carolina — Female 3019, Male 2040
Pennsylvania — Female 2057, Male 6000
Washington — Female 10784, Male 6500
Wisconsin — Female 1413, Male 900

Median PAC Contributions

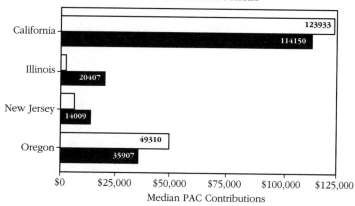

HIGH REVENUE STATES

California — Female 123933, Male 114150
Illinois — Male 20407
New Jersey — Male 14009
Oregon — Female 49310, Male 35907

Median PAC Contributions

Note: PAC contributions include direct corporation and labor contributions. Contested races are those in which the candidate receives at least 10 percent, but less than 90 percent, of the general election vote. All primary losers have been excluded.

131

Surprisingly, females did very well in raising money from PACs and other organized interests, as shown in Figure 7-6. In five of the seven citizen legislatures (Idaho, Mississippi, Montana, North Carolina, and Wyoming), the median contributions received by females were significantly greater (i.e., more than 10 percent larger) than those received by males. In Utah and Maine parity existed, although hardly any money was contributed by PACs and other organized interests in the latter state. In the hybrid legislatures women did very well in four of the six contests (i.e., Delaware, Minnesota, Oregon, and Washington); parity existed in Missouri, and men did significantly better in Kansas. It is in the professional legislatures that the men still hold an advantage, significantly outraising women in three states (Illinois, New Jersey, and Pennsylvania); parity prevails in California and women are advantaged in Wisconsin.

Of course, most PAC funds are distributed to incumbents, not to challengers or open-seat contestants. Figure 7-6 shows such receipts for all general election candidates, regardless of candidate status. In Figure 7-7 the situation for incumbents who face a challenge in the general election is isolated. These results are markedly different than those in Figure 7-6. First, in all eighteen states, the median figures for males and females are larger than for the corresponding gender-state combination in Figure 7-6. Second, whereas females had the advantage in ten states in Figure 7-6, this number dwindles to six when just incumbents are compared. Patterns are reversed in terms of type of legislature. Now, females do better in professional legislatures, outperforming males in three states (New Jersey, Pennsylvania, and Wisconsin), being outperformed in California, while parity prevails in Illinois. On the other hand, males do significantly better in three citizen legislatures (Maine, Mississippi, and North Carolina), while female incumbents receive significantly more contributions in Idaho and Utah; parity exists in Montana and Wyoming. The modal pattern in the hybrid legislatures is parity (Delaware, Kansas, and Missouri), with women predominating in Oregon and men doing so in Minnesota and Washington.

Another potentially significant donor is the political party. The data in Figure 7-8 show that female candidates do very well, compared to men, in obtaining contributions from the parties. In fourteen of the eighteen states, the median party contribution is significantly greater for women than for men. In only two states (Illinois in 1988, and Montana) did men receive significantly more funds, and parity prevailed in two states (Maine and California). This is no surprise. Parties contribute to candidates "strategically," giving money where they think it will do the

Figure 7-7   *Median PAC Contributions to Incumbents by Gender, in Contested General Elections*

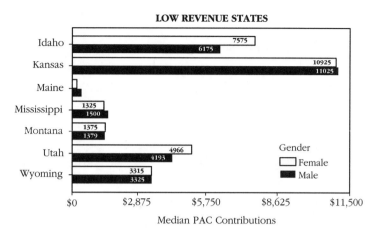

LOW REVENUE STATES

Idaho — Female 7575, Male 6175
Kansas — Female 10925, Male 11025
Maine
Mississippi — Female 1325, Male 1500
Montana — Female 1375, Male 1379
Utah — Female 4966, Male 4193
Wyoming — Female 3315, Male 3325

Gender
☐ Female
■ Male

$0 $2,875 $5,750 $8,625 $11,500

Median PAC Contributions

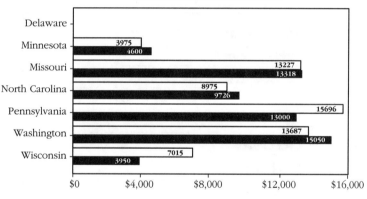

MODERATE REVENUE STATES

Delaware
Minnesota — Female 3975, Male 4600
Missouri — Female 13227, Male 13318
North Carolina — Female 8975, Male 9726
Pennsylvania — Female 15696, Male 13000
Washington — Female 13687, Male 15050
Wisconsin — Female 7015, Male 3950

$0 $4,000 $8,000 $12,000 $16,000

Median PAC Contributions

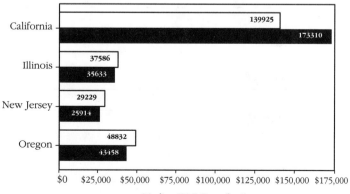

HIGH REVENUE STATES

California — Female 139925, Male 173310
Illinois — Female 37586, Male 35633
New Jersey — Female 29229, Male 25914
Oregon — Female 48832, Male 43458

$0 $25,000 $50,000 $75,000 $100,000 $125,000 $150,000 $175,000

Median PAC Contributions

Note: PAC contributions include direct corporation and labor contributions. Contested races are those in which the candidate receives at least 10 percent, but less than 90 percent, of the general election vote. All primary losers have been excluded.

Figure 7-8   *Median Political Party Contributions by Gender, All Candidates in Contested General Elections*

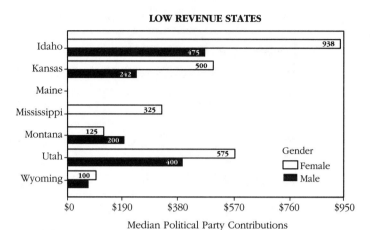

LOW REVENUE STATES

Idaho — 938 / 475
Kansas — 500 / 242
Maine —
Mississippi — 325
Montana — 125 / 200
Utah — 575 / 400
Wyoming — 100

Gender
☐ Female
■ Male

$0 $190 $380 $570 $760 $950
Median Political Party Contributions

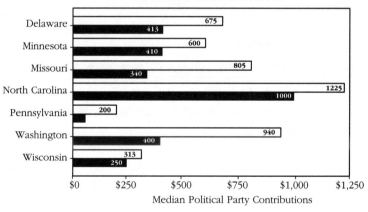

MODERATE REVENUE STATES

Delaware — 675 / 413
Minnesota — 600 / 410
Missouri — 805 / 340
North Carolina — 1225 / 1000
Pennsylvania — 200
Washington — 940 / 400
Wisconsin — 313 / 250

$0 $250 $500 $750 $1,000 $1,250
Median Political Party Contributions

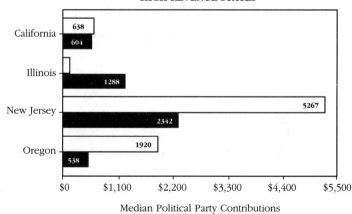

HIGH REVENUE STATES

California — 638 / 604
Illinois — 1288
New Jersey — 5267 / 2342
Oregon — 1920 / 538

$0 $1,100 $2,200 $3,300 $4,400 $5,500
Median Political Party Contributions

Note: Contested races are those in which the candidate receives at least 10 percent, but less than 90 percent, of the general election vote. All primary losers have been excluded.

most electoral good. Most of our data are from 1992, the Year of the Woman, and the odds were clearly on the quality female candidates, regardless of incumbency status. California provides a particularly good example of the strategic contributions of political parties. Most candidates (69.8 percent of the men, 68.9 percent of the women) received less than $10,000 in party contributions. But 22.2 percent of the female candidates received party contributions in excess of $100,000. Only 11.9 percent of the male candidates received $100,000 or more from their party. Clearly, there were some quality female candidates in 1992, and the parties backed them with substantial resources.

CONCLUSION

In general, we find no evidence that female candidates are unable to attract contributions at the same level as male candidates. To the contrary, in 1992 female candidates actually outperformed male candidates, as a group, in raising money. While this is true as a general observation, there is an important qualification to this statement: the professionalism of the legislature matters. Women candidates do well in citizen- and hybrid-type state legislatures. As is pointed out in chapter 3, there is a fairly clear—and perfectly logical—relationship between legislative professionalism and campaign costs. Where costs are lower, a candidate can rely more on her own personal network of contributors. Where costs are higher—as in professional legislatures—PACs, political parties, and other organized interests become more important as revenue sources. As traditional "outsiders," women previously had less access to these sources. This discrepancy in funding was still apparent in 1992 in professional legislatures, both in terms of incumbents and open-seat contestants.

On the other hand, the funding advantage that male incumbents, compared to female incumbents, have in professional state legislatures is, we believe, actually an artifact of leadership status. The existence of leadership PACs and intercandidate transfers (from legislative leaders to other candidates) is a phenomenon far more likely in professional than other types of legislatures. And most people in leadership positions are still men—especially in the professional legislatures where working one's way up the leadership ladder requires extended tenure in office. Of course, term limits soon may have a significant effect on this pattern in some states.

It is important to reiterate that 1992 was a particularly good year for women as candidates. The funding advantage that women enjoyed in

1992 may have been unusual, but more so, we expect, at the *national* than *state* level. As viable candidates, more women have been on the political scene for a longer time at the state legislative level than at the congressional level. But even if women were not advantaged in a "normal" electoral year, there is little reason to think they are systematically *disadvantaged* in this day and age.

APPENDIX

The dependent variable is the total revenue raised by candidates in contested elections. Independent variables include a series of dummy variables for gender (1 = female, 0 = male), leadership (1 = presiding officer, party leader, committee chair; 0 = no such position held), legislative professionalism (dummies for citizen and professional legislatures) and region (1 = western region, 0 = nonwest). Three separate regressions were run, one for each candidate type (incumbent, open seat, and challenger).

Table 7A-1 *Regression Analysis of Total Revenue, All Candidates in Contested General Elections*

Independent Variable	Unstandardized Coefficient	Standardized Coefficient	T-Value	Significance Level
Challengers				
Gender	5,171.8	.040	1.31	.192
Citizen Legislature	−14,723.9	−.120	−3.43	.001
Professional Legislature	22,794.8	.202	5.71	.000
Western Region	30,679.6	.249	7.83	.000
N = 982				
Adj. R2 = .100				
Incumbents				
Gender	−10,002.3	−.027	−.93	.354
Leadership	34,165.3	.103	3.53	.000
Citizen Legislature	−40,388.1	−.117	−3.54	.000
Professional Legislature	91,507.3	.291	8.69	.000
Western Region	93,391.7	.272	9.01	.000
N = 1,002				
Adj. R2 = 167				
Open Seats				
Gender	4,788.1	.023	.712	.477
Citizen Legislature	−25,470.4	−.130	−3.57	.000
Professional Legislature	85,170.4	.405	11.17	.000
Western Region	69,448.9	.340	10.41	.000
N = 665				
Adj. R2 = .318				

NOTES

1. There are a few exceptions. One is the study by Gierzynski and Budreck (1995), which analyzes transfers of campaign funds from women candidates to other candidates in three states. They do not, however, address questions of overall funding levels for female candidates compared to male candidates. Another exception is the information occasionally provided by the Center for the Study of American Women and Politics. Finally, our own previous comparative study (Thompson, Moncrief, and Hamm, 1993) will be discussed in the data analysis section of this chapter.
2. In an eleven-state study of the 1988 campaign cycle, female candidates held a clear advantage in only one state (Idaho). Male candidates held a distinct advantage in three states (California, Pennsylvania, and Wisconsin—all professional state legislatures). The remaining seven states exhibited relative parity between male and female candidates.

REFERENCES

Berch, Neil. 1996. " The 'Year of the Woman' in Context." *American Politics Quarterly* 24: 169–193.

Burrell, Barbara. 1985. "Women's and Men's Campaigns for the U.S. House of Representatives, 1972–1982." *American Politics Quarterly* 13: 251–272.

Burrell, Barbara. 1990. "The Presence of Women Candidates and the Role of Gender in Campaigns for the State Legislature in an Urban Setting: The Case of Massachusetts." *Women & Politics* 10: 85–102.

Carroll, Susan. 1985. *Women as Candidates in American Politics*. Bloomington: Indiana University Press.

Center for the American Woman and Politics. 1997. "Fact Sheet: Women in State Legislatures, 1997." Rutgers University, Eagleton Institute.

Clucas, Richard. 1995. *The Speaker's Electoral Connection: Willie Brown and the California Assembly*. Berkeley, Calif.: University of California, Institute of Governmental Studies.

Darcy, Robert, M. Brewer, and J. Clark. 1984. "Women in the Oklahoma Political System." *Social Science Journal* 21: 67–78.

Darcy, R., S. Welch, and J. Clark. 1994. *Women, Elections, and Representation*, 2nd ed. Lincoln: University of Nebraska Press.

Gaddie, Ronald K., and Charles Bullock III. 1995. "Congressional Elections and the Year of the Woman: Structural and Elite Influences on Female Candidacies." *Social Science Quarterly* 76: 749–762.

Gierzynski, Anthony, and Paulette Budreck. 1995. "Women Legislative Caucus and Leadership Campaign Committees." *Women & Politics* 14: 23–36.

Green, Joanne Connor. 1996. "The District and Female Candidacies: A District Level Test for a Differential Value for Campaign Resources." Paper presented at the annual meeting of the American Political Science Association, San Francisco.

Herrick, Rebekah. 1995. "A Reappraisal of the Quality of Women Candidates." *Women & Politics* 15: 25–38.

Herrick, Rebekah. 1996. "Is There a Gender Gap in the Value of Campaign Resources?" *American Politics Quarterly* 24: 68–80.

Kurtz, Karl. 1992. "Understanding the Diversity of American State Legislatures." Newsletter from the Legislative Studies Section of the American Political Science Association.

McGlen, Nancy, and Karen O'Connor. 1995. *Women, Politics, and American Society.* Englewood Cliffs, N.J.: Prentice Hall.

O'Connor, Robert. 1984. "Parties, PACs, and Political Recruitment." Paper presented at the annual meeting of the Midwest Political Science Association.

Roberts, Susan L. 1991. "Women's PACs: Candidate Assistance Strategies and Successes." Paper presented at the annual meeting of the Southern Political Science Association, Tampa, Florida, November 7–9.

Root, Jeraine. 1994. "Congressional Campaign Funding: A Re-examination of Gender Bias." Paper presented at the 1994 annual meeting of the Southwestern Political Science Association.

Thaemert, Rita. 1994. "Twenty Percent and Climbing." *State Legislatures* (January): 28–29.

Thompson, Joel, G. Moncrief, and K. Hamm. 1993. "Gender Differences in State Legislative Campaign Finances." Paper presented at the annual meeting of the Southwestern Political Science Association, New Orleans, La., March 17–20.

Thompson, Joel, K. Kurtz, and G. Moncrief. 1996. "We've Lost That Family Feeling: The Changing Norms of the New Breed of State Legislators." *Social Science Quarterly* 77: 344–362.

Uhlander, Carole, and Kay Schozman. 1986. "Candidate Gender and Congressional Campaign Receipts." *Journal of Politics* 48: 30–47.

Wilhite, Allen, and John Theilmann. 1986. "Women, Blacks, and PAC Discrimination." *Social Science Quarterly* 67: 283–298.

CHAPTER EIGHT

Minorities and Campaign Contributions

Robert E. Hogan and Joel A. Thompson

In the previous chapter, it was noted that women are underrepresented in state legislatures in comparison to their proportion of the population. This occurs even though the primary structural barriers to participation and election were removed many decades ago. History, tradition, and candidate attributes, more so than electoral structure or bias in fund raising, seem to explain this phenomenon.

Minorities and women share some of the same historical obstacles regarding political participation. For a long period in their political histories within the United States, blacks and Hispanics were effectively prohibited from voting, gaining full participatory rights several decades later than women. Neither women nor minorities were socialized to participate nor encouraged to seek political office. Because they were considered unlikely to be elected, women and minorities were rarely the targets of party recruitment efforts.

There are, however, important differences in the political ethos of women and minorities in the United States. Women were fully enfranchised more than seventy-five years ago. Since then, they have not faced other forms of overt discrimination that have kept them from participating. As a result, women have reached parity with men in voting and continue to make gains in election to office.

Although ostensibly franchised before women, blacks (Bullock 1992, Thompson 1986) and Hispanics (Garcia 1986) have faced a litany of discriminatory barriers to political participation. Only within the past two to three decades, and primarily as a result of an increased federal role (Bullock 1992), have minorities effectively been involved in the political process. The result has been a shorter period of participatory socialization, less experience in campaigning for office, and continued underrepresentation relative to the general population.

The historical legacy of blacks and Hispanics complicates an examination of campaign finance. A contemporary analysis must be sensitive to this legacy, which has produced certain structural and electoral conditions that differentiate minority campaigns from those of nonminorities.

RACE AND POLITICAL PARTICIPATION

The legislative districts from which many blacks and Hispanics are elected today are a product of the political struggle for equal rights. Prior to the mid-1960s, few blacks held political office. Devices such as the white primary, literacy tests, discriminatory registration requirements, economic threats, and intimidation effectively prohibited blacks from voting and seeking electoral office (Thompson 1986). In response, the federal government initiated a series of policies to remove these impediments. These included adoption of the Voting Rights Act of 1965 and enforcement of the preclearance provisions in 1969, which requires jurisdictions to preclear all voting changes with the U.S. District Court for the District of Columbia or the Department of Justice (Bullock 1992). Provisions of the act were extended in 1970 and 1975 to include parts of the Southwest, primarily to non–English-speaking minorities (Garcia 1986).

The Voting Rights Act was instrumental in increasing registration and voter turnout among blacks and Hispanics, which was an essential step toward the election of minority officeholders (Garcia 1986; Thompson 1986). Another important step was the creation of majority-minority districts (i.e., districts in which a majority of the constituents are black or Hispanic). Partly as a reaction to the increase in participation by minorities, officials in some jurisdictions converted to at-large elections and/or created multimember districts in an attempt to dilute minority voting strength. The federal response was enforcement of the preclearance provisions of the Voting Rights Act. The result was that new reapportionment plans, developed under the supervision of the Justice Department, created a number of predominantly minority districts. The impact of these efforts has been impressive. The number of black state legislators increased from virtually none in the mid-1960s to 172 in 1969, and to 514 by 1993 (Bullock 1992, 41–42; Joint Center for Political and Economic Studies, various years). Similarly, the number of Hispanics serving in state legislatures increased from only 67 in 1973 (Garcia 1986, 56) to 158 by 1995 (Alma-Bonilla and Tomes 1996). However, in most states, both groups remain underrepresented relative to their populations (Stanley and Niemi 1994). But there are notable regional variations. For example, blacks are slightly overrepresented relative to population in California, Florida, Ohio, and a few smaller states. Hispanics, while not overrepresented in any state, approach parity with their population in Colorado, Arizona, and New Mexico (Stanley and Niemi 1994).

The federal initiatives have gone a long way toward leveling the political playing field for minority candidates. In some cases—such as majority-minority districts—this has actually given minority candidates an advantage. Given that most overt obstacles to minority participation have been eliminated, an interesting question now is to what extent, if any, are minority candidates disadvantaged by other political factors? One of these factors is political money.

MACRO LEVEL FACTORS: THE DISTRICT

An investigation of minority candidate financing must take into account the structural and electoral factors mentioned above. One of these factors is the type of electoral district in which a candidate runs for office. For example, previous research consistently has shown that blacks are advantaged by running in single-member districts (SMDs). In contrast, female candidates are helped by multimember districts (MMDs) (Moncrief and Thompson 1992). A preponderance of single-member districts was created as a direct result of redistricting plans developed under the preclearance provisions of the Voting Rights Act. Another factor relative to the advantage given minorities in these districts is that they are majority-minority districts.

It is not surprising then that Grofman and Handley (1991) attribute the increase in office holding by blacks to the elimination of MMDs and their subsequent replacement with SMDs, especially SMDs with 60 percent or greater minority population. A similar conclusion was reached by Bullock (1992). In addition to these conditions, Moncrief and Thompson (1992) and Nelson (1991) find black representation related to urbanization. Of course, there is an obvious link between urbanization and concentrations of minorities, which in turn produces a greater potential for the creation of minority districts.

There are fewer studies of Hispanic representation and the results are not as consistent. Garcia (1986, 55) found that in Arizona a disproportionate number of representatives come from predominantly minority districts. Bullock (1992, 45) found that increases in representation after reapportionment cycles are generally smaller for Hispanics than blacks. Lenz and Pritchard (1989) conclude that a major factor related to increases in Hispanic legislators is not the greater number of minority districts created during earlier reapportionments but rather population shifts after reapportionment.

District level characteristics can affect political money. For example, studies have indicated that campaign costs are higher in multimember districts, since they are often more populous (see chapter 4). The cost in these districts may be compounded by urbanization, meaning that minority candidates may be doubly disadvantaged in the money race. On the other hand, if a district is predominantly minority, it may be less competitive and a safer seat for minority candidates, meaning that he or she would not need to raise and spend as much money as candidates running in other nonminority MMDs and/or urban districts.

MICRO LEVEL FACTORS: THE CANDIDATE

Studies of campaign funding and race are rare. In part, this is no doubt related to the fact that there have been few minority candidates available for study at both the national and subnational levels. At the state and local levels, where more candidates run, investigations have been limited by the lack of multistate data; the problem is compounded by the difficulty of identifying minority candidates, especially those who are not elected.

The few studies that have been done offer mixed results. At the congressional level, Whilhite and Theilmann (1986, 295) found that black candidates were significantly hampered in their ability to raise money. They reported that the evidence shows a consistent pattern of discrimination against blacks in all categories of political action committee (PAC) contributions, and this bias seemed to persist regardless of a candidate's visibility.

But time and conditions change, especially at the state level. As speaker of the California Assembly, Willie Brown certainly had little trouble garnering vast financial resources (Clucas 1994). Moreover, in a study of state and local races in Louisiana, Hadley and Nick (1987, 69) found that some black candidates were able to attract funds or in-kind support from unconnected, primarily black political organizations. Finally, an analysis of campaign contributions to candidates for the Texas House of Representatives found that there were several powerful and influential minority candidates who had strong financial backing from PACs (Theilmann and Dixon 1994, 502). Moreover, they found that powerful Hispanic candidates actually netted more money from individual large donors than non-Hispanic candidates (504).

These studies point to a dilemma for most minority candidates similar to that faced by female candidates. As Gierzynski points out in chapter 2, money flows to political power. Most minority candidates lack the legislative attributes that make them powerful. Minorities are under-represented, so there are fewer incumbents to attract a disproportionate share of PAC funds (see chapter 9). With few exceptions, minorities have not been elected to powerful leadership positions in the legislature. With only a limited number of minority legislators, few are available to serve as committee chairs. Such conditions would appear to make it difficult for minority candidates to raise campaign funds. However, because many minorities run in districts that are majority-minority and hence face less electoral competition, large levels of funding may not be necessary. It is this combination of macro-level advantages and micro-level disadvantages that makes an analysis of minority campaign finance so intriguing.

Focus of the Research

As previous chapters have suggested, availability of funding is a major advantage for candidates running for the state legislature. Those with greater levels of funding generally do better on election day than those with fewer financial resources (see chapter 6). Money appears to be a necessary though not sufficient ingredient of electoral success, especially for candidates running as challengers or open-seat contenders. Questions involving variations in available funding, then, necessarily center on questions of access to political institutions. Variations in funding based on racial differences among candidates pose a challenge for equality of representation. Past difficulties experienced by minority candidates in the United States, coupled with the increased role of money within the candidate-centered political system, make a focus on campaign finances among different racial groups an important topic of study.

The questions addressed by this analysis are straightforward: Are minority candidate campaigns financially disadvantaged relative to those of non-Hispanic white candidates? If they are, what factors are responsible? In order to answer these questions, we rely on campaign finance data compiled on state legislative candidates running in four states. A major focus of this chapter is on the total amount of revenue raised by candidates. However, the funding sources of candidates should also be considered. How much of their funding is provided by political parties? How much is provided by interest groups and political action committees? It is assumed that candidates who receive a large share of their funding from these sources have a somewhat easier time at fund raising than candidates who must bankroll their own campaign or raise it from individual contributors.

DATA

Our analysis is restricted to the contribution patterns of candidates running for the lower houses of the legislature in four states: California, Illinois, New Jersey, and Pennsylvania. Three of the states held their elections in 1992; New Jersey's elections are held in odd-numbered years, so election results from 1991 are used in this analysis. These states were chosen based on several criteria, the most important of which is that each contains a sizable minority population. In addition, this mix of states provides variation on a number of district-level features. For example, the average population of eligible voters in each district ranges from a low of about 45,000 in Pennsylvania to a high of more than 250,000 in California. Each state also contains a number of districts where there are few minorities as well as others where minorities constitute a majority of district population. Finally, there are differences in electoral structure across the states, with New Jersey providing variation in its use of multimember districts.[1]

In addition to the data on campaign finances and district characteristics, information on each candidate's general election performance, candidate status (incumbent, challenger, or open-seat contender), and racial/ethnic background is also included. The racial/ethnic data were the most difficult to obtain. For incumbent candidates, this information is easily obtained from sources such as the *National Roster of Hispanic Elected Officials* (National Association of Latino Elected Officials), the *Handbook of Black Elected Officials* (Joint Center for Political and Economic Studies), and legislative manuals. For challengers and open-seat candidates who did not win, however, such information is not as readily available. In these cases, a variety of sources was used, including newspaper articles and voter guides. Sitting incumbents, members of their staff, and party operatives at the state or county level who were familiar with candidates who ran in that year were contacted directly. Overall, the racial and ethnic characteristics of approximately 95 percent of major party candidates who ran in the general election in the four states were identified.

An inherent difficulty in the study of minority candidates is the small number who run in any given year. We have attempted to obtain a useable number of cases by focusing the analysis on states where a large number of minorities reside and frequently run. But even so, a relatively small number of cases were identified: 81 minority candidates and 755 non-Hispanic white candidates from the four sample states. Of the minority candidates, 53 were black, 24 were Hispanic, three were Asian, and one was Filipino. Approximately 70 percent of these candidates were Democrats and 30 percent were Republicans.

Ideally, we would like to compare the contributions of minority candidates with those of non-Hispanic white candidates in head-to-head contests. In other words, what is the average disparity (if any) in contributions between minorities and non-Hispanic white candidates who run against one another? Such comparisons are complicated by the small number of available cases. About half the minorities in the sample ran against non-Hispanic white candidates. However, to make meaningful comparisons, candidate status must inevitably be controlled for since incumbent candidates raise so much more than challengers. Doing so, however, reduces the number of cases so much that comparisons become unreliable. For this reason we have chosen to compare contributions for groups of minorities and non-Hispanic white candidates as they run under similar conditions.[2]

Studies with small sample sizes pose other challenges as well, especially when one case is different from the others. Our sample contains one such case: Willie Brown, who ran in 1992 as the incumbent speaker of the California Assembly. His campaign committees garnered a great deal of money and distributed much of it to other legislators. For the 1992 election cycle alone, Brown's campaign received more than $4 million in contributions, making his total very different from typical minority candidates. In order to prevent his massive fund-raising effort from skewing the results, his totals were removed from the analysis.[3]

ANALYSIS

Differences in Contributions

What is the relative amount of money raised by minority and non-Hispanic white candidates running for the state legislature? The data in Table 8-1 provide an estimate of the mean and median amounts raised by three groups of candidates: all candidates (even those without opposition), candidates with competition in the general election (even third-party and independent candidate opposition), and candidates in highly competitive races where the candidate received between 40 and 60 percent of the general election vote.

Displayed in this fashion, the mean level of contributions for minority candidates is higher than the mean for non-Hispanic whites across each grouping of candidates. Among all candidates running, minorities on average received about $100,000, while non-Hispanic whites took in about $88,000. The disparities are even larger among candidates who had general election competition. Minorities in these races raised approximately $120,000, while non-Hispanic whites raised about $90,000. However, the differences are smaller among candidates in high

Table 8-1   *Mean and Median Revenue Raised, by Race/Ethnicity*

Candidate Type	Non-Hispanic White Candidates	Minority Candidates
All candidates[a]		
Mean	$88,097	$99,938
Median	$33,329	$27,664
N=	(755)	(81)
Candidates with competition[b]		
Mean	$89,640	$120,134
Median	$34,767	$38,349
N=	(715)	(63)
Candidates with high competition[c]		
Mean	$136,523	$160,933
Median	$60,786	$59,358
N=	(277)	(21)

Note: Data are from 1992 elections in California, Illinois, and Pennsylvania and from 1991 elections in New Jersey.

[a] Includes candidates without competition.

[b] Includes third party and independent competition.

[c] Those races in which a candidate received between 40 and 60 percent of the general election vote.

competition races. In these contests the typical minority candidate raised about $161,000 while non-Hispanic white candidates raised about $137,000.

Examining only the mean differences in contributions among candidates may not lead to an accurate assessment of revenue differences if there are several candidates who have very low or very high levels of contributions that skew the averages. One way to solve this problem is to focus on the median level of resources available to candidates. The median value represents the middle category, where one-half the values fall above and the other half below. Such a measure is less sensitive to outliers than the mean.

As the data in Table 8-1 show, focusing on median values results in a somewhat different perspective on candidate funding. Among all candidates, the median contribution for minorities is $27,664, while the median for non-Hispanic whites is $33,329. Minority candidates spend slightly more than non-Hispanic white candidates in campaigns with competition ($38,349 and $34,767, respectively). Among candidates with high competition, contribution levels for the two groups are similar. The median value for minority candidates is $59,358, while the median for non-Hispanic white candidates is $60,786. A focus on the median values shows that the differences among non-Hispanic white and minority candidates are not nearly as great as one would conclude if mean contribution values were the sole basis for comparison.

District Characteristics

A problem that occurs when comparing mean and median receipts is that levels of contributions and expenditures are higher in some states than in others. As noted in chapter 4, levels of spending vary dramatically across districts and states. A number of factors associated with differences in spending were found, but none more important than the number of eligible voters to be contacted. Candidates in some states may need more money to contact a larger number of voters. If minorities in the sample are disproportionately located in states with highly populated districts, then the results could be skewed. To control for this, we have calculated total contributions for each candidate per eligible district voter. This enables us to control for the need for political contributions in a given legislative district.

Another district characteristic that should be considered is the racial/ethnic makeup of the district. Is the district a majority non-Hispanic white district or is it a majority-minority district? It is likely that minority candidates face less electoral competition (particularly from non-Hispanic white candidates) in majority-minority districts than in majority non-Hispanic white districts. Therefore, minority candidates running in majority-minority districts may not raise much money simply because they do not need to. In order to compare the relative levels of funding among non-Hispanic whites to those of minorities, their levels of funding must be examined under similar conditions. Therefore, minority candidates have been divided into two groups based upon the type of district where they run: in majority non-Hispanic white districts and in majority-minority districts.[4]

The average revenue raised per eligible voter across the different groups under varying levels of electoral competition is displayed in Table 8-2. By taking contributions per eligible voter into account, it appears that the mean level of revenue raised per voter by minority candidates does not outstrip the amount raised by non-Hispanic white candidates. In fact, the mean level of contributions per eligible voter for minority candidates running in both types of districts is lower than the mean value for non-Hispanic white candidates in every category. Among all candidates, for example, non-Hispanic white candidates collect about $0.73 per eligible voter, minority candidates in non-Hispanic white districts collect $0.64, and minorities in majority-minority districts collect $0.55. Median contribution levels follow a similar pattern. However, among candidates with competition, minority candidates in majority-minority districts appear to raise as much as non-Hispanic white candidates.

The generally lower levels of contributions to minority candidates running in majority-minority districts are not surprising, given the small

Table 8-2   *Mean and Median Revenue Raised Per Eligible Voter,*
by Race

| Candidate Type | Non-Hispanic White Candidates | Minority Candidates | |
		In Non-Hispanic White Districts	In Majority-Minority Districts
All candidates [a]			
Mean	$0.73	$0.64	$0.55
Median	$0.51	$0.36	$0.32
N=	(755)	(36)	(45)
Candidates with competition [b]			
Mean	$0.74	$0.66	$0.68
Median	$0.52	$0.36	$0.52
N=	(715)	(34)	(29)
Candidates with high competition [c]			
Mean	$0.99	$0.73	$0.58
Median	$0.82	$0.40	$0.77
N=	(277)	(18)	(3)

Note: Data are from 1992 elections in California, Illinois, and Pennsylvania and from 1991 elections in New Jersey.

[a] Includes candidates without competition.

[b] Includes third party and independent competition.

[c] Those races in which a candidate received between 40 and 60 percent of the general election vote.

number of minority candidates who face strong competition in these districts. In this sample, only three candidates fall into the highly competitive category. While it appears that their mean level of contributions is higher than for minorities running in majority non-Hispanic white districts, it is important to point out that it is difficult to make many inferences from such a small number of cases.

The critical aspect to consider in Table 8-2 is the relative levels of funding available to non-Hispanic white candidates and minority candidates running in non-Hispanic white districts. It is in these districts that minority candidates are more likely to face non-Hispanic white opponents. Across all three candidate groupings, non-Hispanic white candidates spend more than minority candidates. The disparity is particularly large in highly competitive non-Hispanic white districts where the median values indicate that non-Hispanic white candidates outraise minority candidates by more than a 2 to 1 margin.

Candidate Status

Why do minority candidates appear to raise less money than non-Hispanic white candidates running under similar circumstances? A number of explanations have been provided by political observers, with the most often cited explanation focusing on candidate status. As the argument goes, because there are fewer minority incumbents and because incumbents raise larger amounts of money than nonincumbents, it appears in the aggregate as if minorities are underfunded. However, seldom is this proposition tested. An appropriate method of evaluating this hypothesis is to compare funding levels of non-Hispanic whites and minorities by candidate status (incumbent, challenger, and open-seat contestants). Fortunately, this sample provides a fairly good distribution of minorities across these types of candidates. Table 8-3 displays the mean and median contribution levels of non-Hispanic white and minority candidates across these three different candidate types.

Among the incumbent candidates, the mean levels indicate that minority candidates running in non-Hispanic white districts are better funded than other minorities or even non-Hispanic white candidates. However, if we consider median values (which lessen the influence of outliers), it appears that non-Hispanic white candidates are better funded than minority candidates regardless of the district characteristics. These results seem to suggest that incumbency is not the only factor driving differences in levels of funding between minority and non-Hispanic white candidates. Clearly, incumbents on average raise more than challengers or open-seat candidates. However, among incumbent candidates it seems that minorities are still underfunded.

Table 8-3   *Mean and Median Revenue Raised Per Eligible Voter, by Race and Candidate Type*

Candidate Type	Non-Hispanic White Candidates	Minority Candidates	
		In Non-Hispanic White Districts	In Majority-Minority Districts
Incumbents			
Mean	$1.06	$1.39	$0.88
Median	$0.78	$0.60	$0.38
N=	(284)	(7)	(13)
Challengers			
Mean	$0.36	$0.16	$0.21
Median	$0.16	$0.03	$0
N=	(255)	(18)	(5)
Open-seat candidates			
Mean	$0.79	$1.08	$0.64
Median	$0.54	$1.18	$0.74
N=	(176)	(9)	(11)

Note: Data are from 1992 elections in California, Illinois, and Pennsylvania and from 1991 elections in New Jersey. Data are for all candidates who had at least some competition in the general election.

Additional findings are provided by the contribution levels of challenger and open-seat contestants. Among challengers, minority candidates raise less money than non-Hispanic white candidates regardless of district makeup. For example, if the funding levels of minorities running in non-Hispanic white districts are compared with the levels raised by non-Hispanic white candidates, minorities appear to be substantially underfunded. On average minority candidates spend less than one-half as much as the typical non-Hispanic white candidate.

However, a different situation exists among open-seat candidates. When competing for open seats, minorities running in non-Hispanic white districts generally raise more than non-Hispanic whites. The mean level of contributions for minorities is $1.08, while the mean is only $0.79 for non-Hispanic whites; at the median level, the difference remains ($1.18 versus $0.54). In fact, the median level of contributions for minority candidates in majority-minority districts is higher than it is for non-Hispanic white candidates ($0.74 versus $0.54, although it is slightly less at the mean level: $0.64 versus $0.79).

To this point, the results suggest that the ability to attract campaign funds is influenced by candidate status and district type. One other point needs to be made in reference to the findings in both Tables 8-2 and 8-3. One of the primary concerns in this analysis is whether minority candidates are disadvantaged in the political process by their inability to compete financially. Although conclusive evidence cannot be drawn from this relatively small sample, the best available evidence is derived from comparisons of the first two columns in each table. The third column represents something of a special case—a situation where minority candidates run in majority-minority districts. We know that minorities can and do get elected in these districts. Because of other social networks and organizations, minority candidates simply do not need to raise and spend funds like their counterparts who run in non-Hispanic white districts.

If these cases are included in an analysis that attempts to answer the question posed above, they would significantly overestimate any minority bias in the campaign finance system. Among incumbents and challengers in Table 8-3, median values for minority candidates in majority-minority districts are lower in each case. To estimate any minority bias, the first two columns—where white candidates and minority candidates run in non-Hispanic white districts—must be compared.[5] A comparison of these two columns produces interesting, and mixed, results. The averages for incumbent minority candidates lag their nonminority counterparts, but not by a wide margin. The medians are reversed, but again, not by a wide margin. Minority candidates in open-seat races actually do better, while the largest discrepancies are found among minority candidates who challenge a sitting incumbent. Of course, candidates of any race are more often than not disadvantaged when they challenge incumbents.

Leadership

Another explanation often provided for why minorities are under-funded is that they seldom hold leadership positions in the legislature. Leaders have an easier time raising funds than rank-and-file incumbents. To test for this, levels of campaign contributions are compared in Table 8-4 across three candidate categories: nonincumbent candidates

Table 8-4   *Mean and Median Revenue Raised Per Eligible Voter, by Race, Candidate Type, and Degree of District Competition*

District Competition/ Candidate Type	Non-Hispanic White Candidates	Minority Candidates
LOW COMPETITION		
Challengers/open seat		
Mean	$0.34	$0.39
Median	$0.14	$0.13
N=	(262)	(25)
Incumbent nonleaders		
Mean	$0.69	$0.67
Median	$0.61	$0.55
N=	(134)	(9)
Incumbent leaders		
Mean	$1.75	$1.41
Median	$0.89	$0.25
N=	(42)	(8)
HIGH COMPETITION		
Challengers/open seat		
Mean	$0.83	$0.60
Median	$0.68	$0.40
N=	(178)	(17)
Incumbent nonleaders		
Mean	$1.31	$0.18
Median	$1.03	$0.18
N=	(71)	(1)
Incumbent leaders		
Mean	$1.19	$1.49
Median	$1.15	$1.51
N=	(28)	(3)

Note: Data are from 1992 elections in California, Illinois, and Pennsylvania and from 1991 elections in New Jersey. Data are for all candidates who had at least some competition in the general election. Leaders are those holding a position such as speaker, assistant speaker, majority or minority leader, or committee chair.

(challengers/open seat), incumbents who are not legislative leaders, and incumbent leaders. Leadership is defined here rather broadly and includes those holding a position such as speaker, assistant speaker, majority or minority leader, or committee chair. These categories have been arrayed by competitiveness of the race in order to provide an opportunity to examine the multiple effects of these factors on the funding of non-Hispanic white and minority candidates.

The data in Table 8-4 show that a leadership position does matter, but that its effects vary based on the competitiveness of the district. As one might expect, incumbent candidates of either racial grouping generally raise more money on average than challengers and open-seat candidates regardless of district competitiveness. In addition, leaders raise more than nonleader incumbents among both minority and non-Hispanic white candidates. But what is most interesting is that while minority candidates appear to raise less money on average in districts with low competition, minority leaders seem to raise more than their non-Hispanic white counterparts in highly competitive races. But these findings are probably related to district type once again. Low competition districts more than likely include the majority-minority districts, where minority candidates do not need to raise or spend as much. Hence, the relative parity of candidates in this category is even more interesting. The highly competitive districts more than likely exclude most minority-majority districts, indicating that the few minority leaders in the sample do very well, while minority challengers and open-seat contestants lag their white counterparts, but not by a great deal. We cannot draw any inferences from our lone incumbent nonleader.

Care should be taken when interpreting these results. Many of the cells have a very low number of cases and conclusions about the role of leadership should be made with caution. However, these results point to several observations. One is that minority candidates are not always underfunded. Under some conditions, in fact, minorities receive a higher level of funding than non-Hispanic white candidates in similar situations. A second point is that candidate status and leadership position affect contribution patterns and the fact that fewer minorities possess these characteristics may partially explain why minorities generally have lower levels of funding than non-Hispanic whites.

PAC and Party Contributions

Another explanation often provided for differences in contribution levels involves the source of candidate revenues. One possibility is that minority candidates receive less help than non-Hispanic white candidates from parties and interest groups in funding their campaigns. Table 8-5

Table 8-5   *Campaign Revenue Raised from Political Parties and*
Interest Groups, in Percentages

	Interest Groups/PACs		Political Parties	
	Non-Hispanic White Candidates	Minority Candidates	Non-Hispanic White Candidates	Minority Candidates
All candidates[a]				
Mean	31%	45%	14%	8%
Median	30	45	3	1
N=	(729)	(73)	(729)	(73)
Candidates with competition[b]				
Mean	30	40	15	8
Median	29	41	4	1
N=	(689)	(55)	(689)	(55)
Candidates with high competition[c]				
Mean	29	32	21	10
Median	29	32	9	2
N=	(276)	(21)	(276)	(21)

Note: Data are from 1992 elections in California, Illinois, and Pennsylvania and from 1991 elections in New Jersey. Party contributions include total contributions from political parties on all levels.

[a] Includes candidates without competition.

[b] Includes third party and independent competition.

[c] Those races in which a candidate received between 40 and 60 percent of the general election vote.

provides some evidence that may help answer this question by presenting the percentage of funding received from party and interest group (PAC) sources.[6]

How are minorities funded by interest groups and PACs? In all cases the mean and median values exceed 30 percent of the contributions. The data in Table 8-5 also appear to indicate that minority candidates receive a slightly larger share of their funding from interest groups and PACs than do non-Hispanic white candidates, and this pattern holds across competition levels.

The results from Table 8-5 also suggest that minority candidates are not allocated a proportionate share of funds from political parties. Across all three categories of competition, minority candidates receive on average only about 8 to 10 percent of their funds from political parties, while non-Hispanic whites receive about 14 to 21 percent.

Since party funds are relatively small in comparison to PAC funds, this discrepancy might not be too detrimental to campaign efforts. But it is interesting as to why party operatives are not more strategic in allocating party funds. Several factors may be at play here, one of which is partisanship. Generally, Republican party organizations have more money to distribute, and fewer minorities run as Republicans. In a similar vein, Democratic strategists may not allocate party funds to minority candidates running in safe minority districts. However, in nonminority districts, party money may be important as seed money for building early support among potential contributors and may be more helpful than interest group funding, which tends to come later in the campaign season.

CONCLUSION

Once differences in districts and candidate attributes have been taken into account, it appears that minority candidates are funded at a lower rate than non-Hispanic white candidates, but not by wide margins. The disparity appears to be most prevalent among campaigns where there is a high level of competition. Even after controlling for population of the district, candidate status, and leadership position, minority candidates generally attract less money, although this finding is somewhat clouded by the presence of majority-minority districts. There are exceptions to this pattern among candidate types (minority candidates in open-seat races raise more on average than non-Hispanic white candidates), and there is some evidence that minority leaders are more successful in highly competitive races. However, the general pattern is that minority candidates, for the most part, raise and spend less than non-Hispanic white candidates.

Several explanations for this pattern were explored. Attempts were made to link these differences to the fact that fewer minority candidates are incumbents or legislative leaders and some support was found for these propositions. In addition there is evidence that minority candidates are disadvantaged with regard to where they receive their funding. Minority candidates receive a lower percentage of funding from political parties than non-Hispanic white candidates, but they receive a larger share from interest groups.

What is to be made of these findings? Are these differences important? Given the current candidate-centered political environment and the need for money to communicate effectively with voters, those who lack financial resources ostensibly lack an ability to gain access to the legislature. The findings presented here would seem to indicate that the allocation of resources vary by racial category and that this may be one reason why minorities are underrepresented in legislative institutions.

One might argue that funding disparities among candidates do not matter much given that many minorities run in districts that are drawn as majority-minority districts. Evidence presented here does in fact show that minorities running in such districts seldom face stiff competition. However, such a conclusion is misguided for two reasons. One is that about half of the minority candidates in this study ran against a non-Hispanic white candidate. If minorities are running against non-Hispanic white candidates and are systematically underfunded, this may be a contributing factor for why minorities are often underrepresented. Evidence indicates that minority challengers who run in majority non-Hispanic white districts are indeed underfunded compared to non-Hispanic white candidates. A second reason why such a conclusion seems misguided is that the Supreme Court in recent years has begun to limit the use of race as a criteria for drawing electoral districts. If fewer majority-minority districts result, many more minority candidates will find themselves running in majority non-Hispanic white districts. As a result, any bias in the campaign finance system will only exacerbate the underrepresentation of minority groups in the legislature.

Finally, a word of caution is in order. Much more research is needed in this area. The findings presented here are based on an analysis of four states at one point in time. In order to more fully understand the nature of the relationship between campaign finances and the success of minority candidates, a larger sample of candidates across a wider array of institutional settings needs to be examined. By examining minority groups in a variety of contexts, we can determine how institutional factors might play a role. For example, all four states used in this analysis are considered to have "professional" legislatures, which generally have higher costs associated with elections (see chapter 3). How might the ability of minority candidates to raise funds differ in less professional settings? In lower cost states? How well do minority candidates fare in other regions of the country, particularly in southern states? These and other important questions need to be explored before we can develop a complete picture of minority representation.

NOTES

1. Each member of New Jersey's lower house is elected from a two-member at-large district where the top two vote-getters become the winners.
2. From the sample of 81 minority candidates, we were able to identify 37 that ran against non-Hispanic white candidates. There may be more, but it was not always possible to identify the race/ethnicity of all the opponents. Of these 37 candidates, 18 were challengers, 8 were incumbents, and 11 were open-seat contenders. While comparisons could be made with these candi-

dates, the situation is complicated further by the fact that many of them ran in New Jersey's multimember districts. It is not altogether obvious what constitutes a head-to-head contest in such districts.

3. We have not removed the contributions of non-Hispanic white leaders for two reasons. One is that no other leader takes in nearly as much as Brown (only Michael Madigan, speaker of the Illinois house comes close in raising $2 million—half as much as raised by the Brown campaign). Second, any one non-Hispanic white candidate in our sample is unlikely to skew the results much in that we have 755 non-Hispanic white candidates in the sample. In contrast, there are only 81 minority candidates in the sample.

4. In our candidate-level data set, a district is considered a majority-minority district if the minority candidates' race/ethnicity matched that of the majority-minority population.

5. Actually a better method would be to compare head-to-head races between whites and minority candidates in both types of districts. Unfortunately, we do not have enough cases for meaningful comparisons.

6. Money from interest groups and PACs are combined in this table since some states allow interest groups to contribute directly to candidates.

REFERENCES

Alma-Bonilla, Y. I., and J. Tomes. 1996. "Latinos Set Pace as Hispanics Gain 11 Seats in '97 State Legislatures." *Hispanic Link Weekly Report* 14 (December 2): 1–2.

Bullock, C. 1992. "Minorities in State Legislatures." In *Changing Patterns in State Legislative Careers,* edited by G. Moncrief and J. Thompson. Ann Arbor: University of Michigan Press.

Clucas, R. 1994. "The Effect of Campaign Contributions on the Power of the California Assembly Speaker." *Legislative Studies Quarterly* 19: 417–428.

Garcia, J. A. 1986. "The Voting Rights Act and Hispanic Political Representation in the Southwest." *Publius: The Journal of Federalism* 16: 49–66.

Grofman, B., and L. Handley. 1991. "The Impact of the Voting Rights Act on Black Representation in Southern State Legislatures." *Legislative Studies Quarterly* 16: 11–128.

Hadley, C., and R. Nick. 1987. "The Two Step Flow of State Campaign Funds: PACs as Donors and Receivers in Louisiana." *Western Political Quarterly* 40: 65–77.

Joint Center for Political and Economic Studies. Various years. *Handbook of Black Elected Officials.* Washington, D.C.

Lenz, T., and A. Pritchard. 1989. "The Effects of Changing from Single-Member to Multi-Member Districts: The Case of Florida." Typescript. Boca Raton, Fla.: Florida Atlantic University.

Moncrief, G., and J. A. Thompson. 1992. "Electoral Structure and State Legislative Representation." *Journal of Politics* 54: 246–257.

National Association of Latino Elected Officials. Various years. *National Roster of Hispanic Elected Officials.* Washington, D.C.

Nelson, A. J. 1991. *Emerging Influentials in State Legislatures.* New York: Praeger.

Stanley, H. W., and R. G. Niemi. 1994. *Vital Statistics on American Politics,* 4th ed. Washington, D.C.: Congressional Quarterly.

Theilmann, G., and D. Dixon. 1994. "Explaining Contributions: Rational Contributors and the Elections of the 71st Texas House." *Legislative Studies Quarterly* 19: 495–520.

Thompson, J. A. 1986. "The Voting Rights Act in North Carolina: An Evaluation. *Publius: The Journal of Federalism* 16: 139–153.

Wilhite, A., and J. Theilmann. 1986. "Women, Blacks, and PAC Discrimination." *Social Science Quarterly* 67: 283–298.

CHAPTER NINE

Patterns of PAC Contributions to State Legislative Candidates

William E. Cassie and Joel A. Thompson

As discussed in chapter 1, it is widely perceived in contemporary American politics that campaign costs are ever-increasing. In chapter 3, Gary Moncrief noted that growth in campaign expenditures is not uniform across states and appears to be associated with several factors, including legislative professionalism, the electoral cycle, and the competitiveness of the race. Other scholars have investigated factors that contribute to this trend and have concluded that inflation (Neal 1992), party control of chambers (Moncrief and Patton 1993), and the growing use of more expensive campaign techniques (Neal 1992) are related as well.

Campaign expenditures are a function of the pool of political money that is available in a constituency in any given election. Political action committees, or PACs, contribute to this pool of money and often contribute quite heavily. While systematic data across states are not available, case studies offer evidence of a correlation between the growth in the number of PACs and the rise in campaign expenditures. Herbert Alexander has noted that, at the national level, the number of PACs increased from 2,551 in 1980 to 4,172 in 1990—an increase of 64 percent (1992, 59). At the state level, the number of PACs doubled in Wisconsin between 1976 and 1984, quadrupled in New York between 1978 and 1984, and more than quintupled in Arizona between 1974 and 1982 (Jones 1986). We found a similar trend in North Carolina, where the number of registered PACs increased from 106 in 1976 (the first year data were available) to 454 in 1988 (Thompson and Cassie 1990).

Given the dramatic rise in the number of political action committees over the past two decades, an examination of their activities is warranted. This chapter will describe trends and analyze patterns of contributions by political action committees to state legislative candidates.

Among the questions to be explored are: How much do PACs contribute in various states? What system-level variables explain differences in the amount of money contributed by PACs? Is the perception that PACs contribute a major proportion of candidate funds accurate? Do legal restrictions on contributions affect the level of PAC funding? How does PAC money vary by candidate attributes, such as incumbency and leadership status? Is there a partisan bias in PAC contributions? Does the type of PAC affect contribution strategy?

THEORETICAL CONSIDERATIONS

In addition to the aggregate factors associated with the classification of states presented in chapter 1, an analysis of PAC behavior must be guided by the findings of previous research relative to individual level attributes. The theoretical work concerning the actions, motivations, and influences of PACs is also helpful. Generally, this work has taken one of two perspectives. Some studies have employed individual PACs as their unit of analysis and attempted to explain the *motivations or incentives* that govern PAC behavior. A second approach has utilized individual candidates as the unit of analysis and examined the impact of various *candidate attributes* on the amount of PAC funds received. Both of these approaches will be used in this analysis.

PAC Motivations and Incentives

In one of the earliest works at the congressional level, Gopoian (1984) identified four broad categories of incentives that influence PAC decision making. He theorized that these incentives may be a function of relatively narrow and parochial issue concerns, broad policy or ideological positions, the desire for access to decisionmakers, or desire for political power.

Each of these incentives may lead PACs to pursue different strategies. For example, a PAC primarily interested in specific policies may target members of relevant legislative committee for support (see, for example, Grier and Munger 1991, Hall and Wayman 1990, Munger 1989, Romer and Synder 1994). For other types of PACs, broader ideological considerations may outweigh particular issue concerns, prompting these PACs to support candidates of one party over another (see, for example, Su, Neustadtl, and Clawson 1995; Welch 1979). Access to decisionmakers is perhaps the most common goal attributed to PAC behavior (Hansen 1991, Herrnson 1992). Quite often, PACs desire access not only to keep the communication channels open (Gopoian 1984, 262), but also as a defensive measure to "avoid having something done" to them (Greenwald 1977, 144). This strategy provides a political action committee with the incentive to contribute to likely winners who, more often than not, are incumbents. Finally, a PAC's desire to influence policy outcomes may be tempting enough for it to risk contributing to an incumbent in electoral jeopardy, with the hope that its contribution is helpful (if not decisive) in sustaining a winning coalition, thereby increasing the PAC's clout with that member (see, for example, Wright 1985).

Other studies by Grenzke (1989), Grier and Munger (1986, 1993), and Poole and Romer (1985) have found evidence of relationships between PAC contributions and various measures of incentives, including committee assignments, party and leadership positions, voting records, seniority, electoral security, and political party affiliation *at the congressional level*. These studies point to a clear linkage between PAC incentives that guide contribution strategies and certain candidate attributes that help determine whether and how these candidates fit within the PACs' legislative game plan.

Few state legislatures, however, are models of Congress. Given the substantial variation in legislative professionalism and party control at the state level, not all of these linkages may be operative. While there is evidence to suggest that some of these decision rules may apply, they must be explored in a comparative analysis. Some candidate-level variables that previous studies suggest are important determinants of PAC strategy are outlined below. These linkages are then tested within the varying legislative arenas of the states.

Candidate Attributes

There has been a paucity of multistate studies of PAC behavior at the state level. Previous studies by the authors found some similarity with congressional studies (see Thompson and Cassie 1996; Thompson, Cassie, and Jewell 1994). In general these studies found that candidate attributes, especially incumbency and party, were important determinants of PAC contributions.

A recent six-state analysis of the tobacco industry by Monardi and Glantz lends support to Gopoian's incentive theory. Their analysis of contributions in California, Colorado, Massachusetts, Ohio, Pennsylvania, and Washington found that tobacco interests tended to "support the party in power regardless of whether it was the Democrats or Republicans" (1996, 3). Also, they noted that tobacco PACs were likely to contribute larger sums to leaders "who were able to influence the overall policy making process" (1996, 3). They concluded that tobacco PACs are more opportunistic than ideological in making campaign contributions.

From these and a number of case studies, several factors have emerged as consistent correlates of PAC contributions. These include:

Incumbency

One constant from previous studies is the power of incumbency, and as Gierzynski points out in chapter 2, money flows to power. Studies consistently have found that PACs favor incumbents over challengers at both the congressional and state legislative levels (California Commission on Campaign Financing 1985; Cassie 1991; Eisenstein 1984; Eismeier and Pollock 1986; Jacobson 1980; Jones and Borris 1985; Sabato 1985; Sorauf 1988; Thompson and Cassie 1992; Thompson, Cassie, and Jewell 1994). This relationship is driven primarily by PACs' motivation for access. Consequently, they contribute funds to those most likely to occupy legislative seats in general and certain committee assignments in particular. Given their high reelection rates, incumbents are the logical choice for most PACs since these are the candidates most likely to win election. This is their best strategy to gain access, to keep the channels of communication open, and to receive an early warning on potential problems (Jacobson and Kernell 1983; Sabato 1985; and especially Gopoian 1984).[1]

Party

A linkage between party and PAC contributions is suggested by both the access and ideological motivation theories of PAC behavior. Previous research has observed such biases but has been unable to explore this relationship in detail because of data limitations (Cassie 1991; Thompson, Cassie, and Jewell 1994).

The access motivation would suggest a linkage between PACs with specific issue concerns and candidates of the majority party, especially in one-party dominant states. Since majority parties provide not only access but potentially more clout for the PAC's money (more partisan and programmatic "bang for their bucks"), we would expect PACs with issue concerns to seek favor with members of the predominant party. Of course, all PACs have issue concerns—that is why they exist—but some have more narrowly focused interests than others (i.e., the NRA contrasted with the AFL-CIO). Access keeps the PAC in the line of communication, affording opportunities for input into the rule-making process.

PACs with broader agendas, like business and labor PACs, may be more interested in ideological and partisan alignments than majority/minority status. Thus, their contribution strategies would vary accordingly. For example, given the general ideological tendencies that exist in the United States, this logic would predict that, all other things being equal, pro-labor PACs would likely give predominantly to Democrat incumbents while pro-business PACs would contribute to Republican candidates. However, the existence of linkages will vary across states, depending upon the nature of the economy and the strength and organization of the political parties. In other words, such a labor-Democrat or business-Republican linkage may be more prevalent in Michigan than in Montana.

Leadership

Incumbents who hold leadership positions in the legislature provide the greatest degree of access and political clout. Van Der Slik states this point succinctly: "When it comes to the end of the session, with settlement of the big issues, the question is: Who's going to be at the table?" (quoted in Fitzgerald and McDermott 1997, 123). For these reasons, leaders are generally favored by most PACs, unless they are known opponents of the PAC's issue position or ideological domain. Under this rubric, leaders would include the usual cast of partisan leaders as well as chairs of relevant substantive committees. Previous research has found some support for this relationship in North Carolina (Thompson and Cassie 1992), California (Clucas 1992), and Illinois (Fitzgerald and McDermott 1997). However, the relationship between leadership position and PAC contributions remains untested in the broader context of variations in legislative professionalism and party control.

System-Level Variables

We have reviewed several possible explanations for variations in PACs' strategic contributions across the states and assessed previous studies that identify factors linked to variations in candidates' PAC receipts, such as party status, incumbency, electoral vulnerability, committee assignment, and leadership position. While these studies are instructive in guiding this analysis, they are limited, primarily because of a lack of multistate data. It is not known to what extent these factors differ in professional versus amateur bodies or whether they are consistent in one-party dominant states versus competitive states. The impact of legal restrictions on candidates' PAC revenues is also not known.

There is reason to expect differences across states due to legislative professionalism[2] and partisan alignments. For example, professional legislatures have more resources available for members. Thus, members of these bodies may not be as reliant upon groups for information, technical expertise, or other resources. On the other hand, obtaining or retaining a seat in a professional legislatures is often a high-cost endeavor, placing a premium on candidates' ability to raise enough revenue to run competitive campaigns. Which of these (and other) factors are more important in explaining variations in PAC contributions? Similarly, the inclination of some types of PACs to align with a political party (e.g., business interests with Republicans) may be different in two-party versus one-party states. These forces have been found to be important determinants of spending by legislative campaign committees (Rosenthal 1995). Are they related to PAC spending? If so, in what ways? Our data will allow us to explore some of these questions.

In order to answer the questions raised above, the patterns of PAC contributions to general election candidates in seventeen states will be examined.[3] The goals of this analysis are to discern the common patterns of PAC contributions across states and to identify factors that may explain variation among states.

VARIATIONS IN PAC REVENUES

Macro-Level Factors

The average total PAC contribution and percent of total funds derived from PACs, broken down by incumbents, challengers, and open-seat candidates, are displayed in Table 9-1. Vast differences in PAC money across the states can be observed. Average contributions for incumbents range from a low of about $1,000 in Montana to a high of more than $200,000 in California. Similar variations exist for candidates vying for open seats (from $513 in Montana to $125,126 in California) and challengers ($538 in Montana to $40,178 in California). To what extent can these variations be explained by macro-level variables, such as legislative professionalism, party competition, overall costs of campaigns, or legal restrictions?[4]

Legislative Professionalism

Figure 9-1 displays PAC contributions for incumbents. It is organized by level of professionalism, ranging from most professional on the left to least professional on the right. California stands alone with average PAC contributions to incumbents that are approximately four times greater than those of the nearest state (and primarily for this reason the PAC data are displayed on a logarithmic scale). Incumbents in professional states generally receive larger amounts of PAC money than other states, although Oregon and Washington (hybrid legislatures) rival the amounts in professional states. The level of PAC money in Wisconsin is noticeably lower than other professional states, and Minnesota has lower levels of PAC funding than most of the hybrid states. Both of these states utilize public financing, which may lead to less reliance on PAC funding. Citizen legislatures generally have much smaller average PAC contributions.

Table 9-1   *Average PAC Contribution and Percentage of Funds from PACs, by Candidate Status*

State	Incumbents		Challengers		Open Seat	
	Average PAC Contribution	% of Funds from PACs	Average PAC Contribution	% of Funds from PACs	Average PAC Contribution	% of Funds from PACs
California	$200,220	42.34%	$40,178	32.71%	$125,126	44.72%
Illinois	51,912	52.68	4,048	16.13	24,320	30.46
New Jersey	31,629	27.49	9,482	19.94	20,375	15.36
Pennsylvania	15,593	43.73	2,233	19.09	7,411	20.67
Wisconsin	4,449	19.77	541	3.52	1,992	7.94
Delaware	7,085	44.79	2,014	17.69	4,981	24.70
Kansas	10,373	66.11	1,967	26.74	4,594	39.31
Minnesota	4,569	11.49	620	4.36	1,963	8.47
Mississippi	2,044	61.55	592	37.07	1,586	33.86
North Carolina	9,112	50.84	1,221	9.69	3,275	21.98
Oregon	46,277	53.08	18,505	42.97	45,392	60.39
Washington	31,691	54.04	6,556	31.81	18,922	39.36
Idaho	5,120	64.74	1,724	28.22	3,646	43.07
Maine	1,422	30.42	701	23.43	1,009	23.11
Montana	1,066	24.46	538	13.49	513	10.91
Utah	4,526	70.14	2,104	38.07	3,250	51.88
Wyoming	2,740	60.33	1,154	28.24	1,930	39.88

Note: States are grouped by legislative professionalism: California, most professional to least professional.

Figure 9-1   *Average Incumbent PAC Revenue, by Professionalism*

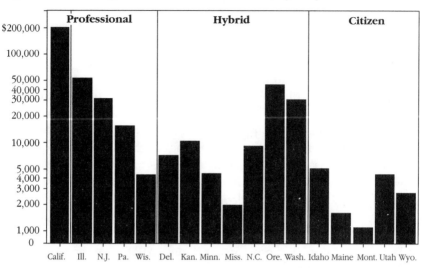

Note: States are grouped by legislative professionalism: California, most professional to least professional. PAC revenue is displayed on a logarithmic scale so that all states are visible in the figure.

It appears that professionalism accounts for some of the variation in PAC revenues. Citizen legislatures have averages that tend to fall well below hybrid or professional states. At this point it cannot be determined whether this is a direct or an indirect relationship. This question will be pursued in more detail as other factors that may explain variations among states are considered.

Party Competition

We have suggested that increased party competition may lead to greater PAC activity. When parties are vying for control of the legislature we expect to observe renewed efforts by candidates to raise money in order to gain/maintain control. This is likely to involve the party organizations as well as the party leadership in the government. If this relationship exists, we should observe higher levels of PAC funding in competitive states and less PAC involvement in the less competitive states.

Our sample includes four states—Idaho, Mississippi, Utah, and Wyoming—that are categorized by the Ranney index[5] as being one-party states (Bibby and Holbrook 1996) and six states—Idaho, Maine, Mississippi, Montana, North Carolina, and Wyoming—where the majority party holds more than 60 percent of the seats prior to the election being considered. Combining these two measures yields seven states that may be characterized as less competitive and where it is unlikely that the majority party will lose control in the upcoming election.

Five of these states have citizen legislatures and two (Mississippi and North Carolina) have hybrids. As already noted in Figure 9-1, average PAC totals for candidates in citizen legislatures are considerably lower than those in hybrid and professional states. Mississippi, which has the lowest level of PAC funding among the hybrid states, fits the pattern as well. The one atypical state is North Carolina—a state whose one-party Democratic dominance disappeared with the 1994 election. Collectively, the PAC totals for these states lend credence to the notion that less party competition is associated with decreased PAC involvement in elections. However, since professionalism and party competition are so intertwined in our sample, their independent effects cannot be sorted out.

Costs of Campaigns

While some explanations for variations in PAC funding have been identified, we cannot say with certainty that professionalism and party competition directly influence PAC behavior. A plausible explanation is that PACs *react* financially to the political environment of a state, an environment that includes professionalism, party competition, and the overall costs of elections. Strategically, PACs may determine what it takes to achieve their goals and contribute this amount and no more. If the candidates in a state are forced to raise a larger war chest to be competitive, then PACs respond with larger average contributions. In low-cost states, PACs can achieve their goals with smaller contributions. In other words, it costs less to do political business in Montana than in California. The key is to give enough to achieve the goal of access and then pursue the organization's agenda after the election.

The level of PAC funding coincides nicely with the overall costs of elections (see Table 3-1). The six states with the highest level of incumbent PAC funding in Table 9-1 are the six with the most expensive elections (California, Illinois, Oregon, and Washington from Table 3-1, in addition to New Jersey and Pennsylvania from our analysis). Similarly, the states with the least amount of PAC money are also those with the least expensive elections. Our analysis (not shown) also indicates that the *growth* in PAC money over time (1986–1992) corresponds with the *increase* in election costs demonstrated in Table 3-3. These findings may be interpreted as evidence that PAC money is a major force in driving up election costs. However, we believe a different interpretation is true—PACs are *reacting* to escalating costs and greater demands for money. Candidates must find additional funding and PACs are one source to which they turn with greater frequency. PACs react to the greater demand by contributing larger sums. Their increased contributions are simply a recognition that the cost of doing political business is going up, like every other commodity.

To explore this premise more thoroughly we examined the relationship between PAC funding and the amount of money donated by other types of contributors. Figure 9-2 displays the average PAC contribution for incumbents, but ordered by the average total revenue from sources other than PACs. If PACs react to the overall costs of elections, then we should observe a linear pattern indicating that PAC revenues are greater in states where other revenues are higher and less in states where other revenues are lower. This is exactly the pattern observed. There is a strong relationship between these two variables ($r = .97$), which supports the hypothesis that PACs react to the state's political environment by developing a contribution recipe that varies by state. In Maine a dash of PAC money may do, but California requires a full cup (or more).

These findings may also help us understand the relationship between professionalism and party competition. The relationship between these variables and PAC contributions may be indirect. Both factors may influence the costs of elections, which in turn influences the amount of PAC activity. If correct, this notion would go far in explaining variations in PAC revenues across states.

Figure 9-2   *Average Incumbent PAC Revenue, by Total Non-PAC Revenue*

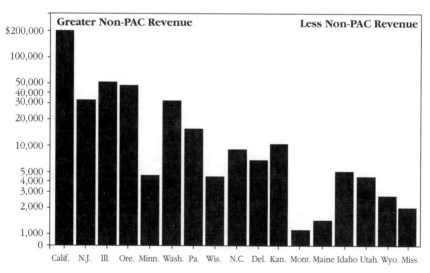

Note: PAC revenue is displayed on a logarithmic scale so that all states are visible in the figure.

Legal Restrictions

A final systemic variable—legal restrictions on campaign contributions—will be examined to see if these regulations impact the flow of political money into campaign coffers and, thus, help explain some of the variation seen across the states. One of the most popular reforms currently being discussed is placing restrictions, or greater restrictions, on contributions from political action committees. The obvious theory behind this proposal is that greater restrictions will reduce the amount of PAC money and, by extension, PAC influence. The states provide a unique arena for examining this linkage since the states vary considerably in terms of their legal restrictions.

About half the states in this study have some form of legal restrictions on PAC contributions to candidates. Five of the states (Delaware, Kansas, Minnesota, Montana, and Wisconsin) have fairly restrictive laws that limit contributions to $1,000 or less. Two states (Maine and North Carolina) are less restrictive, with ceilings ranging from $4,000 to $5,000.[6] The other ten states did not limit PAC contributions at the time of this study.

Referring again to Table 9-1, these restrictions do not appear helpful in explaining the overall amount of PAC money contributed to candidates, especially incumbents. While it is true that the states with the greatest amounts of PAC money are also states with little or no restrictions, before we conclude that this is a causal relationship we must consider the implications of the totals in Table 9-1. Montana ranks as the state with the least amount of PAC money flowing into legislative coffers, and it has the most rigid restrictions (a $300 limit). However, it is doubtful that the low level of PAC funding is actually due to the restrictions, since it would take only four PACs contributing the maximum to exceed the average noted. Undoubtedly, the average Montana incumbent receives funds from more than four PACs. In fact, they receive on average about eight PAC contributions. A more likely explanation is that the cost of doing political business in Montana is comparatively low.

In contrast, Maine has a liberal $5,000 limit on PAC contributions, yet incumbents average less PAC money than most other states. In fact, Maine incumbents receive an average of only $1,422 from PACs. Similar statements can be made with regard to candidates in Wyoming and Mississippi. Our analysis indicates that both states have comparatively lower levels of PAC money despite having no restrictions.

Generally, the level of PAC money obtained in states with limitations could be achieved with only a small number of maximum contributions. Even in the most extreme state, California, incumbents would need to receive $5,000 from just forty PACs to attain the state's "average."[7] It is unlikely that the average incumbent in California receives money from so few PACs. Given these findings, we conclude that PACs, in general, contribute less than the amount allowed by law. This suggests that PACs limit themselves, probably to an amount related to the "cost of doing political business" in a state and that statutory limits are not the primary factor in setting the price.

Micro-Level Factors

Incumbency

Candidate-level variables may contribute to patterns of PAC contributions. Given the results of congressional studies and state-level case studies, it should come as no surprise that incumbents are the primary recipients of PAC funds. In every state in our analysis, incumbents average more PAC money than challengers and open-seat candidates. The results in Table 9-1 suggest that the order of priority for PACs is incumbents, open-seat candidates, and finally challengers. These findings support the notion that PACs, in the aggregate, are access oriented and, as a result, contribute to likely winners—incumbents and candidates competing for open seats.

The differences between PAC contributions to incumbents and challengers may be seen more clearly if the ratio between these two variables is considered. Figure 9-3 displays these ratios. It is clear that challengers,

Figure 9-3   *Ratio of Incumbent-to-Challenger PAC Revenues*

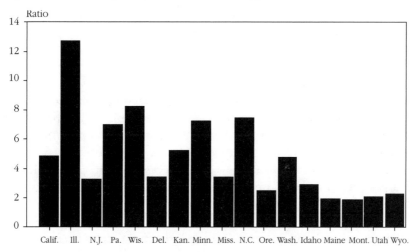

Note: States are grouped by legislative professionalism: California, most professional to least professional.

on average, are at least 2 to 1 underdogs in the PAC money race and, in most cases, are even greater underdogs. There are two major groupings of states. Nine states have incumbent-to-challenger ratios of less than 4 to 1, while eight states have ratios of more than 4 to 1. Illinois stands alone, where incumbents are favored by PACs at a ratio of more than 12 to 1. These findings indicate that PACs play a major role in the overall funding advantage of incumbents, as discussed in chapters 3 and 6. They also indicate that PACs play a greater role in some states than others.

Generally, states with smaller ratios are those with overall lower levels of PAC funding for incumbents. These are states with less party competition, less professional legislatures, and lower overall election costs. The one exception is Oregon, which is one of the states with the highest level of PAC money. Here the ratio is close because challengers in Oregon are, relatively speaking, fairly successful in attracting PAC money (see Table 9-1), perhaps due to the intense competition for control of the legislature. It is also interesting that Wisconsin and Minnesota are two of the highest ratio states, yet are states with lower levels of PAC funds for incumbents compared to similar states. The obvious explanation is that challengers in these states take advantage of available public funds, thereby closing the gap some between themselves and their incumbent opponents.

Percent of Funds from PACs

As shown by the data in Table 9-1, PACs often provide a major proportion of the total funds for incumbents. PACs provide more than 40 percent of average incumbent revenues in twelve of the states and a majority of the funds in nine of these states. Utah and Kansas are the extreme cases, with PACs contributing approximately 70 percent of incumbent funding. Minnesota and Wisconsin are the only states where the percentage of total incumbent funds coming from PACs is less than 20 percent. As noted, these states utilize limited public financing of elections, which would lower the proportional impact of other types of contributors. Less PAC money in these states may also be a reflection of public attitudes against "big money" from interest groups. Among the other states, there appears to be little, if any, relationship between the proportion of PAC funds and level of professionalism, party competition, contribution limits, or election costs.

Competitiveness of the Election

Another interesting question relating to incumbency is whether PACs behave differently toward candidates in competitive and noncompetitive elections. We have suggested that contributions to more vulnerable incumbents may be indicative of a "policy" motivation. It is also logical that challengers in competitive elections, compared to other challengers, may find PACs to be more generous since these candidates are more likely to win and subsequently provide "access."[8]

The findings in Table 9-2 indicate that candidates in competitive elections (winner receiving 60 percent of the vote or less), regardless of incumbency status, generally receive more PAC money than their counterparts in less competitive elections. This finding is interesting, since incumbents in less competitive races are generally considered as safe bets to win. However, this may indicate that vulnerable incumbents simply work harder at raising funds, while those virtually assured of reelection simply do not need to do so. Oregon represents the extreme case, with incumbents in competitive races averaging more than $22,000 more from PACs than incumbents in less competitive races. Again, this finding is probably related to the intense competition for control of the chamber, with candidates and parties being active fund-raisers.

In the case of challengers, PAC money clearly goes to those in competitive races, often at a ratio of about 10 to 1. California challengers in competitive elections average almost $70,000 more than other challengers. The difference is dramatic (in dollar amount) for Illinois and Oregon as well. It should be noted, however, that the amount of PAC money for competitive challengers is still well below the amount given to their incumbent opponents. The pattern for open-seat candidates is similar to that observed for incumbents. In about half the states there is no significant difference between the categories, but in the states where there is a difference the contribution amounts usually favor candidates in competitive races.[9]

These findings, taken collectively, indicate that incumbents are the primary target of PAC funds. This lends strong support for the incentive theory relating to "access" or "communication." Political action committees clearly favor likely winners. This is beneficial to incumbents and open-seat candidates, but leaves likely losers (challengers) trailing well behind. In chapter 6 we discussed the relationship between the incumbency advantage and election results. The findings here indicate that PACs are a major player in creating the financial advantage enjoyed by incumbents and that the inability of challengers to be competitive in many races is at least partially due to their inability to obtain PAC funding.

Partisan Bias

It is also possible that, in pursuing their programmatic agendas, PACs demonstrate partisan bias. Certain types of PACs may prefer one party over the other for ideological or issue-related reasons. Another possibil-

Table 9-2 Average PAC Contribution, by Competitiveness and Incumbency

State	Incumbents		Challengers		Open Seat	
	Competitive	Safe	Competitive	Safe	Competitive	Safe
California	$177,817	$222,623	$93,145	$25,862	$160,916	$84,668
Illinois	60,529	50,592	15,626	1,669	34,229	16,393
New Jersey	32,806	30,822	13,349	5,497	27,560	15,586
Pennsylvania	16,757	15,381	6,399	1,450	7,597	7,030
Wisconsin	4,073	4,557	1,127	143	1,626	2,376
Delaware	6,738	7,205	3,139	1,234	4,292	5,808
Kansas	11,752	9,539	2,746	1,314	4,567	4,768
Minnesota	4,101	4,826	1,198	299	1,959	1,979
Mississippi	3,696	1,727	1,493	75	2,305	867
North Carolina	11,905	7,269	1,598	151	3,422	3,116
Oregon	61,386	38,723	33,197	6,406	52,510	25,622
Washington	35,527	29,035	13,794	1,072	21,527	8,073
Idaho	6,681	4,428	2,628	764	4,640	2,776
Maine	1,577	1,309	1,097	405	1,070	920
Montana	1,344	906	689	358	622	369
Utah	4,702	4,326	2,307	1,842	3,591	2,796
Wyoming	3,561	1,620	1,422	150	2,448	1,140

Note: States are grouped by legislative professionalism: California, most professional to least professional. Competitive races are those in which the winner received 60 percent of the vote or less; safe races are those in which the winner received more than 60 percent of the vote.

ity is that the majority party will be favored by most PACs, particularly if there is a clearly dominant party in the state. The rationale is that the majority party controls the decision-making process, thereby providing a means of greater access and success.

Table 9-3 presents the average PAC contributions when categorized by incumbency status and political party. The incumbency advantage remains regardless of party affiliation. The differences between parties, within the same category of candidates, are the focus of analysis here.

Incumbents are clearly the primary recipients of PAC funds. Democratic incumbents are preferred over Republican incumbents in six states, while Republicans have an advantage in another six. The remaining five states show virtually no difference between Democrat and Republican incumbents.

If PACs show a bias toward the majority party, incumbents of that party should be receiving more PAC money than incumbents of the minority party. In competitive states, we would expect to see little, if any, difference. The data in Table 9-3 show some support for the majority party hypothesis, but the pattern is not consistent. Democrats held strong majorities in Maine, Montana, and North Carolina, yet there is no bias in favor of Democrats. There are also three states controlled by Democrats (New Jersey, Mississippi, and Washington), and two by Republicans (Utah and Wyoming), where the bias goes in the opposite direction. The other nine states are consistent with the hypothesis: seven display the predicted bias and two are competitive states with no apparent bias (Kansas and Wisconsin).

There may be something to be gleaned from further examination of three states that did not fit the expected pattern. North Carolina and Mississippi are southern states that had clear Democratic majorities leading into the elections. However, Republicans have been making major inroads in these states; Republicans actually gained control of the North Carolina House in the subsequent election of 1994. New Jersey was controlled by the Democrats, yet Republican candidates were clearly favored by PACs. Interestingly, the Republicans won a clear majority in the following election. A similar pattern was found in 1987, but with the parties in opposite positions (Cassie, Thompson, and Jewell 1992). These findings suggest that PACs are not only good at supporting candidates who can provide maximum access, but they are very adept at reading the state's political winds as well.

Leadership

While these findings indicate that incumbents are the primary targets of PAC funds, all incumbents are not equal in other ways. In several of

Table 9-3   Average PAC Contribution, by Political Party and Incumbency

State	Majority Party	Incumbents		Challengers		Open Seat	
		Democrat	Republican	Democrat	Republican	Democrat	Republican
California	D	$216,648	$174,406	$24,286	$50,961	$81,789	$170,269
Illinois	D	56,130	46,199	6,146	2,454	23,884	24,866
New Jersey	D	30,194	33,297	5,154	12,589	18,958	22,264
Pennsylvania	D	18,401	12,073	3,523	1,281	7,265	7,557
Wisconsin	D	4,544	4,332	282	500	1,048	1,232
Delaware	R	6,138	7,645	2,609	1,153	6,417	3,259
Kansas	D	10,305	10,445	1,899	2,030	3,983	5,295
Minnesota	D	5,584	2,726	1,571	138	2,861	1,132
Mississippi	D	1,878	2,890	192	963	1,916	1,197
North Carolina	D	9,086	9,178	1,285	1,190	3,508	3,002
Oregon	R	43,859	48,274	22,068	14,179	43,239	47,545
Washington	D	30,251	34,051	9,786	4,722	16,821	20,894
Idaho	R	3,833	5,883	1,447	2,225	2,436	4,705
Maine	D	1,440	1,393	454	843	880	1,154
Montana	D	1,340	1,318	638	965	674	1,001
Utah	R	5,457	3,985	2,672	1,370	4,069	2,278
Wyoming	R	3,309	2,488	1,156	1,152	2,193	1,634

Note: States are grouped by legislative professionalism: California, most professional to least professional. The majority party is the party with greater than 50 percent of the state legislative seats; D = Democrat, R = Republican.

the states incumbents in competitive elections averaged more PAC money than those in less competitive races. Similarly, incumbents from one party are sometimes favored over the other party's incumbents.

Another factor that may differentiate among incumbents is leadership position. Regardless of whether a PAC's interests are narrow or broad, it is likely that leaders will attract a great deal of attention from PACs. These are the people who greatly influence or control the decision-making process in the legislature. In order to examine the relationship between leadership and PAC contributions to incumbents, the data in Table 9-4 have been organized into three categories: party leaders (speaker, majority and minority leaders), committee leaders (committee chairs), and nonleaders (rank-and-file members). The results indicate that leadership influences PAC strategy. Party leaders are the overwhelming favorites. They are clearly favored over the other two categories in twelve states. In several states these differences are great, with Illinois leading the way (but see note 3 in chapter 8, which may explain the large totals for party leaders in Illinois). In many states, the speaker of the house is the major recipient of PAC funds, but majority and minority leaders benefit as well (data not shown). In four states (New Jersey, Kansas, Minnesota, and Idaho) the committee leaders average more than other incumbents. In Montana there is little difference between

Table 9-4   *Average Incumbent PAC Revenues, by Leadership*

State	Party Leader	Committee Leader	Nonleader
California	$341,927	$185,830	$192,768
Illinois	566,497	40,446	35,575
New Jersey	29,921	31,167	23,645
Pennsylvania	54,876	20,084	13,731
Wisconsin	7,950	3,967	4,034
Delaware	25,430	4,810	6,000
Kansas	10,275	12,730	9,953
Minnesota	5,849	7,010	3,530
Mississippi	5,600	2,159	1,920
North Carolina	29,409	8,561	6,491
Oregon	83,764	42,696	45,449
Washington	55,438	32,681	24,083
Idaho	3,161	5,810	4,101
Maine	4,103	1,371	1,372
Montana	1,432	1,000	783
Utah	13,325	3,551	3,549
Wyoming	4,800	2,113	2,411

Note: States are grouped by legislative professionalism: California, most professional to least professional. Party leaders are speaker and majority and minority leader positions; committee leaders are committee chairs; nonleaders are rank-and-file members.

party leaders and committee chairs, but both receive more PAC money than nonleaders.

There is additional evidence to support the hypothesis that PACs prefer leaders. In several cases where one category of leadership appears to be favored there is also a noticeable difference between the other leadership category and nonleaders. The difference between party leaders and committee chairs (when one exists) may be due to the perceived or real location of power in the legislature. PACs seeking power and broad influence would logically target the holders of power in the legislature. If power in the chamber is more fragmented (i.e., resides at the committee level), then the money is targeted to committee leaders. If power is concentrated in the hands of the party leaders, those individuals are the beneficiaries of large PAC contributions.

VARIATION BY TYPE OF PAC

It has been suggested that different types of PACs may have distinct contribution patterns related to their particular motivations. For example, business PACs may contribute disproportionately to Republicans and labor PACs to Democrats if their issue positions match with the ideological position of the party. In this section different types of PACs will be examined, particularly business, labor, and professional and trade.[10] We have some preconceptions about business and labor PACs, but those representing professional and trade interests present an area that rarely has been studied.

Business PACs

Table 9-5 presents information for the three types of PACs, broken down by party. There are two important points to be made concerning business PACs. First, business PACs are clearly the largest contributors of the three types. Regardless of political party, incumbents generally receive more money from businesses than they do from other types of organizations. The only exceptions are found in Minnesota (for both parties) and Wyoming (for Democrats only), where professional and trade PACs are the largest contributors.

The second point is that business PACs favor Republican candidates. They contribute noticeably more to Republican incumbents in all but two states (Illinois and Minnesota). In these states there is virtually no difference between contributions to Democrats and Republicans. This finding fits well with the idea that business interests pursue broad ideological goals that are consistent with traditional Republican policies. We should note, however, that the Republican advantage generally is not

Table 9-5   Average PAC Contributions to Incumbents, by Type of PAC and Party

State	Democrat Business	Democrat Labor	Democrat Prof./Trade	Republican Business	Republican Labor	Republican Prof./Trade
California	$112,164	$45,460	$45,529	$119,849	$11,740	$28,051
Illinois	34,339	9,852	9,880	34,144	1,917	8,123
New Jersey	25,243	3,211	1,199	25,699	4,082	520
Pennsylvania	7,220	4,944	3,615	8,458	644	1,912
Delaware	2,565	1,350	1,832	4,709	695	1,739
Kansas	5,635	1,947	2,070	7,554	163	2,229
Minnesota	1,132	1,231	2,281	934	209	1,172
Mississippi	1,177	122	418	1,983	80	450
North Carolina	5,979	101	2,372	6,780	0	1,274
Oregon	25,118	5,839	10,014	38,635	955	6,001
Washington	16,876	7,321	4,799	26,639	2,278	4,226
Idaho	2,161	1,468	110	4,770	394	288
Maine	825	382	75	1,153	35	118
Montana	589	243	422	939	26	145
Utah	2,351	1,268	1,342	2,809	632	405
Wyoming	988	650	1,545	1,976	0	384

Note: States are grouped by legislative professionalism: California, most professional to least professional. Wisconsin has been eliminated for this analysis because contributions in that state from PACs and non-PACs could not be separated.

great, indicating that business interests hedge their bets somewhat (i.e., they are also sensitive to access irrespective of party). Previous research has suggested this tendency among business interests (Alexander and Bauer 1991).

The variation in the amount of money per state is consistent with the overall variation in PAC contributions noted previously. Business PAC contributions are larger in the more competitive and more professional (and high-cost) states, and notably less in the other states. However, the trend relative to partisan differences follows a somewhat different pattern. Here we find that the difference between business contributions to Republicans and Democrats is generally greatest (in terms of ratio) in states controlled by the Republicans (Delaware, Idaho, Oregon, and Wyoming). The exceptions to this pattern are Utah, a Republican state with little difference between parties, and Washington, a competitive Democratic state with a notable difference between the parties.

Following this reasoning, it is logical that business PACs would demonstrate significant support for Republican incumbents when their party also controls the legislature. However, it would be unwise for business interests to ignore Democrats in states where they control the legislature. Our findings are consistent with this logic.

Labor PACs

Labor PACs appear to have greater partisan bias than business PACs. In every state but one (New Jersey), labor PACs prefer Democrats. Most of the time the difference between labor contributions to Democrats and Republicans is much more noticeable than that observed for business. Democrats generally receive at least twice as much labor money as Republicans, quite often much more. It is also clear from Table 9-5 that labor PACs lag well behind business PACs in the amount of money they contribute. Despite this lag, labor PACs may be critical in understanding the overall partisan bias discussed earlier. If labor PACs help offset the advantage Republicans have with businesses, then Democrats may experience an overall advantage, particularly since businesses have shown a willingness to support Democratic candidates as well.

Professional and Trade PACs

It is apparent from Table 9-5 that professional and trade PACs are a force to be reckoned with in the world of political money. These PACs generally equal or exceed the amount of money contributed by labor PACs. These PACs are the largest source of funds for Democrats in two states (Minnesota and Wyoming) and for Republicans in one (Minnesota). When there is any partisan difference, Democrats are generally the winners. Democrats have a distinct advantage in ten of the states, with little difference observed in the other six.

We cannot conclude with any certainty why this bias toward Democrats exists. We can speculate that it is a result of strong involvement by lawyer and teacher groups that may find Democrats more ideologically compatible. These groups have been identified as influential in many states, which undoubtedly translates into them being a major source of campaign funds (Thomas and Hrebenar 1996). These preliminary findings suggest that future studies of PAC behavior should be directed toward a more in-depth examination of professional and trade PACs.

SUMMARY AND IMPLICATIONS

This chapter has examined the contribution patterns of political action committees to candidates in seventeen states. Our findings are consistent with previous research that has found a strong link between PAC money and incumbency. Also, we have confirmed findings from case studies that suggest that PACs contribute heavily to legislative leaders and candidates of the majority party.

This analysis has expanded our understanding of PAC strategy and behavior by considering certain macro-level factors. PACs are more active in states with higher levels of legislative professionalism and in states in which the parties are in contention for control of the legislature. Theoretically, however, we believe that professionalism and competitiveness indirectly influence PAC funding. The major factor in explaining variation across states is the overall cost of elections. PACs are more active in states where candidates must raise a lot of money to run a competitive campaign. Therefore, it is likely that the collective impact of legislative professionalism and party competition is to drive up the cost of elections, which in turn leads to a greater demand for money. Given their motivations, PACs are happy to oblige.

We also find that PACs are primarily reactive, yet strategic in giving. PACs contribute what they need to in order to accomplish their goals, but generally no more. In low-cost states, they contribute smaller amounts than in high-cost states, where the price of doing political business is greater.

Previous research has speculated that PACs eschew vulnerable incumbents, but our findings suggest that this is not always true. Our evidence indicates that PACs are willing contributors to incumbents in the more competitive elections. In many states, incumbents in competitive elections receive noticeably more money from PACs than their safe-seat colleagues.[11] Given the overall reelection success of incumbents, there is little political risk in backing any incumbent, and the potential rewards are substantial. A legislator who survives a close race may feel especially grateful—and a little beholden when the lobbyist comes calling.

A preliminary look has been given at contributions by type of PAC. Our findings indicate that partisan biases exist among business and labor groups in the states. However, business groups are not as partisan as labor, particularly in states with more professional and competitive legislatures. In this situation labor groups, despite their smaller total of contributions, can offset the Republican advantage with business groups. In some cases, they may even produce an advantage for Democrats.

Professional and trade PACs rarely have been the focus of research, and our analysis suggests that this is unfortunate. These PACs are active contributors, often favoring Democratic candidates. We have speculated that this is due to the influence of legal and education organizations that may feel more ideologically compatible with Democrats. Future research should be directed at gaining a better understanding of these PACs and their contribution patterns.

These findings have implications for many contemporary proposals aimed at reforming the campaign finance system. A commonly suggested reform is to place greater restrictions on the amount of money that may be contributed by PACs. The states provide an excellent test for this argument. Our findings indicate that limitations generally do not influence the total amount of PAC money that is contributed to candidates. Rather, it appears that PACs contribute according to the overall cost of elections.

This creates a problem in determining how limits on PAC money may affect the campaign finance system in other states. For example, Kansas has a rather restrictive limit of $500 per candidate, yet PACs contribute large sums of money to incumbents (comparatively) and PAC funds constitute two-thirds of the funds raised by incumbents. How would similar restrictions affect the flow of money in a high-cost state like California? These and other questions must be explored in greater detail before we fully understand the consequences of various reform efforts.

While we have advanced our understanding of the behavior of political action committees, there are many other questions that cannot be addressed with the available data. We cannot examine the timing of contributions, the relationship between contributions and actual lobbyist access, or the relationship between PACs and other political actors. There is much yet to be explored in the world of campaign finance.

NOTES

1. Political action committees may have other motives than simply access seeking. Jacobson and Kernell (1983) and Eismeier and Pollock (1986) note that PACs may pursue ideological or partisan strategies. However, seeking access would seem to be the predominant strategy employed, and as Alexander and Bauer (1991) point out, PACs that were once more partisan or ideological in nature are shifting toward an access strategy because it is a more rational method of spending their money.

2. See the discussion of the effects of legislative professionalism on campaign costs in chapter 1.

3. The findings are presented for the most recent election for each state listed in Table 9-1. With the exceptions of Mississippi and New Jersey (1991) and Illinois (1988), this is for the 1992 elections. Totals include direct contributions from corporations and unions where allowed.

4. The nature of the interest group system in a state could also affect the level of PAC funding. Unfortunately, measures of interest group strength incorporate other factors than simply the interest groups themselves. Thomas and Hrebenar (1996) note that Wyoming has an underdeveloped interest group system and has little need for PACs, yet the interest groups are rated as "dominant/complementary" for the state. New Jersey is given as an example of one of the most developed interest group systems yet rated as "complementary" because of the strength of other institutions in the state. For this reason the often cited measure of interest group power in the states does not help to explain variations in PAC activity.

5. The Ranney index is a measure of party competition at the state level that is computed from gubernatorial election results and party control of the state legislature.

6. The limitations reported for PACs are per candidate per election. Technically, a PAC could double this amount if it contributed to a candidate in both the primary and general election.

7. Actually the number of PACs necessary would be half this amount if they contributed in both primary and general election cycles.

8. We realize the time order problem that occurs when suggesting that PAC contributions that likely transpired prior to the election could be affected by the actual election results. However, it is our contention that the actual election results are the best indicator available for the expectations about the upcoming election. Certainly, some election results are surprising, but we feel that generally the competitiveness of an election is known in advance, and candidates, parties, and PACs are all aware of this.

9. The average for open-seat candidates in competitive elections may be driven up because both candidates can attract PAC money, since both have a chance to win. PACs would likely give to open-seat candidates in noncompetitive races who were likely to win but avoid the likely loser. This would bring the overall average down for noncompetitive races.

10. We have information concerning nonconnected or ideological PACs, but these PACs generally constitute a much smaller proportion of PAC funds than the other types of PACs and information concerning these PACs are not shown. Generally there is no predictable pattern observed for this type

of PAC. Wisconsin is not included in the analysis in this section because contributions from PACs and non-PACs cannot be separated.
11. Of course, some PACs hedge their bets even more by giving to both candidates, especially in open-seat contests.

REFERENCES

Alexander, Herbert E. 1992. *Financing Politics: Money, Elections, and Political Reform,* 4th ed. Washington D.C.: CQ Press.

Alexander, Herbert E., and Monica Bauer. 1991. *Financing the 1988 Election.* Boulder, Colo.: Westview Press.

Bibby, John F., and Thomas M. Holbrook. 1996. "Parties and Elections." In *Politics in the American States: A Comparative Analysis,* 6th ed., edited by Virginia Gray and Herbert Jacob. Washington, D.C.: CQ Press.

California Commission on Campaign Financing. 1985. *The New Gold Rush: Financing California Legislative Campaigns.* Los Angeles: Center for Responsive Government.

Cassie, William E. 1991. "The Roles and Strategies of PACs and Parties in the Financing of State Legislative Races." Paper delivered at the 1991 annual meeting of the Midwest Political Science Association, Chicago, April 18–20.

Cassie, William E., Joel A. Thompson, and Malcolm E. Jewell. 1992. "The Pattern of PAC Contributions to Legislative Elections: An Eleven State Analysis." Paper delivered at the 1992 annual meeting of the American Political Science Association, Chicago, September 3–6.

Clucas, Richard. 1992. "Legislative Leadership and Campaign Support in California." *Legislative Studies Quarterly* 17: 265–283.

Eisenstein, James. 1984. "Patterns of Campaign Finance in Pennsylvania's 1982 Legislative Elections." Paper delivered at the 1984 annual meeting of the Pennsylvania Political Science Association, Elizabethtown, Pa., March 30–31.

Eismeier, Theodore J., and Philip H. Pollock III. 1986. "Strategy and Choice in Congressional Elections: The Role of Political Action Committees." *American Journal of Political Science* 30: 197–213.

Fitzgerald, Jay, and Kevin McDermott. 1997. "Big Bucks, Political Power: Playing the Political Contribution Game." In *Illinois for Sale: Do Campaign Contributions Buy Influence,* edited by Dana Heupel. Springfield: University of Illinois, Institute for Public Affairs.

Gopoian, J. David. 1984. "What Makes PACs Tick? An Analysis of the Allocation Patterns of Economic Interest Groups." *American Journal of Political Science* 28: 258–281.

Greenwald, Carol S. 1977. *Group Power: Lobbying and Public Policy.* New York: Praeger.

Grenzke, Janet. 1989. "Candidate Attributes and PAC Contributions." *Western Political Quarterly* 43: 245–264.

Grier, Kevin B., and Michael C. Munger. 1993. "Comparing Interest Group PAC Contributions to House and Senate Incumbents, 1980–1986." *Journal of Politics* 55: 615–643.

Grier, Kevin B., and Michael C. Munger. 1991. "Committee Assignments, Constituent Preferences, and Campaign Contributions." *Economic Inquiry* 29: 24–43.

Grier, Kevin B., and Michael C. Munger. 1986. "The Impact of Legislator Attributes on Interest-Group Campaign Contributions." *Journal of Labor Research* 7: 349–361.

Hall, R. L., and F. W. Wayman. 1990. "Buying Time: Moneyed Interests and the Mobilization of Bias in Congressional Committees." *American Political Science Review* 84: 797–820.

Hansen, John Mark. 1991. *Gaining Access: Congress and the Farm Lobby, 1919–1981.* Chicago: University of Chicago Press.

Herrnson, Paul. 1992. "National Party Organizations and the Postreform Congress." In *The Postreform Congress,* edited by Roger Davidson. New York: St. Martin.

Jacobson, Gary C. 1980. *Money in Congressional Elections.* New Haven: Yale University Press.

Jacobson, Gary C., and Samuel Kernell. 1983. *Strategy and Choice in Congressional Elections,* 2d ed. New Haven: Yale University Press.

Jones, Ruth S. 1986. "State and Federal Legislative Campaigns: Same Song, Different Verse." *Election Politics* 3: 8–12.

Jones, Ruth S., and Thomas J. Borris. 1985. "Strategic Contributing in Legislative Campaigns: The Case of Minnesota." *Legislative Studies Quarterly* 10: 89–106.

Monardi, Fred, and Stanton A. Glantz. 1996. "Tobacco Industry Campaign Contributions and Legislative Behavior at the State Level." Paper delivered at the 1996 annual meeting of the American Political Science Association, San Francisco, August 29–September 1.

Moncrief, Gary, and D. Patton. 1993. "Upping the Campaign Ante as Parties Compete to Control the State Legislature." *State and Local Government Review* 25: 39–44.

Munger, Michael C. 1989. "A Simple Test of the Thesis that Committee Jurisdictions Shape Corporate PAC Contributions." *Public Choice* 62: 181–186.

Neal, Tommy. 1992. "The Sky-High Cost of Campaigns." *State Legislatures* (May): 16–22.

Poole, Keith T., and Thomas Romer. 1985. "Patterns of Political Action Committee Contributions to the 1980 Campaigns for the United States House of Representatives." *Public Choice* 47: 63–111.

Romer, Thomas, and James M. Snyder Jr. 1994. "An Empirical Investigation of the Dynamics of PAC Contributions." *American Journal of Political Science* 38: 745–769.

Rosenthal, Cindy Simon. 1995. "New Party or Campaign Bank Account? Explaining the Rise of State Legislative Campaign Committees." *Legislative Studies Quarterly* 20: 249–268.

Sabato, Larry J. 1985. *PAC Power.* New York: W. W. Norton.

Sorauf, Frank J. 1988. *Money in American Elections.* Glenview, Ill.: Scott, Foresman.

Su, Tie-ting, Alan Neustadtl, and Dan Clawson. 1995. "Business and the Conservative Shift: Corporate PAC Contributions, 1976–1986." *Social Science Quarterly* 76: 20–40.

Thomas, Clive S., and Ronald J. Hrebenar. 1996. "Interest Groups in the States." In *Politics in the American States: A Comparative Analysis,* edited by Virginia Gray and Herbert Jacob. Washington D.C.: CQ Press.

Thompson, Joel A., and William E. Cassie. 1990. "Campaign Contributions to State Legislative Candidates in North Carolina." Paper delivered at the 1990 annual meeting of the North Carolina Political Science Association, Salisbury, N.C., March 30–31.

Thompson, Joel A., and William E. Cassie. 1992. "Party and PAC Contributions to North Carolina State Legislative Candidates." *Legislative Studies Quarterly* 17: 409–416.

Thompson, Joel A., William E. Cassie, and Malcolm E. Jewell. 1994. "A Sacred Cow or Just a Lot of Bull?: The Impact of PAC and Party Funds in State Legislative Elections." *Political Research Quarterly* 47: 223–237.

Thompson, Joel A., and William E. Cassie. 1996. "Patterns of PAC Contributions to State Legislative Candidates." Paper delivered at the 1996 annual meeting of the Western Political Science Association, San Francisco, March 13–17.

Welch, William P. 1979. "Patterns of Contributions: Economic Interest and Ideological Groups." In *Political Finance,* edited by Herbert Alexander. Beverly Hills: Sage.

Wright, John R. 1985. "PACs, Contributions, and Roll Calls: An Organizational Perspective." *American Political Science Review* 79: 400–414.

CHAPTER TEN

The Financing Role of Parties

Anthony Gierzynski and David A. Breaux

Money became important to political campaigns largely because of the rise in expensive campaign techniques and the decline in the role of political parties in elections. Parties, which once organized electoral activity for candidates, were pushed to the sidelines in elections with the advent of the direct primary, the loss of party organizational strength and vitality (in part due to the rise of the welfare state and government reforms ending patronage), and the technological advances that made it easier for candidates to communicate directly with voters (mainly the electronic media). These developments led many observers in the 1970s and 1980s to predict the demise of political parties (see Broder 1971). More recently it has been argued that the parties have recaptured some of their role by adapting to the cash economy of the modern candidate-centered campaigns (see Gierzynski 1992, Gierzynski and Breaux 1994, and Herrnson 1988). Specifically, parties have refocused their efforts by acting as centralized campaign fund-raisers, assisting candidates in raising money, and providing other electoral services.

This chapter will investigate the potential impact of political parties by focusing on the role played by various party organizations in financing state house elections. We look at the level of party involvement in financing elections and try to answer how and why that involvement differs from one state to the next. We look at which type of party organizations are involved—national, state, local, and legislative—and the extent of their involvement. We examine what the parties do with their contributions, that is, who gets party money and why. And, finally, we will discuss the impact of party financing on the distribution of money and the competitiveness of races.

PARTY ORGANIZATIONS

Party organizations at the national and local level represent a possible source of campaign revenues to candidates in state legislative races. National party organizations (the national and congressional committees) may give to state legislative candidates for a number of reasons. Probably the two biggest reasons are to support future congressional candidates (like major league baseball teams supporting prospects in the farm system) and to try to control redistricting in key states. After every decennial census states must redraw the district maps for congressional districts to account for shifts in population. This redrawing of district maps can shift the partisan balance in districts and, consequently, can have a significant effect on the number of seats a party controls in Congress.

State party organizations (usually known as state central committees) and legislative party caucus committees are state-level organizations that represent possible sources of revenue for state legislative candidates. Legislative party campaign committees (like the Assembly Democrats in California or the House Republican Caucus Committee in Washington) are party organizations that operate out of the state legislature. In most cases they consist of all the party's legislators in a chamber and are usually led by the party's legislative leaders. Both state and legislative committees are interested in gaining political control of the state government, though in some states the legislative party campaign committees may have a more narrow focus of winning control of their legislative chamber.[1] Finally, local party organizations, which can include district committees, county committees, town committees, and ward committees, may also contribute to candidates whose districts include the local committees.

LEVEL OF PARTY INVOLVEMENT

Even as they appeared to have adapted to the cash economy of candidate-centered campaigns, political parties have not been viewed as major players when it comes to providing direct cash contributions to candidates. This perception comes mainly from the level of party involvement in congressional elections: contributions from congressional campaign committees (in direct and coordinated expenditures) hover around 5 percent of the total funds raised by candidates (though this seems to have changed in the 1996 election with the increase in the use of "soft" or unregulated money that has no contribution limits). At the state level, because of variation in the costs of campaigns (see chapter 3) and variation in the strength of political party organizations, we expect to find variations in the importance of party money in campaigns. This is what has been found with regard to legislative party campaign committees in about ten states (Gierzynski 1992) and overall party contributions in 1988 for eleven states (Gierzynski and Breaux 1994). Table 10-1 presents the total and average party contributions made to candidates by Democratic and Republic parties (national, state, legislative, and local) in seventeen states for the 1991 and 1992 elections.

Clearly there is tremendous variation between the states in the amounts of money contributed by the political parties. The totals range from more than $3.6 million given by Democratic party organizations in California to $900 given by Democratic party organizations in Mississippi. This variation is reflected in the average contribution parties made to their candidates in these states. For example, Democratic candidates in New Jersey received, on average, $15,802 from their party's organizations (third highest average), while Republican candidates in Montana received, on average, $147 from their party's organizations (lowest average among Republican candidates). Because the costs of campaigns vary dramatically from state to state, part of the differences in party contributions must be due to differences in the overall costs of campaigns. To take the overall costs of campaigns in each state into con-

Table 10-1   *Total and Average Party Contributions*

State	Democrats		Republicans	
	Total	Average	Total	Average
California	$3,659,284	$48,148	$1,891,491	$25,911
New Jersey	1,232,526	15,802	555,699	7,124
Pennsylvania	290,001	1,568	541,767	2,882
Wisconsin	76,690	947	197,307	2,530
Washington	207,747	2,258	116,084	1,235
North Carolina	82,555	809	117,160	1,502
Minnesota	106,036	835	121,210	940
Missouri	91,162	651	115,006	958
Oregon	101,419	1,914	266,772	4,940
Kansas	95,758	826	100,909	909
Delaware	24,542	766	15,472	430
Mississippi	900	8	10,085	3,559
Utah	25,800	469	34,032	524
Idaho	19,200	384	62,556	1,097
Maine	90,740	648	82,564	645
Montana	14,600	168	12,783	147
Wyoming	5,052	103	9,576	192

Note: New Jersey and Mississippi data are for 1991; all others are for 1992. States are grouped by legislative professionalism: California, most professional to least professional.

sideration, we calculated the percentage of candidate revenues that came from political parties for each state. The results for 1992 are presented in Figure 10-1.

This figure also shows a great deal of variation not only between states but also within states between the two major parties. The party role in funding elections was largest for the Democratic parties in New Jersey and California and the Republican party organizations in Maine: more than 16 percent of these parties' candidate revenues come from party organizations. The party role was the least for Democrats in Mississippi: only .3 percent of these Mississippi Democratic candidates' revenues came from party organizations. Within a number of states there appear to be significant differences in the importance of party money. In Idaho, for example, Republican candidates receive 12.9 percent of their revenues from party organizations whereas Democrats in that state receive only 5.9 percent of their revenues from party sources. Other states with such intrastate differences include California, where Democratic party sources constitute a substantially greater portion of candidate revenues than Republican party sources, and Mississippi, Missouri, North Carolina, Oregon, Pennsylvania, and Wisconsin, where the Republican party sources constitute a greater share of candidate revenues than Democratic party sources.

The variations found in Table 10-1 and Figure 10-1 raise a number of questions: Why do party organizations of some parties in some states play a greater role in candidates' financing than others? Is the party role in financing stable from one election to the next or does it fluctuate?

The discussion of campaign finance systems in chapter 2 points to a number of possible reasons why the contributions of party organizations varies from state to state, including the cost of campaigns, the party, the level of party competition at the state and district level, legislative professionalism, interest group involvement in the states, and campaign finance laws. Greater party involvement might be found in states in which campaign costs are higher because candidates' need for funds might pressure the party to act. Republicans have outstripped Democrats in fund raising at the national level due to the greater resources of their supporters, and there is no reason not to suspect the same at the state level. The level of party competition in the districts might lead candidates to pressure the party for assistance, and statewide party competition (which includes competition for control of the legislature) should inspire parties to pull together to assist candidates, since gaining or losing control of the state government is always a possibility. One might expect to find more professional party organizations in states with more

Figure 10-1 *Candidate Revenues from Political Parties, in Percentages*

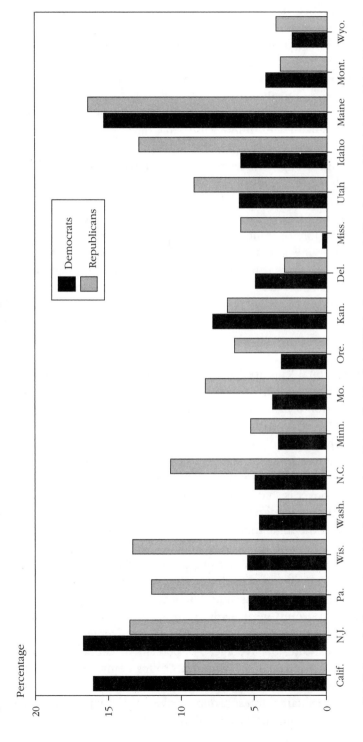

Note: Data are for the seventeen states in our analysis. Totals reflect funds in 1992 elections, except in New Jersey and Mississippi, which held elections in 1991. States are grouped by legislative professionalism: California, most professional to least professional.

"professional" legislatures (that is, legislatures with relatively high pay, staff, and long sessions). One might find that the party's role in financing is greater in states with interest groups that tend to work with other political institutions. Finally, we might expect that the role of parties in financing campaigns flourishes in states whose campaign finance laws are friendly to political parties.

An analysis of the relationship between these state characteristics and the proportion of party funding indicates that campaign spending levels, party, statewide party competition, legislative professionalism, and interest group strength all seem to be associated with the level of party financing, but not always in the way expected. There is a positive correlation between average spending (in competitive races) in the state and the proportion of candidate revenues coming from the parties. The average proportion of candidate revenues from the parties is slightly higher for Republicans than for Democrats, 8.4 percent versus 6.5 percent (a relationship that holds even while controlling for legislative professionalism). The role of the parties is slightly greater in the more competitive states.[2]

The relationship between legislative professionalism and the party role can be seen fairly clearly in Figure 10-1, in which states are ranked by our modified professionalism scale (see chapter 1). In states with the most professional legislatures party contributions make up, on average, 11.5 percent of candidate revenues; this compares to the 5 percent that parties contribute in hybrid legislatures. Party revenues in states with citizen legislatures constitute a little more than 7 percent of candidate revenues. The party role is the least in hybrid legislatures (this relationship holds across levels of statewide party competition). This could be due to two conflicting forces associated with professionalism. One, mentioned above, is that states with more professional legislatures may have more professional political institutions in general, including political parties. At the same time, as a legislature becomes more professional its legislators become more independent. So, while states with hybrid legislatures probably have more professional parties than states with citizen legislatures, they also probably have more independent legislators.

The states that Thomas and Hrebenar (1996) classify as ones in which interest groups work with or are restrained by other institutions are the states where party contribution is, on average, greatest (party revenues constitute, on average, 7.7 percent of candidate revenues in states with "complementary" interest groups compared to 4.1 percent and 5.7 percent for states with dominant/complementary or complementary/subordinate interest groups, respectively). Finally, campaign finance laws that limit party contributions do not seem to account for much of the variation from state to state. Party contributions are limited under various schemes in Delaware, Maine, Minnesota, and Wisconsin.[3] One of these states, Maine, is at the top of states in terms of the proportion of candidate revenue coming from the parties, and the other states by no means rank at the bottom in terms of party contributions.

Table 10-1 and Figure 10-1 leave unanswered the question of whether party contributions are stable across time or whether they have been increasing, decreasing, or fluctuating. To address that question, the data in Table 10-2 present the percent of candidate revenues coming from the parties over time for a subset of our states. Rows that are shaded represent parties that have increased their share of fund raising between the first and last elections for which we have data.

Some parties, such as the Utah, Washington, and Wyoming Democrats, have seen small increases in the financing role of the parties. The role of the New Jersey Democratic party increased substantially between the 1987 and 1989 elections. This may reflect the increase in competition (fed by the actions of then-governor James Florio, a Democrat) that ultimately led to a Republican takeover in that year. The

Table 10-2   *Candidate Revenues from Party Organizations,*
1986–1992, in Percentages

	Democrats				Republicans			
	1986	1988	1990	1992	1986	1988	1990	1992
California		11.2		16.0		19.4		9.7
New Jersey		4.7	23.7	16.7		21.3	20.0	13.5
Pennsylvania		11.4	7.9	5.3		6.6	6.1	12.0
Wisconsin	15.8	6.6	5.0	5.4	20.4	9.7	9.2	13.3
Washington	3.6	3.6	3.9	4.6	4.0	5.7	2.8	3.3
North Carolina		0.1	4.2	4.9		10.4	10.4	10.7
Minnesota	4.5	5.2	3.9	3.3	9.5	7.0	4.5	5.2
Missouri	0.3	0.2	0.7	3.7	3.2	1.8	2.8	8.3
Oregon	2.7	9.4	3.6	3.1	8.2	8.7	8.2	6.3
Kansas	7.2	5.3	7.9	7.8	6.7	7.5	4.3	6.8
Delaware	4.7	5.2	5.3	4.9	8.5	7.1	5.1	2.9
Mississippi		0.2		0.3		8.9		5.9
Utah	3.2	1.2	4.3	6.0	6.0	2.2	2.3	9.1
Idaho	15.1	11.8	6.4	5.9	3.2	2.5	4.6	12.7
Maine	12.5	21.9	19.8	15.3	17.9	24.5	11.5	16.4
Montana	5.5	5.5	4.4	4.2	7.9	6.4	9.7	3.2
Wyoming	1.3	0.8	0.6	2.4	3.1	2.3	2.8	3.5

   Note: Shaded cells represent parties that have increased their share of fund raising between elections. New Jersey data are for 1987, 1989, and 1991; Mississippi data are for 1987 and 1991. States are grouped by legislative professionalism: California, most professional to least professional.

Republican party's level of funding for state legislative candidates jumped in Kansas, Missouri, Pennsylvania, and Utah, especially between 1990 and 1992 (doubling in this time period). These parties may have been beneficiaries of soft money from the presidential race, which would have freed up state party money for state legislative races.

There are a number of cases where party contributions have failed to keep up with the growing costs of campaigns. The party role in financing statehouse elections has declined for Republicans in Delaware and Minnesota, and for Democrats in Idaho, Pennsylvania, and Wisconsin. The key finding of Table 10-2 is that there is no common trend among the states. The party role in financing campaigns is neither increasing nor decreasing across all states. The role of party organizations appears to vary dramatically from one state to the next, a variation that seems to be more idiosyncratic than following any pattern.

TYPES OF PARTY ORGANIZATIONS INVOLVED

Up to this point all party organization contributions to state house candidates have been lumped together. Included in these party totals are contributions from at least four different types of organizations: national party organizations, state party organizations, legislative party caucus campaign committees, and local party committees.[4] Figure 10-2 presents the breakdown of party contributions to Democratic and Republican candidates by the type of party organization, all states combined.

Figure 10-2   *Party Contributions, by Party Organization, in Percentages*

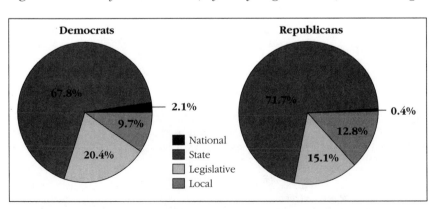

Note: Data are for the seventeen states in our analysis. Totals reflect funds in 1992 elections, except in New Jersey and Mississippi, which held elections in 1991.

The bulk of the party money contributed to state house candidates comes from state party organizations (67.8 percent for Democratic candidates, 71.7 percent for Republicans). Legislative party campaign committees are the second largest source, though more so for Democrats (20.4 percent) than Republicans (15.1 percent). Local parties constituted a larger share of the Republican party contributions (12.8 percent) than those of the Democrats (9.7 percent). While national party organizations contribute to state legislative campaigns in some states, such contributions constituted a small percentage of party funds during the period of our analysis. There is some indication that the role of the national parties may have increased dramatically in the 1996 election.

The breakdown of party contributions by type of organization for each state is shown in Table 10-3. The rows in bold type represent states in which the state party organizations are predominant in funding state house races. The shaded rows represent states in which legislative party campaign committees are the predominant contributors to campaigns. The unshaded rows represent cases where the local party dominates (excluding Wisconsin Republicans, since we only have data on total party contributions and legislative caucus campaign committees).

State parties constitute the greatest proportion of party revenue going to state house candidates in fifteen instances, while legislative party caucus committees constitute the greatest proportion of party revenue in ten. In four cases local party organizations constitute the greatest portion of party revenues. The variation with regard to the relative involvement of the different types of party organizations in funding state house campaigns is quite interesting, especially given the somewhat conflicting conclusions of Gierzynski (1992) and Shea (1995) regarding the role of legislative party campaign committees. Gierzynski concluded that legislative party committees arose because of the absence of help from other party organizations, especially for Democrats. Shea argued instead that legislative party organizations are usurping the still active role of state and local party organizations. It appears from Table 10-3 that both are correct, depending on the state. In many of the states where legislative party campaign committees constitute the greatest proportion of money going to candidates, the state party role is indeed minimal. This is especially the case for Democratic candidates, who seem to rely more on the legislative party campaign committees for funding legislative elections. (If we were to look back to the 1988 and 1986 elections, we would find that California Democrats relied heavily on their legislative campaign committee as well, constituting 46 percent of party money going to assembly candidates; however, Proposition 73 limited the activities of legislative campaign committees after these elec-

Table 10-3   Party Contributions, by Party Organization, in Percentages

	Democrats				Republicans			
	National	State	Legislative	Local	National	State	Legislative	Local
California	2.9	86.6	9.4	1.1	0.5	94.2	1.0	4.3
New Jersey	0.2	49.4	26.6	23.7	0.0	50.1	14.7	35.2
Pennsylvania	0.7	39.1	36.3	23.9	0.0	52.6	39.3	8.1
Wisconsin	n.a.	n.a.	82.3	n.a.	n.a.	n.a.	20.2	n.a.
Washington	0.8	23.1	63.5	12.6	1.3	2.6	77.5	18.6
North Carolina	1.6	27.2	45.7	25.5	2.7	56.0	25.5	15.9
Minnesota	0.0	9.8	40.9	49.3	2.1	1.8	30.9	65.3
Oregon	1.0	0.0	92.5	6.5	0.0	83.1	15.9	1.0
Kansas	0.0	65.9	17.9	16.1	0.0	98.0	0.6	1.4
Delaware	0.0	19.3	19.2	61.6	0.0	22.9	68.3	8.7
Mississippi	50.0	50.0	0.0	0.0	0.0	65.2	0.0	34.8
Utah	3.9	41.1	29.6	25.4	0.0	2.5	59.3	38.2
Idaho	0.0	13.5	49.5	37.0	0.0	82.7	13.1	4.2
Maine	11.0	19.4	40.9	28.7	0.0	51.5	6.8	41.8
Wyoming	0.0	18.0	44.6	37.4	0.0	36.6	0.0	63.4

Note: Rows with bold entries represent states in which the state party funds dominate; shaded rows represent states in which legislative party funds dominate; unshaded rows represent cases where local party funds dominate (excluding Wisconsin Republicans, for which data are insufficient). New Jersey and Mississippi data are for 1991; all others are for 1992. States are grouped by legislative professionalism: California, most professional to least professional. n.a. = not available. Missouri and Montana excluded from this analysis.

tions.) On the other hand, state party organizations and local party organizations are still very active in a number of states.

WHO GETS PARTY MONEY?

What type of candidate benefits from party contributions? Answering the question requires first that we understand the motives of political parties. As argued in chapter 2, one underlying principle of campaign finance is that money flows to the source of power. Power for political parties in legislative elections is control of the state legislature. Consequently, we should suspect that parties give to candidates in such a way as to maximize the possibility of winning control of the state legislature. This would mean protecting vulnerable incumbents and supporting challengers and open-seat candidates in close races. Since most incumbents are not vulnerable, we should find that the parties are likely to be generous with nonincumbents, especially in comparison to political action committees (see chapter 9). Figure 10-3 provides the breakdown of party contributions to Democratic and Republican candidates by incumbency status, all states combined.

Clearly, the parties are generous with nonincumbent candidates. A little less than 50 percent of all Democratic and more than 80 percent of all Republican party money goes to nonincumbents. The greater emphasis of the Republican party on nonincumbents is probably due to the fact that most state house seats were in the hands of Democrats prior to the 1992 election (the houses in twelve of the seventeen states

Figure 10-3   *Party Contributions, by Incumbency, in Percentages*

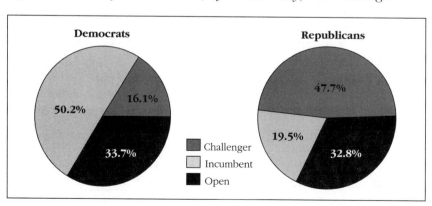

Note: Data are for the seventeen states in our analysis. Totals reflect funds in 1992 elections, except in New Jersey and Mississippi, which held elections in 1991.

in our sample were controlled by the Democrats). It is interesting to note that the Republicans' strategy of generously supporting their challengers and open-seat candidates may have played an important role in their great success in winning seats and legislative chambers in the 1994 election.

Does this analysis mask variations among the states? The answer is found in Table 10-4, which presents the average party contributions to Democratic and Republican candidates by incumbency. The shaded cells represent those cases where party contributions to challengers were on average greater than those to incumbents: this was the case in 29 of the 34 instances. In a number of cases average contributions to challengers were substantially larger than those going to incumbents: in 15 cases the average contribution the party gave challengers was better than twice the average given to incumbents. Kansas Republicans, for example, gave an average of $1,221 to challengers and $286 to incumbents. When examining party contributions over time (data not shown), the same pattern holds. In 107 of 119 cases of party contributions in elections between 1986 and 1992 the average contributions to challengers were more than the average for incumbents. The average contribution to open-seat candidates is universally high. Since no candidate has an incumbency advantage in these races, a change in party control of the district is much more likely; thus, open-seat races are rational places for parties to put their money.

Not only does it make sense for parties to contribute to nonincumbents, but it also seems rational for parties to target their resources to close races. By targeting close races they are much more likely to have an impact on the composition and control of the legislature. Figure 10-4 presents the proportion of party revenue going to Democratic and Republican candidates in competitive (candidates whose vote share was between 40 and 60 percent) and noncompetitive races.

Nearly three-fourths of the money Democratic parties contributed to state house campaigns went to candidates in competitive races, while similar races for Republicans attracted nearly two-thirds of the money contributed. Clearly the parties are concentrating their resources on close races. In Table 10-5 we present the average contributions going to competitive and noncompetitive races in 1992 for each party as well as the ratio of the average contribution for competitive and noncompetitive races.

Average party contributions for both Democrats and Republicans were greater for candidates in competitive races than noncompetitive races in every single state. In 25 of the 34 cases the average contribution to candidates in competitive races was at least twice that given to can-

Table 10-4 *Average Party Contributions, by Candidate Status*

	Democrats			Republicans		
	Challenger	Incumbent	Open	Challenger	Incumbent	Open
California	$18,180	$64,623	$49,220	$32,106	$15,182	$28,069
New Jersey	10,092	18,371	19,941	7,974	5,141	8,089
Pennsylvania	1,095	1,328	3,143	3,862	1,477	3,692
Wisconsin	1,399	574	1,309	3,063	881	4,777
Washington	2,548	917	3,889	1,050	774	1,809
North Carolina	939	760	843	1,557	1,484	1,447
Minnesota	1,010	516	1,483	910	483	1,637
Missouri	1,068	467	659	1,462	369	1,452
Oregon	2,268	378	3,275	8,207	2,344	6,108
Kansas	1,139	462	1,081	1,221	286	1,358
Delaware	852	681	767	689	195	995
Mississippi	25	0	35	235	84	375
Utah	508	290	613	523	402	713
Idaho	473	237	642	2,033	865	996
Maine	563	570	807	563	675	714
Montana	184	113	321	155	130	158
Wyoming	131	103	90	471	111	171

Note: Shaded rows represent those cases where party contributions to challengers were on average greater than those to incumbents. New Jersey and Mississippi data are for 1991; all others are for 1992. States are grouped by legislative professionalism: California, most professional to least professional.

Figure 10-4   *Party Contributions, by Competitiveness of the Race, in Percentages*

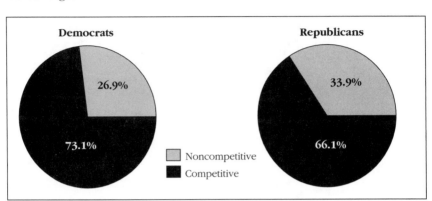

Note: Competitive races are those in which the winner received 60 percent of the vote or less. Data are for the seventeen states in our analysis. Totals reflect funds in 1992 elections, except in New Jersey and Mississippi, which held elections in 1991.

didates in noncompetitive races. In 16 of those cases the competitive race average was more than three times that of the noncompetitive races. The Republican party in Oregon demonstrated the greatest level of targeting close races with an average contribution to candidates in competitive races nearly nine times that of the noncompetitive races. This pattern holds when we analyze party contributions over a series of elections (data not shown). In only 1 case (Maine Republicans in 1988) of 119 instances of party contributions recorded between 1986 and 1992 did the average contribution to candidates in noncompetitive races exceed the average contribution in competitive races.

It seems clear that the beneficiaries of party money in elections are candidates in close races, including nonincumbents as well as incumbents. This finding is in line with previous research in this area. Given the differing role of state, legislative, and local party organizations in the states, one question remains: Is there a difference between the type of party organization and how these organizations distribute their money? Given the common interest in gaining or maintaining control of the state legislature, one would expect that state party organizations and legislative caucus campaign committees would follow similar strategies: focusing on close races and giving to nonincumbents as well as incumbents. Local party organizations might not be expected to target their resources, since their aim may be more local than statewide (i.e., sup-

Table 10-5 Average Party Contributions, by Competitiveness of the Race

	Democrats			Republicans		
	Noncompetitive	Competitive	Ratio	Noncompetitive	Competitive	Ratio
California	$15,534	$101,006	6.5	$16,596	$37,202	2.2
New Jersey	11,312	21,318	1.9	6,957	7,329	1.1
Pennsylvania	1,379	2,120	1.5	1,322	7,839	5.9
Wisconsin	573	3,842	6.7	573	3,842	6.7
Washington	630	3,511	5.6	276	2,079	7.5
North Carolina	443	1,222	2.8	507	2,194	4.3
Minnesota	475	1,401	2.9	475	1,401	2.9
Missouri	339	1,234	3.6	635	1,511	2.4
Oregon	611	3,168	5.2	1,078	9,409	8.7
Kansas	460	1,260	2.7	325	1,596	4.9
Delaware	553	1,123	2.0	272	746	2.7
Mississippi	5	21	4.2	67	390	5.8
Utah	330	569	1.7	438	659	1.5
Idaho	193	648	3.4	504	2,285	4.5
Maine	527	780	1.5	463	838	1.8
Montana	78	277	3.6	135	164	1.2
Wyoming	74	120	1.6	104	241	2.3

Note: Competitive races are ones in which candidates received between 40 and 60 percent of the vote. Ratio compares the average contribution to competitive candidates versus the average contribution to noncompetitive candidates. New Jersey and Mississippi data are for 1991; all others are for 1992. States are grouped by legislative professionalism: California, most professional to least professional.

porting local candidates). In Table 10-6 the average contribution made by state, legislative, and local parties to challengers, incumbents, and open-seat candidates are presented. Rows are shaded for parties whose average contribution is greater for challengers than incumbents.

The data in Table 10-6 show that there are differences among the party organizations in supporting challengers and those differences depend upon which party you are talking about. For Republicans, state and local party organizations do the best job at targeting nonincumbent candidates. Republican state and local party organizations generally outspend the legislative organizations on contributions to challengers. For Democrats, the legislative party campaign committees are more likely than the state or local parties to support nonincumbents. Legislative parties have higher average contributions to challengers than to incumbents in more instances than state parties. While the number of instances in which the average party contribution for challengers exceeds that for incumbents is about the same for local and legislative Democratic parties, the magnitude of the difference is much greater among legislative parties.

In terms of competitive versus noncompetitive races, state and legislative organizations of both parties do a better job focusing on competitive races (Table 10-7). The magnitude of the differences between the average contribution to competitive and noncompetitive races is much greater for state and legislative parties than for local parties. Legislative party contributions to competitive races are twice that of their average contribution to noncompetitive races in sixteen cases compared to four such cases for local party organizations. For Democrats it seems that, once again, the legislative party does the best job of targeting close races.

IMPACT OF PARTY MONEY ON LEGISLATIVE ELECTIONS

The analysis in this chapter has shown the role national, state, legislative, and local political parties play in directly financing state house elections. The size of that role varies from state to state, as does the type of party organization most involved in that role. The analysis also demonstrates, once again, that party organizations make contributions in such a way as to gain or maintain a majority in the legislature (i.e., giving mostly to competitive races and nonincumbents), a tendency that sets them apart from other contributors.

This party role in financing elections has implications for legislative races. By focusing their resources on competitive races and funding nonincumbents, political parties are having an impact on the distribution of

Table 10-6   Mean Contributions from Party Sources, by Incumbency

	Democrats								
	State			Legislative			Local		
	Challenger	Incumbent	Open	Challenger	Incumbent	Open	Challenger	Incumbent	Open
California	$14,670	$55,836	$43,627	$2,877	$6,653	$2,852	$ 340	$ 768	$ 366
New Jersey	5,076	9,561	9,013	3,876	3,364	5,924	1,149	5,413	4,904
Pennsylvania	639	686	354	84	302	2,245	373	318	544
Washington	188	25	1,435	1,969	672	2,098	390	183	349
North Carolina	83	311	272	477	420	392	574	156	324
Minnesota	68	87	84	303	164	881	639	265	517
Oregon	0	0	0	2,114	675	3,086	154	90	131
Kansas	698	256	823	339	72	81	102	134	177
Delaware	123	179	133	85	231	100	644	271	533
Mississippi	79	0	28	none	none	none	none	none	none
Utah	150	158	276	173	53	189	136	73	147
Idaho	91	0	75	280	44	433	102	193	133
Maine	100	127	139	239	221	341	224	145	220
Montana	3	2	0	22	7	10	174	120	73
Wyoming	25	0	36	55	56	35	100	50	16

(continued)

Table 10-6 (continued)

	State			Republicans Legislative			Local		
	Challenger	Incumbent	Open	Challenger	Incumbent	Open	Challenger	Incumbent	Open
California	30,216	15,054	25,782	0	0	813	1,854	123	1,123
New Jersey	4,294	2,085	4,074	1,512	367	925	2,168	2,689	3,090
Pennsylvania	2,192	972	1,081	1,479	259	2,297	188	247	314
Washington	14	12	70	867	481	1,432	142	281	292
North Carolina	1,029	1,099	741	312	611	455	349	210	199
Minnesota	12	26	17	211	39	829	688	377	754
Oregon	7,793	1,648	4,758	377	675	1,250	37	20	100
Kansas	1,053	222	1,216	0	0	15	168	64	127
Delaware	178	27	270	406	150	725	105	18	0
Mississippi	190	60	200	none	none	none	45	24	210
Utah	29	11	0	203	311	425	294	81	288
Idaho	1,749	703	737	100	150	225	184	12	33
Maine	254	416	349	19	51	65	289	208	300
Montana	27	4	9	21	0	0	236	146	284
Wyoming	0	83	38	0	0	0	298	250	98

Note: Shaded rows represent parties whose average contribution is greater for challengers than incumbents. New Jersey and Mississippi data are for 1991; all others are for 1992. States are grouped by legislative professionalism: California, most professional to least professional. Missouri and Wisconsin excluded from this analysis.

Table 10-7   Mean Contributions to Safe and Close Races, by Party Organization

| | State | | | | Legislative | | | | Local | | | |
| | Democrats | | Republicans | | Democrats | | Republicans | | Democrats | | Republicans | |
	Non-competitive	Competitive	Non-competitive	Competitive	Non-competitive	Competitive	Non-competitive	Competitive	Non-competitive	Competitive	Non-competitive	Competitive
California	$12,276	$89,378	$15,197	$35,547	$1,630	$9,173	$ 0	$ 591	$ 668	$ 317	$1,248	$ 958
New Jersey	3,677	12,888	2,931	4,361	4,773	3,499	646	1,540	2,838	4,874	3,381	1,429
Pennsylvania	488	982	604	4,416	553	614	559	2,951	331	503	159	467
Wisconsin	n.a.	n.a.	n.a.	n.a.	202	1,873	90	1,307	n.a.	n.a.	n.a.	n.a.
Washington	51	885	7	55	367	2,253	98	1,713	175	369	148	303
North Carolina	362	164	259	1,351	150	716	288	524	29	499	99	364
Minnesota	71	95	17	17	68	688	64	577	245	623	496	758
Kansas	240	906	240	1,434	115	187	0	10	105	167	83	152
Delaware	66	283	42	213	83	254	197	488	404	585	33	46
Mississippi	0	21	67	248	none	none	none	none	0	0	0	180
Utah	163	213	4	21	88	175	242	404	79	147	192	235
Idaho	15	104	384	1,953	113	296	112	209	66	248	8	122
Maine	92	162	226	445	181	357	24	64	117	262	213	329
Oregon	0	0	847	7,879	524	2,972	217	1,440	88	159	15	91
Wyoming	21	17	67	72	33	53	none	none	20	49	37	169

Note: Competitive races are ones in which candidates received between 40 and 60 percent of the vote. Mississippi and New Jersey data are for 1991; all others are for 1992. States are grouped by legislative professionalism: California, most professional to least professional. Missouri and Montana excluded from this analysis. n.a. = not available.

campaign money and the competitiveness of races. Whereas PACs, corporations, and individuals tend to contribute to the advantage incumbents have in campaign fund raising (see chapter 9), political parties' contribution patterns make it possible for some challengers to have the money to run competitive races. The ability of political parties to have a significant impact on the distribution of campaign money and the competitiveness of races is limited, however, by the fact that their resources in many states have been limited. This, however, may have changed in the 1996 election.

The 1996 election was a watershed for "soft money" (that is, unregulated money with no limits as to who can contribute or how much can be contributed). Soft money is raised by the national party committees for purposes of party building. More specifically, soft money is used for paying a portion of state party overhead; for campaign activity that benefits federal, state, and local elections (e.g., voter registration and get-out-the-vote drives); issue advocacy; and generic party advertising. The 1995–1996 election cycle saw a soft money explosion. The Democratic national party committees spent $121.8 million in nonfederal soft money, a 271 percent increase over 1992! Republicans spent $148.7 million, a 224 percent increase over 1992! For Democrats, $64.6 million of this money was transferred to state party committees and $4.4 million was contributed directly to state and local candidates. The Republicans transferred $50.2 million of this money to state parties and contributed $5.2 million to state and local candidates (Federal Election Commission 1997).

These numbers represent a substantial jump in the resources of the political parties, including state and local parties, and raise new questions about party involvement in the financing of elections. How much of this money filtered down to state legislative campaigns? How did the party committees that benefited from this national party largess spend this money? Did they follow previous patterns of contributing to non-incumbents and competitive races as shown in this chapter, or did they begin to act more like PACs? Did this influx of money upset the pattern of which parties were most involved in financing state house races?

The answers to such questions will, unfortunately, have to wait until the campaign records of the 1996 election are processed. The implications of what might be found are very important, especially considering what this chapter has shown about the distribution of party money and the attack that has been mounted against soft money. If the parties are found to allocate this new found wealth much as they did in the past, then it is possible that the benefits derived from how the parties use the money may balance out the costs of allowing unlimited contributions in the system. This may, at least, balance out the costs of a system that allows some form of regulated soft money to exist.

NOTES

1. See Gierzynski (1992) and Shea (1994) for a more detailed discussion of these types of party organizations.
2. We used Bibby and Holbrook's (1996) update of the Ranney index. Party revenues in states categorized as competitive two-party states were, on average, higher than those in modified one-party Democratic or Republican states.
3. In Delaware, Maine, and Minnesota party contributions in 1992 were limited to $5,000 per candidate in the general election. In Wisconsin candidates may not receive more than 65 percent of their revenues from all political party committees; party committees that make independent expenditures on behalf of candidates are limited in their direct contributions to $500 (Council of State Governments 1993).
4. We focus here on official party organizations, excluding party affiliated clubs such as the Lincoln Clubs, Young Republicans, party affiliated caucuses like the DFL Women's Caucus in Minnesota, etc., which also give direct contributions to candidates. Legislative party caucus campaign committees exclude transfers from other candidates of the same party (which in some states are substantial).

REFERENCES

Bibby, John F. and Thomas M. Holbrook. 1996. "Parties and Elections." In *Politics in the American States: A Comparative Analysis,* 6th ed., edited by Virginia Gray and Herbert Jacob. Washington: CQ Press.

Broder, David S. 1971. *The Party's Over: The Failure of American Politics.* New York: Harper and Row.

Council of State Governments. 1993. *GOGEL Blue Book,* 9th ed. Lexington, Ky.: Council of State Governments.

Federal Election Commission. 1997. "FEC Reports Major Increase in Party Activity for 1995–96." Washington, D.C., press release.

Gierzynski, Anthony. 1992. *Legislative Party Campaign Committees in the American States.* Lexington: University Press of Kentucky.

Gierzynski, Anthony, and David Breaux. 1994. "The Role of Parties in Legislative Campaign Financing." *American Review of Politics* 15 (Summer): 171–190.

Herrnson, Paul S. 1988. *Party Campaigning in the 1980s.* Cambridge, Mass.: Harvard University Press.

Shea, Daniel M. 1995. *Transforming Democracy: Legislative Campaign Committees and Political Parties.* Albany: State University of New York Press.

Thomas, Clive S., and Ronald J. Hrebenar. 1996. "Interest Groups in the States." In *Politics in the American States: A Comparative Analysis,* 6th ed., edited by Virginia Gray and Herbert Jacob. Washington: CQ Press.

Part IV

CONCLUSION

CHAPTER 11

Can the Legislative Campaign Finance System Be Reformed?

Malcolm E. Jewell and William E. Cassie

The 1996 election broke all records for the cost of presidential and congressional campaigns and focused public attention on the techniques used by both Democrats and Republicans to raise campaign funds and to reward the largest contributors. The election reopened the debate over the best ways to reform the campaign finance system. But this debate did not shed much light on the complex problems of campaign financing nor lead to any break in the deadlock over priorities for reform.

While the issues of campaign finance reform at the national level received most of the attention in the media, many of the same problems occur in the financing of state gubernatorial and legislative elections. As state legislatures continue to play a more important role in policy making, the financing of state legislative campaigns has assumed greater importance. A clearer perspective can be obtained on the issues of campaign finance at the state level because state legislatures vary in many ways: the cost of campaigns, the level of competition for seats and the electoral advantages of incumbents, and the role that parties and interest groups play in campaign financing.

The financing of campaigns, at both the national and state levels, is a complex process, and proposals for reform are often complex. But the basic issue raised by critics of campaign financing is a simple one: Does the campaign finance process, at the state and national levels, seriously undermine the democratic, representative system? Voters in a representative system should be free to choose the candidates that they believe are most capable and most likely to serve their interests. If elections can be "bought" by the candidate who can raise and spend the most money in a campaign, then the representative system is flawed.

In a democracy, representatives should be accountable to the voters, but if incumbents are almost always reelected because they can raise much more money than challengers, accountability may be more myth than reality. If candidates are heavily dependent on special interests and their political action committees (PACs) to raise enough money to win, those who are elected may be more accountable to these interests than to most of the constituents in their district.

There is obviously some truth to these charges, and to the more specific criticisms that reformers make of campaign finances. But, as often happens in the world of politics, pinning down exactly how the financing of campaigns affects the electoral and representative process requires more careful analysis.

Is the cost of legislative campaigns escalating in most states, or in only a few, and does the sheer cost of campaigning damage the democratic process? We know that the winners of legislative races usually spend more than the losers; but do they win *because* they have more funding, or do the candidates who are most likely to win because of their political strength attract the most campaign money? Are female or minority candidates less able than others to attract funding, or can they raise just as much money if they have comparable political strengths? Do PACs keep incumbents entrenched and make elections less competitive by giving most of their funding to incumbents, particularly those from the safest districts? Are political parties both willing and able to make elections more competitive by providing significant funding to candidates, including challengers, in close races?

To answer such questions, we will review what has been learned from previous research and particularly from the findings reported in this book on campaign finance and legislative elections in eighteen states. These findings will be used both to evaluate the accuracy of criticisms leveled by reformers at campaign finance systems and to make judgments about whether proposed reforms are likely to bring about the results that the reformers expect. The effectiveness of some of the reforms already adopted in the states will also be evaluated. For example, does tougher regulation of campaign financing make any difference?

The states vary in the way they regulate campaign financing and in the reforms that some have adopted. States differ in the limitations placed on contributions by individuals and PACs; some permit corporations and/or labor unions to contribute directly to candidates and some ban them; some regulate political party fund raising and contributions and others do not. Some states have established systems of public financing for campaigns by candidates or political parties, and a very few of these extend public financing to legislative candidates.

In many states there is a recurring debate over campaign finance reform, and in some of them significant changes have been made in the campaign finance laws during the 1980s and 1990s. The prospects for continuing reforms in campaign financing appear much more likely at the state level than in Washington.

THE RISING COSTS OF LEGISLATIVE ELECTIONS

Criticism of Costs

Many of those who criticize the existing campaign finance system in the states stress that the costs of campaigns are too high and are rising too fast. Sometimes this is little more than a general argument: politicians raise too much money and spend too much, wasting it particularly on huge amounts of television advertising. Public perceptions of high costs may be based mostly on presidential, congressional, and gubernatorial races, as well as scattered examples of unusually expensive state legislative races.

Critics who are better informed about the problems of campaign financing and more articulate about the need for reform focus their attention on two aspects of expensive campaigns. First, as the costs of campaigning increase, it is difficult or impossible for some candidates to compete for office effectively. A candidate with some political experience who could raise $10,000 for a legislative race from his or her own resources and from friends and supporters might find it impossible to raise $50,000 for the race. This situation often arises for those challenging an entrenched incumbent. But even incumbents are concerned about the time and effort it takes to raise large sums of money.

The second reason for being concerned about rising campaign costs is that this trend forces many candidates to raise most of their funds from large contributors and interest groups, and not just from friends and supporters. Most of these contributors want something in return from the legislators. The larger the amount of money that must be raised, the greater the pressure on legislators to pass the bills and provide the benefits that these contributors want.

There are several reasons why campaign costs might be expected to rise, even faster than the rate of inflation. The costs of advertising as well as various modern campaign techniques (such as the use of polls and consultants) may drive campaign expenditures upward. In some states an increase in competitiveness may affect costs. As the competition for a state's legislature increases, we would expect the costs of campaigns to increase as well. For example, as the Republicans become more competitive in the southern states, it is likely that the Republicans will attract more money and likewise the Democrats will have to counter with more funding themselves.

Evidence of Rising Costs

The conventional wisdom is that the costs of running for political office are climbing steadily, much faster than the rate of inflation. Certainly the cost of congressional campaigns has been rising, though more slowly that it did in the early 1980s. Between the 1986–1988 elections and the 1994–1996 elections, the total cost of campaigns increased by almost 80 percent in the U.S. House—more than twice the rate of inflation. But in the Senate costs increased by slightly more than 35 percent, which is less than the inflation rate (Ornstein, Mann, and Malbin 1996, 81; *New York Times* 1997).

There are large differences among the states in the rate at which campaign spending has been increasing (see chapter 3). Between the 1986 and 1994 elections, the increase in the median spending of candidates in contested races in fourteen states ranged from 13 percent to 159 percent. It averaged about 67 percent, almost twice the 34.5 percent rate of inflation. The increase was considerably higher than inflation in ten states and less in four. (In two of the four other states being studied the increase through 1992 was above the rate of inflation.)

We have suggested that one of the problems created by rising costs is the increasing difficulty challengers are likely to have in raising enough money to run a credible race. The funding gap between incumbents and challengers is particularly large in the more professional legislatures, which usually have larger districts and thus higher costs (chapter 3). The glaring example is California, where challengers raise only about 6 percent of what incumbents do. But there is no consistent trend among the states of this gap getting larger, in percentage terms.

Implications for Reform

The most obvious implication of these findings is that the need for controlling costs is much greater in some states than in others. It is not inevitable in every state, or in every time period, that the costs of campaigning will rise much faster than the rate of inflation. In those states where the costs are rising most rapidly, the incumbents' advantage over challengers and the pressures on candidates to raise funds from large contributors and PACs are problems that are growing more serious.

Whether campaign costs are rising rapidly or slowly, reformers who want to place an absolute limit on the amount a candidate can spend face the same problem. A compulsory limit on candidate spending is unconstitutional, according to the U.S. Supreme Court. This is why those who are concerned about the cost of campaigns often propose voluntary limitations, accompanied by financial incentives to those candidates who accept limitations, such as some form of public funding or free time or reduced rates on television.

THE ADVANTAGE OF INCUMBENCY

Goals of Reformers

Two closely related goals of reformers are to create a "more level playing field" among candidates and to encourage closer competition in legislative races. Because it is widely assumed that incumbents are able to raise and spend much more than challengers, this goal often translates into reducing the financial advantage enjoyed by incumbents.

An incumbent's greater ability to raise funds affects the competitiveness of elections in several ways. Most obviously, if the incumbent raises a lot more money than the challenger, he or she can spend much more money on advertising; with this, the voters have more knowledge about the incumbent (including name recognition as a minimum) and are therefore more likely to vote for the incumbent. In addition, if the incumbent is perceived to be likely to win because of this money-raising advantage, individuals and particularly groups will be more willing to contribute to this perceived winner and less likely to financially support the challenger. Finally, the perception that the incumbent can raise as much as is necessary to win often discourages candidates, or at least viable candidates, from challenging the incumbent.

Better Funded Incumbents

We need to look more closely at the evidence about the financial advantage of incumbents. First, do incumbents usually win? Do they usually outspend challengers? If so, how large is that financial advantage? How much do challengers have to raise to run a competitive race against an incumbent? Under what conditions do challengers actually raise enough to be competitive?

State legislative incumbents enjoy a high rate of success, and have done so for many years. For the elections from 1968 through 1988, 92.3 percent of all representatives and 90.3 percent of all senators who were seeking reelection and won renomination were elected. There was a rise of about three percentage points between the first and second half of this period. There is obviously some variation from state to state in the reelection rate, but in three-fourths of the states the range for house races has been only from 88 to 96 percent (Jewell 1994).

In our study of elections from 1988 through 1992, between 77 and 98 percent of the incumbents having opponents in the eighteen states won, and in ten of the states the figure was at least 90 percent (chapter 6). There is also evidence that the electoral margins for incumbents have been increasing since the late 1960s (Jewell and Breaux 1988; Garand 1991; Weber, Tucker, and Brace 1991).

Most experts think that a major reason for the success of incumbents is that they enjoy a large advantage over challengers in raising and spending funds. We have found that in all states in our study at least 66 percent of incumbents outspend challengers, and in almost half of them at least 90 percent spend more. Incumbents are much more likely to outspend challengers in the more professional states and those with higher cost elections (categories that often overlap).

In California, where the average incumbent spent more than $500,000 on the campaign, three-quarters of the challengers spent less than 25 percent as much as the incumbents. Not surprisingly, in states where legislative campaigns usually cost less, challengers can more often afford to spend almost as much or even more than incumbents. Clearly challengers can often keep up with incumbent spending when costs are low, but as costs increase challengers are usually left behind, sometimes far behind.

Why Do Incumbents Usually Win?

Most winners outspend most losers, and we are tempted to conclude that money was the major cause of these victories, but we cannot simply jump to that conclusion. Political scientists who have tried to measure exactly how much incumbents benefit from having more money to spend in their campaigns have run into several dilemmas. In most election campaigns incumbents start out with nonmonetary advantages over challengers. Incumbents often need less money to get elected, but are able to raise—and usually spend—more. Challengers need more money but usually have less.

According to Jacobson (1980, 1990) and other students of congressional elections, the more challengers spend, the closer the race is; at the same time, the more incumbents spend, the closer the race is. The reason for this paradox seems to be that congressional incumbents usually spend only what seems necessary to win. Most incumbents are able to raise as much as is needed, but they are less likely to raise a lot, and particularly to spend a lot, if they face a weak opponent with limited funding.

Research on congressional elections has suggested that, for the reasons just listed, challenger spending has a stronger positive relationship with the candidate's vote than does spending by the incumbent (Jacobson 1980, 1990). Would the results be the same in state legislative races? Gierzynski and Breaux (1991), in a study of nine states, conclude that in each of them spending by challengers has a greater effect than spending by incumbents.

The closer a state legislative challenger can come to spending as much as the incumbent, the better chance he or she has of being competitive. We have found that challengers have a good chance of being competitive if they can spend half as much as the incumbents. In the most professional states they may have to spend more than that, and in the least professional states they may be competitive even though spending less than half what incumbents spend (see chapter 6). Spending enough to be competitive does not, of course, guarantee victory; it simply creates the opportunity for a skillful, hard-working candidate to win.

There is evidence that, except in the most professional states, a challenger has more than a 50 percent chance of becoming competitive if he or she can raise as little as $3,000 to $5,000 (chapter 6). On the other hand, we must remember that when a challenger succeeds in raising and spending enough to become competitive, the incumbent often reacts by spending more money on his or her campaign.

Implications for Reforms

It is clear that in many state legislatures, particularly the more professional ones in larger states, the playing field between incumbents and challengers is not level. In addition to their nonmonetary advantages, most incumbents can spend considerably more than challengers. A relatively small proportion of challengers are able to raise enough money to be competitive, and even fewer can raise as much as the incumbent. It is certainly rare for a challenger who lags far behind an incumbent in funding to win the election.

Achieving the goal of a more level playing field is one of the more difficult problems facing anyone seeking to reform campaign finance laws. It is uncertain whether any feasible change in the laws regulating campaign finance can accomplish this and make elections more competitive. The dilemma arises not only because incumbents can usually spend more money than challengers, but also because incumbents usually are much better known than challengers at the start of the campaign, particularly in the more professional states, and thus have a huge head start.

Reformers have proposed low limits on total spending by each candidate for the legislature in an effort to narrow the gap between incumbents and challengers. Such absolute limits have been ruled unconstitutional by the U.S. Supreme Court, however, as a violation of free speech.

Reformers have tried to accomplish the same objective by imposing lower limits on what individuals or groups can contribute to legislative candidates. This would make money raising more difficult and might in fact reduce the average gap between what incumbents and challengers can spend. But it might make it more difficult for challengers to win, because they usually are less experienced in money raising and also have to spend substantial amounts of money in order to have a reasonable chance of beating an incumbent.

There are both legal and practical problems with putting limits on spending. The key to making races more competitive seems to be to improve the challenger's opportunities to raise more money. Therefore, the most realistic reform strategy may be to develop methods of helping challengers gain substantially more campaign resources. One such method might be to reduce legal restrictions on those groups, such as political parties, that are most likely to fund the campaigns of challengers.

FEMALE AND MINORITY CANDIDATES

A campaign finance system would appear to weaken the representative process if female or minority candidates have a smaller chance of raising enough money to run competitively. When significant numbers of women began to run for state legislatures, there was evidence that they had more difficulty in raising adequate funding than other challengers, but in recent years women have been able to compete with men in money raising. It is more difficult to determine how minority candidates are faring in fund raising, and the evidence is mixed.

A large majority of incumbents are men and, as would be expected, they are able to raise much more money than female challengers. But female incumbents are also able to raise more than male challengers, and the gap is actually larger in a number of states. In open-seat contests between men and women, men have a financial advantage in some states and women do in others. In the more professional states, where the gap between incumbent and challenger spending is greatest, female challengers lag far behind male incumbents, but once a woman gains incumbent status, she is far ahead of a male challenger. Multiple regression analysis shows that there are no significant differences in the ability of male and female candidates to raise funds when all other variables (such as incumbency status) are controlled (see chapter 7).

The financial status of black, Hispanic, and other minority candidates is much less clear, partly because of political differences among the states and the small number of examples of minority candidates running in some states. Because the racial characteristics of districts are so important in these races, an analysis of funding must be put into a district context. In districts where a majority of voters belong to racial minorities, the level of competition is usually low in general elections, and therefore a minority candidate often needs only a modest amount of funding to win. In districts where a minority of voters are black or Hispanic, minority candidates often must run against non-Hispanic white candidates and need substantial funding to be competitive, particularly if they are challengers. The evidence suggests that, in such districts, minority candidates are often at a fund-raising disadvantage, and that it is often a major obstacle for minority challengers (see chapter 8).

If minority candidates are often at a financial disadvantage, there is no obvious solution to be found through reforming the campaign finance system. Public financing might distribute revenues more evenly, but there is still a shortage of evidence on its effects. Efforts to limit campaign costs might turn out to be counterproductive, because minority candidates may need large campaign resources to win outside of minority districts. The electoral prospects of minority candidates depend more on how districts are drawn than how elections are financed.

The Role of Political Action Committees

Criticism of PACs

The political action committees established by interest groups are criticized for a number of reasons. Many citizens want to abolish PACs, believing that organized interests should not be permitted to give funds to candidates or parties because this gives them an unfair advantage over individuals. Many well-informed observers are concerned that, by using PACs to make contributions, particularly to the more influential legislators, organized interests have gained too much influence over the legislative process. They see this as a particularly serious problem in legislatures where the cost of running a viable campaign is high and thus there is greater dependence on PAC contributions.

Another major criticism made by reformers against PACs is that they contribute a large proportion of their funds to candidates most likely to win (incumbents and some candidates for open seats). PACs have little to gain, and perhaps much to lose, by contributing to probable losers. Therefore, the giving strategy followed by PACs is perceived as helping to enlarge the financial gap between incumbents and challengers.

These concerns often lead reformers to argue that PAC contributions should be limited more strictly or eliminated altogether. In this study, we do not have the data that would be required to make a judgment about how much influence PACs have over legislative decision making. However, we can draw conclusions about the strategies followed by PACs in allocating resources among legislators and particularly the proportion of PAC funding going to incumbents and challengers. We can also examine the impact of existing state regulation on PAC contributions.

Patterns of PAC Contributions

In most states PACs contribute considerably more funding to party leaders than to rank-and-file legislators. Obviously they recognize that party leaders have more influence over a wider variety of bills than do most legislators. This contrast is greatest in the legislatures with high-cost campaigns. In only about one-third of the states, however, do committee chairs receive significantly more funding than the average legislator. PACs contribute disproportionately to the majority party in several state legislatures, including those in three states with particularly high campaign costs and Democratic majorities: California, Illinois, and Pennsylvania.

One of the clearest findings is that PACs consistently give more funding, often much more, to incumbents than to challengers. The ratio is about 2 to 1 in six states, around 4 to 1 in five states, and 6 to 1 or more in six states, including a ratio of more than 12 to 1 in Illinois. PACs give more to incumbents because incumbents are most likely to be reelected, and because many of them have a track record of supporting the positions taken by PACs on particular issues. In most states the levels of PAC funding for open-seat candidates fall between those for incumbents and for challengers. PACs have the highest ratio of preference for incumbents in states with greater party competition and professionalism, those with higher costs, and those with the highest levels of PAC spending for incumbents.

Does it make any difference to PACs whether incumbents face strong or weak opposition in the election? When incumbents face a strong challenger, they usually have to raise more campaign money and very often turn to PACs for increased help. PACs may be willing to respond to such requests in the belief that incumbents facing a close race will be particularly grateful for help. But the data show that in only about one-third of the states is PAC funding clearly higher in the more competitive races.

In all states PACs give more funding to those challengers who are running in competitive races, usually by a margin of at least 4 to 1. The reason is obvious. If PACs are going to support any challengers, they will concentrate on those who appear to have some chance of winning. Moreover, the ability of a challenger to raise money is one criteria used by PACs, and other potential contributors, to identify viable candidates.

The conclusion seems obvious that political action committees help to create a funding advantage for incumbents, making the playing field more uneven. Even those challengers who seem to have the potential for being competitive usually get less funding from PACs than incumbents. This is one of the most important reasons why challengers are often at such a competitive disadvantage.

Implications for the Regulation of PACs

The evidence that PACs contribute significantly to the imbalance of funding between incumbents and challengers and that they often give disproportionately to the more powerful legislators provides support for reformers who want to place greater restrictions on campaign contributions by PACs. In none of the states in our study do we have an example of PACs being prohibited from making campaign contributions, but there are variations in the limits placed on PACs. Five states (Delaware, Kansas, Minnesota, Montana, and Wisconsin) set a ceiling of $1,000 or less for PAC contributions to legislative candidates, and two others (Maine and North Carolina) have less restrictive limits of $4,000 to $5,000. The other ten states did not impose any limits in 1992, the election covered in our study of PAC contributions (see chapter 9).

This variation in the size of limits (or lack of limits) on PAC contributions to candidates seems to have had little impact on the total PAC contributions received by incumbents—the legislative candidates most likely to get PAC funding. All of the states with a PAC limit of $1000 or less, except Montana, had higher average PAC contributions than Idaho, Mississippi, and Wyoming—states with no restrictions. Six of the states with the highest average contribution from PACs (California, Illinois, Oregon, New Jersey, Pennsylvania, and Washington) are among the states with no limits on PAC contributions.

It appears that the size of the state, the professionalism of its legislature, and the cost of campaigns in the state are more important than legal limitations in determining how much incumbents receive from PACs. PACs may determine that there is a financial threshold that represents the minimum cost for doing political business in a state. That minimum would obviously be higher in the high-cost states than in the low-cost ones, and it would presumably increase over time as the cost of campaigns increases. If states that now have no limits for PACs, or have relatively generous ones, were to impose a legal limit that was lower than the current threshold, that change could bring about a reduction in PAC spending, or perhaps encourage the PACs to distribute funds more broadly among potentially viable candidates.

Another reform that is sometimes suggested is to place a limit on the proportion of a candidate's total funding that comes from PACs, in an effort to make legislators less dependent on PACs and thus less indebted to interest groups. Some plans, for example, have set that limit at 25 or 50 percent of total funding. Incumbents received more than 50 percent of their funding from PACs in five states, more than 25 percent in another seven states, and less 25 percent in only five states. A 25 percent limitation would obviously produce a significant reduction in the amount of many legislators' aggregate funding from PACs. It might, however, lead PACs to increase the amount of independent spending made by PACs on behalf of legislative candidates, particularly incumbents.

The evidence from the states suggests that political action committees may be part of the problem, but the commonly proposed restrictions on contribution levels do not appear to work, although aggregate limits on candidate receipts from PACs could have some effect. The solution for reformers may not be to try to take more money away from incumbents, but to get more money in the hands of challengers. However, it is not clear how PACs could be induced to take more interest in funding challengers.

The Role of Political Parties

Criticism and Support of Parties

Among those who want to reform legislative campaign financing, there are different and often contradictory views about the role that political parties[1] should play. Some would like to minimize the contributions that parties can make to candidates, primarily in order to limit their influence over legislators (similar to the goal of limiting interest group influence).

Some reformers also believe that the majority party has access to more resources and thus can fund its candidates more generously than can the minority party—thereby weakening rather than strengthening party competition. Some reformers are particularly critical of contributions made by party caucuses or leaders in the legislature (Rosenthal 1989, 85–89). The California Commission on Campaign Financing (1985, 105) believes that the contributions of funds from legislative leaders to candidates significantly raise the costs of campaigns.

Some reformers are concerned about the sources of party funding at the state level, particularly for legislative races. Both state party organizations and legislative party campaign committees often turn to PACs as major sources of funding, and critics are concerned that the parties (and particularly at the legislative level) will come under increasing pressure from these interest groups when bills come before the legislature. In the most recent elections, the transfer of large quantities of "soft money"[2] to state parties has intensified this concern about the sources of party funding.

Other reformers believe that the limits on contributions by party organizations and legislative caucuses should be increased, in an effort to encourage party cohesion, strengthen the position of legislative leaders, and encourage responsible party government. They may also be motivated by a belief that political parties will provide funds to both incumbents and challengers and will give priority to close races, thus reducing the incumbent advantages and encouraging competition. This partisan strategy is often contrasted to that of political action committees, which are perceived as wanting to support sure winners (which usually means incumbents).

To assess some of these arguments, we need to determine what actually is the strategy of party organizations. Do they concentrate their funding on close races and, controlling for this factor, do they treat incumbents and challengers alike? We also need to measure the level of funding provided by the majority and minority parties in order to assess their impact on legislative elections.

Political Party Funding Strategies

It is important to remember that funding for the legislative races included in our study has come from state and local party organizations, legislative party campaign committees, and, in a very limited way, from national parties. (The infusion of soft money from the national level in the 1994 and 1996 elections has presumably changed this balance.) For the elections covered in this study (in most cases from 1986 through 1992), about two-thirds of party funding has come from state parties, more than one-sixth from legislative party campaign committees, and somewhat less than that from local parties. But there are fourteen parties, mostly Republican, where the state party organization provides most of the funding and ten others, mostly Democratic, where the legislative party campaign committee is the major source of funds.

The first question about party strategy is how much funding do the parties provide, measured as a percentage of all funding for legislative candidates? The data from both parties in seventeen states (chapter 10) show that less than half the state parties have made major contributions to legislative candidates, measured as a proportion of all funds these candidates received. Both parties in California, Maine, and New Jersey, and the Republicans in North Carolina, have nearly always contributed 10 percent or more of candidates' funding; some parties have reached

20 percent on occasion. Both parties in Pennsylvania, Wisconsin, and Idaho have contributed as much as 10 percent. One or both parties have come close to that level in several other states.

On the other hand, eight of the parties have consistently contributed 5 percent or less of the total funding for its legislative candidates. It is difficult to believe that parties contributing so little can make much of an impact unless they concentrate their funding on a few close races. In any assessment of the role that political parties play in financing campaigns, we must recognize that many of them do not consistently provide enough funding to have much impact on legislative races.

It might be expected that if one political party is making substantial contributions, then the other party must try to match these funds, but that is not consistently true. Both parties in Maine and California, for example, consistently gave a substantial share of legislative candidates' contributions. But in North Carolina the minority Republican party consistently provided a considerably larger share of its candidates' funding than did the Democrats in all three elections from 1988 through 1992. In 1994 Republicans outspent Democrats by almost 3 to 1. In Pennsylvania both parties spend heavily in terms of dollars, but the Democratic funds, as a proportion of all funds for their candidates, has been falling while the Republican percentage has risen.

In 1992 the Democratic party gave more funding to the average challenger in nine states, more to the average incumbent in two states (California and New Jersey), and there was little difference in the other six states in the study. The Republican party gave more to challengers in twelve states, with little difference in the other five. There are a variety of reasons why a party in a particular election year may give more funding, on average, to incumbents or challengers. It may depend on whether the party sees a greater risk of losing seats it holds or a greater chance of capturing new seats. A minority party that is close to winning a legislative majority may give higher priority to funding viable challengers. In California the Democrats gave more to incumbents in 1992 presumably because they were trying (successfully) to hold their majority in the assembly, while the Republicans gave more to challengers and open- seat candidates in an effort to make gains.

Political parties consistently contribute substantially larger amounts of money to candidates in competitive races (defined as those won by less than 60 percent) than to those in safe races, usually by a margin of at least 2 to 1. This was true in almost every state election from 1986 through 1992. A party's incumbents who face strong opponents need more funds to avoid defeat. Most parties target seats held by the opposition that are considered vulnerable and try to find and financially support strong candidates as challengers. In some states where the party plays a major role in campaign funding, the funds are heavily concentrated on close races. In the 1988 California Assembly elections, for example, the party contribution averaged more than $300,000 for 27 close races and $16,000 for 124 safe races (Breaux and Gierzynski 1992).

In nearly all the thirty-two parties in the sixteen states for which we have data on contributions from both parties and PACs in 1992, the funding from parties was less, and often much less, than the funding from PACs. Every state party (except the New Jersey Democrats) contributed less, often much less, to its incumbents than PACs did; for more than half of the parties, the ratio of PAC giving to party giving was 10 to 1 or more. For challengers and open-seat candidates, however, the ratio was usually 3 to 1 or less, and there were six parties that gave more than PACs to challengers and open-seat candidates. In none of the cases where state parties gave more to challengers than to incumbents did they give enough to offset the advantage that incumbents received from PACs.

Implications for Reform

The obvious conclusion to be drawn from this analysis is that if party funding were substantially increased, compared to funding from other sources, then the financial advantage enjoyed by incumbents would be decreased and a higher proportion of funds would be concentrated on close races. Both of these developments should make legislative races more competitive, although if the parties targeted their spending too narrowly on the closest of races, there would be less benefit to challengers running in those districts traditionally dominated by the other party.

The strategy followed by parties encourages more competition and often helps candidates challenging incumbents, while the strategy of most PACs favors incumbents and thereby tends to weaken competition. As long as PACs contribute much more money to legislative candidates than parties do, the combined effect of these two types of contributions will be to weaken competition and help incumbents hold their jobs.

We have seen that, in some states, it would probably not require a large infusion of cash in a number of races to make the challenger competitive. In many cases, except in the most professional states, several thousand dollars might be enough to accomplish that purpose. Stronger party financial support for a challenger might make him or her appear to be more viable and encourage other individuals and groups to contribute.

The next question is whether the political parties would be likely to substantially increase their funding of legislative races if the legal limitations were raised on both contributions by party organizations to candidates and contributions by individuals and PACs to the parties. As of the 1992 election, in about three-fourths of the states in this study, there were no limitations on contributions by political parties to legislative candidates in the general election. There is no clear evidence that the limitations on party contributions to legislative candidates in the other states, usually about $5,000 per candidate, deterred party contributions. Where such limits applied, the average party contribution was no less than in other states with similar levels of professionalism. Many of these states do not place any limits on contributions by individuals or by PACs to political parties.

We conclude that increased party funding of legislative races would probably make many of them more competitive, but that in most states the campaign finance laws are not a major barrier to such increases. On the other hand, if reformers made a successful effort to impose much tighter limitations on contributions to parties or on contributions to legislative candidates by state, local, or legislative parties, the result could be the creation of more serious obstacles to challengers and a decline in legislative competition.

It is also likely that legislative candidates in 1994 and 1996 have benefited, at least indirectly, from the increasing use of soft money by state political parties and from court decisions that permit political parties to make "independent expenditures"[3] on behalf of candidates. The official campaign finance records do not provide the information necessary to measure how soft money has been spent in ways that would benefit state legislative candidates. If legislation were passed at the state or national level curtailing or abolishing the use of soft money, then state parties would presumably have fewer resources to spend on legislative races, and thus less opportunity to aid challengers and increase the number of competitive races.

PUBLIC FINANCING

The Argument for Public Finance

One reform that is often mentioned is public financing for campaigns. The positive aspect of public financing is that it allows for spending limitations to be placed on all those who agree to accept public funds. This could serve as a means of holding down costs and reducing the importance of large contributors. Ultimately, public financing would increase the competitiveness of elections by equalizing the amount of funding available to all candidates.

A public financing system will function as designed only if most candidates agree to accept public funding and the spending limit that accompanies it. Candidates who are sure that they can raise as much as they need, or at least more than the limit, have little incentive to utilize public funding. A challenger, for example, might benefit from public funding but be handicapped because the incumbent, who rejected public funding, was able to spend much more. Public funding works well only if the spending limits are set high enough so that most candidates accept the funding and spending limits.

Evaluation of Public Finance

There are only two states that provide for public financing of legislative elections (Minnesota and Wisconsin). This very limited number of cases makes it difficult to assess the impact of public financing as it could apply to other states. We can, however, make some preliminary evaluations of public financing in these two states.

Previous research has considered both states as case studies, but not in a comparative design. Interestingly, the previous research comes to opposite conclusions. The public financing in Minnesota apparently has provided more funding to incumbents than challengers, yet Donnay and Ramsden (1995) conclude that public financing has served to make elections more competitive. Mayer and Wood (1995) argue that, while public financing in Wisconsin has served to close the spending gap between incumbents and challengers, it has not made elections more competitive. These different conclusions would appear to be the result of differing research designs and conceptualizations.

Our findings indicate that Minnesota's system continues to benefit incumbents, while challengers in Wisconsin average more public funds than incumbents. As an example, in 1992 Minnesota incumbents averaged $5,280 in public funds, while challengers averaged just $3,540. Conversely, in Wisconsin the averages were: incumbents $2,000, challengers $4,060. The difference is due to the way in which funds are distributed. It would be tempting to conclude that Wisconsin's system works while Minnesota's does not. This requires further examination.

Another means of comparing these two states is to examine the ability of challengers to compete financially with incumbents, as well as the actual percentage of competitive challengers. Unfortunately, this does not provide a clear answer about the effects of public financing. The data show that Wisconsin challengers do not face as large a financial gap as do Minnesota challengers, and that Wisconsin challengers are much more likely to raise the amount spent by the average incumbent. The data also show, however, that there is almost no difference in the overall percentage of challengers who are competitive in the two states.

There is not enough evidence from two states to conclude that public finance would succeed or fail in meeting the goals of reformers. We could learn more if more states extended public financing to legislative races. However, the results in Wisconsin suggest that public financing may be a way of reducing money as a road block to competitiveness.

CONCLUSION

The cross-state research done in recent years on state legislative campaign financing does not directly answer the normative questions about campaign financing reform. But it does give us more information about the accuracy of assumptions underlying some of the proposals for reform, as well as some basis for estimating what would be the consequences of such proposals. Unless the diagnosis is correct and the prescription is appropriate and realistic, reforms will not work.

Although critics of campaign finance often focus on the high and increasing costs, we know that costs vary widely among the states. The states with higher, and more rapidly increasing, costs tend to be the larger ones with more professional legislatures. This is where we usually find the largest gap, in percentage terms, between what is spent by incumbents and challengers. Consequently, this may be where the need for reform is greatest.

An incumbent who is experienced, politically skilled, and hardworking, and who knows the district well, has major advantages over most challengers, and the head start is even greater if the district is one where the incumbent's party usually enjoys a comfortable lead. In addition to these advantages, most incumbents are able to raise and spend more campaign funds than most challengers. The small minority of challengers who are able to spend about as much or more than incumbents are the most likely to run a competitive race, and they have the greatest chance of beating the incumbent.

This does not necessarily mean that money is the deciding factor in most legislative elections. Some challengers are able to run competitive, or even winning, races even though they spend less. A more important factor is that the incumbents who are most skillful and hard working are likely to raise the most money, and that those who are perceived as being solid choices to win have little trouble raising as much as they need. Moreover, those challengers who outspend incumbents and sometimes win are likely to be the ones who are the most skillful and experienced—the ones perceived as viable in the race. The real question, and a hard one to answer, is: To what extent is money crucial to the outcome? Do relatively weak incumbents win because they have more money? Do relatively strong challengers fail because they lack money?

We can conclude that the incumbents usually spend more, often much more, than challengers and this financial edge is a major ingredient in their victory. In order for challengers to be competitive and have some realistic chance of winning, they usually must be able to substantially narrow or sometimes eliminate the spending gap.

It is difficult to devise a reform plan that would neutralize or minimize the incumbent's advantage. Imposing an absolute limit on candidate spending would run into constitutional obstacles and might seriously handicap those challengers who have the political strength and experience to raise enough money to challenge an incumbent effectively.

Can the playing field be made more level, not by imposing spending limits, but by encouraging more funding of challengers? It would be difficult, and probably unconstitutional, to accomplish this by raising the amount that individuals or groups can give to challengers or lowering the limit for giving to incumbents. However, it might be possible to change the laws regulating groups that contribute differentially to incumbents and challengers.

Because PACs give much more to incumbents than to challengers, one might impose lower limits on the amount PACs can give to a candidate. The evidence from our research raises doubts about whether this strategy would be effective in practice. What about the notion of entirely eliminating PAC contributions to candidates? This might not be constitutional, and it might not prevent PACs from spending independently on campaigns or prevent their current contributors from finding other ways to contribute to campaigns. It would make it more difficult to provide public information about such spending.

We know that political parties (state, local, or legislative) give priority to candidates in close races and often give priority to challengers. But in many states the amount of giving by parties is relatively small, certainly less than what PACs contribute. Would raising the legal limits on party contributions to candidates make a difference? This is doubtful, because many states have no limits, and in those states with limits parties often contribute less than they are permitted to. There may be some cases where such limits prevent parties from spending large amounts on a relatively small number of close races. It is likely that reforms designed to impose stricter limits on spending by state, local, or legislative parties might significantly curtail the parties' ability to help challengers and to spend abundantly in close races.

Public financing is an option to reform financing and negate some of the advantages of incumbency. Our evidence indicates that this can occur, but it is not guaranteed. If public financing is set up to reward past electoral results, then incumbents will have a distinct advantage. Public financing does not guarantee competitive elections but if instituted properly it can reduce the financial roadblock to competing. Another option is to institute total public financing and eliminate all outside contributions, a proposal that has received some support in Wisconsin.

There are at least three serious obstacles to any plan that would use public financing to pay a major part of the cost of legislative campaigns. First, it would be expensive because there are so many legislators—more than one hundred in most states. Second, incumbent legislators will be reluctant to make drastic changes in the financing system under which they were elected, particularly a public financing plan that they would perceive as primarily helping challengers. Third, and perhaps most important, today there is a high level of public cynicism about politics and politicians. Polls suggest that many voters have serious doubts about underwriting the cost of any campaigns. They perceive this as simply a way to bail out candidates and not as a program that would provide them with a better choice of viable candidates, weaken the grip of incumbents on their seats, and reduce the influence of special interests—goals that we might expect them to favor.

Political scientists have long known that reform legislation often fails to accomplish its goals and often has unintended consequences. Campaign finance reform is no exception, and what evidence we have makes us cautious about predicting that new laws can solve many of the problems that have been identified. A number of states are grappling with the issues and are adopting a variety of approaches to reform. In the years ahead, as we watch these experiments in many of the states, we will learn much more about how reforms actually affect the reality of campaign financing.

POSTSCRIPT: WHERE DO WE GO FROM HERE?

At the end of any research project, unanswered questions remain. A major purpose of research and writing is to raise questions for both scholars and students to try to answer. Much of our analysis has compared states with different political, campaign, and legislative characteristics. We have also described the changes over time in campaign financing between 1986 and the 1992–1994 period. In the years ahead, it is important to pay more attention to trends over time. This should be more feasible as campaign finance data become more regularly available, particularly in computer records.

Trends over Time

Several types of over-time studies deserve high priority. We have mentioned that numerous states are adopting a variety of reforms in campaign financing. It is important to compare the effects of these varied reforms by looking at the realities of campaign financing under old and new rules. Do politicians and lawyers always find ways to evade many of the purposes of campaign finance laws? What kinds of reforms actually produce change, and what kind of change is it? Do some real changes resulting from reform have an effect on the outcome of elections? To what extent do states copy the new reform ideas that seem to work best in other states?

At the same time that we are examining reforms, we need to look at changes in the strategy of campaign financing in legislative races. If there are more restrictions on raising and spending money, will candidates find ways to campaign with less money or spend it more effectively? Will there be more or less use of television, more emphasis on issues, or greater use of attack advertising?

Political scientists are already examining various consequences of the term limits movement as it begins to take effect. By reducing the number of incumbents running, do term limits make races more competitive? Does such a trend raise the cost of campaigns? Do less experienced candidates have less success in raising money? If term limits weaken legislative party leaders, are they less able to raise funds for candidates?

In the South, where politics has been changing more than in other parts of the country, legislative races are becoming much more competitive. One obvious question is whether this is leading to higher campaign costs. As the partisan balance in many southern legislatures grows closer, we would expect both Democratic and Republican legislative parties and/or state party organizations to be targeting close races and providing more funding for their candidates in such districts. We need to describe and analyze the process in considerable detail.

The Role of Political Parties

We have learned that legislative and/or state political parties in most states throughout the country are providing funding to legislative candidates, that they concentrate on close races, and usually give challengers and open-seat candidates as much or more help than incumbents. We need to track this process in greater detail. What specific criteria do parties use in selecting candidates to help? Do they concentrate funding on just a few races? What is the timing of their financial support? How much of this support is in cash and how much in services, and what difference does that make? How and why are there variations in the relationship between legislative parties and state parties in providing this support? We must understand more precisely how soft money works. We need to find out how much financial support comes from national to state parties and how much of this benefits legislative candidates directly or indirectly. If the use of soft money is restricted or banned by federal legislation, what impact might this have on legislative candidates?

Case Studies

Now that we finally have a large-scale study covering more than one-third of the states, it may seem strange to call for more in-depth studies of individual states. But now we can identify states that appear to be outliers: states, for example, where elections cost much less or where incumbents have a much smaller financial advantage in campaigns than in states with similar characteristics. Political scientists who are particularly familiar with one state have a good opportunity to test our broad conclusions against their knowledge of legislative races in that state. This is particularly important in the states not covered by our study.

We also need studies below the state level. What factors cause particular legislative districts to grow more competitive over time, or less competitive, and are these trends caused in some way by the realities of campaign financing? We need more surveys and interviews of individual legislative candidates to understand their political and financial strategies. How do they make choices about raising money or investing their own funds in a campaign? Why are some willing to run for a seat when they have no realistic chance of raising enough money to win or even be competitive? How do some candidates, particularly challengers, succeed in winning or coming close while being outspent by wide margins? It might even be interesting for those conducting research to summarize some of the major findings of this study and ask legislative candidates what they think about them.

In the field of legislative campaign finance, as in all fields of state politics, the opportunities for significant research are limited only by our imagination, our resources, and our ability to get access to the data.

NOTES

1. When the term *party* or *parties* is used, in discussing funding sources, it includes both state and local party organizations and legislative party campaign committees.
2. "Soft money" refers to unlimited and unregulated funds that are given to political parties for party-building activities.

3. Independent expenditures are those activities, such as television advertisements, that support or oppose a candidate but are made independently of the candidate's campaign.

REFERENCES

Breaux, David A., and Anthony Gierzynski. 1992. "The Role of Parties in Legislative Campaign Financing." Paper presented at the annual meeting of the American Political Science Association, Chicago, September 3–6.

California Commission on Campaign Financing. 1985. "The New Gold Rush: Financing California's Legislative Campaigns." Los Angeles: Center for Responsive Government.

Donnay, Patrick D. and Graham P. Ramsden. 1995. "Public Financing of Legislative Elections: Lessons from Minnesota." *Legislative Studies Quarterly* 20: 351–364.

Garand, James. 1991. "Electoral Marginality in State Legislative Elections." *Legislative Studies Quarterly* 16: 7–28.

Gierzynski, Anthony, and David Breaux. 1991. "Money and Votes in State Legislative Elections." *Legislative Studies Quarterly* 16: 203–217.

Jacobson, Gary C. 1980. *Money in Congressional Elections.* New Haven, Ct.: Yale University Press.

Jacobson, Gary C. 1990. "The Effects of Campaign Spending in House Elections: New Evidence for Old Arguments." *American Journal of Political Science* 34: 334–362.

Jewell, Malcolm E. 1994. "State Legislative Elections: What We Know and Don't Know." *American Politics Quarterly* 22: 483–509.

Jewell, Malcolm E., and David Breaux. 1988. "The Effect of Incumbency on State Legislative Elections." *Legislative Studies Quarterly* 13: 495–514.

Mayer, Kenneth R., and John M. Wood. 1995. "The Impact of Public Financing on Electoral Competitiveness: Evidence from Wisconsin, 1964–1990." *Legislative Studies Quarterly* 20: 69–88.

New York Times, "Gingrich Tops Spending List in Campaign for House," January 3, 1997, A8.

Ornstein Norman J., Thomas E. Mann, and Michael J. Malbin. 1996. *Vital Statistics on Congress, 1995–96.* Washington: Congressional Quarterly.

Rosenthal, Alan. 1989. "The Legislative Institution: Transformed and at Risk." In *The State of the States,* edited by Carl E. Van Horn. Washington: CQ Press, pp. 69–102.

Weber, Ronald E., Harvey J. Tucker, and Paul Brace. 1991. "Vanishing Marginals in State Legislative Elections." *Legislative Studies Quarterly* 16: 29–47.

Data-Gathering Issues

Anthony Gierzynski

Anyone who wants to study the financing of state legislative campaigns faces two key problems: obtaining the campaign finance records of candidates and creating comparable data sets out of those records (which then will allow for comparative study). Thanks to a grant from the National Science Foundation, we were able to overcome those obstacles in researching this book. Some of the difficulties we faced are discussed in this appendix.

OBTAINING THE DATA

The first problem with studying the financing of state legislative elections is just getting the records of the candidates. There is no uniform procedure for maintaining such records. Some states, such as North Carolina and New Mexico prior to 1994, did not even require all candidates to file their records in the state capital; this meant we had to travel to local courthouses to obtain some of the records. Some states make obtaining the information easy. Minnesota, Washington, and Oregon, for example, publish books that itemize or list the contributions for all legislative candidates. Some states (e.g., Idaho and Washington) now make the data available on disk. Other states make obtaining the data much more difficult. In Illinois one has to fill out three separate forms to look at each candidate's records. Furthermore, records in Illinois, as well as Bernallio County, New Mexico (the Albuquerque area), are on microfiche, which is difficult to read, especially for long periods of time. California records used to be easily accessible and in excellent form (with pages detailing the contributors to each candidates). The management of their records was then privatized and access to the itemized records of candidates following 1990 is only available if one is willing to pay a large sum of money, or has access to LEXIS/NEXIS. Other states, such as Maine, maintain candidate records on file that can be photocopied at a per-page rate. In Maine, the records can be copied for 10 cents a page or a staff member will do the photocopying for 20 cents a page. In Kansas we rented a photocopying machine and wheeled it into the state building to copy the records! For the most part, the staff of the various agencies and departments that maintained the data were extremely helpful.

The ease of obtaining the records seems to depend on the political culture and recent politics of the state. The most open states (e.g., Minnesota, Wisconsin, Oregon, Washington, and even Maine—if they had greater resources) tended to be the states from Elazar's moralistic political subculture (Elazar 1984). Those with less accessible records (e.g., Illinois and New Mexico) tend to be from either individualistic or traditionalistic subcultures. Recent politics played a role in shifting California records from very open to less open (the legislature did not, apparently, appreciate the good work of the California Fair Political Practices Commission and removed the responsibility of maintaining campaign finance records from them).

COMPARABILITY

After obtaining the data one then has to ask questions about the comparability of data from state to state. Each state has its own unique way of requiring candidates to report their finances—some require reports of expenditures over certain amounts, some require several reports a year, others require only one or two, and so on. Because many of our conclusions about campaign finance in this volume stem from comparing finance behavior in the states, these differences could affect the conclusions we reach in our research. Therefore, it is important to discuss the issue of comparability.

Reporting Period

The time periods covered by campaign finance data vary because candidates are required to file reports at different times and because the agencies that aggregate the data do so for different periods. But does it differ enough to cause problems for comparative analysis of campaign finance behavior? Table A-1 provides information on the reporting periods and requirements for the states that are part of the analysis in this book and by the Federal Election Commission (FEC).

The filing requirements seem to vary significantly among the states and with the federal government. Federal candidates are required to re-

Table A-1   *Campaign Finance Recording Practices in Eighteen States*

	Reporting Period for Candidates and Committees		Separate Primary Report	Itemization of Contributions Larger Than:
	Preelection[a]	Postelection[b]		
Federal	12	30	no	$200
California	45, 17	July 31 or January 31	yes	250
Delaware	20	December 31	yes	0
Idaho	7	30 and January 31[c]	no	50
Illinois	15	semiannually	no	150
Kansas	8	January 10 annually	yes	50
Maine	6	42	no	50
Minnesota	10	January 31 annually	no	100
Mississippi	7	none required	no	200
Missouri	40, 7	30 and January 15[c]	yes	100
Montana	5	20 and close	no	35
New Jersey	29, 11	20, every 60	no	100
North Carolina	10	annually[d]	no	100
Oregon	29, 39	30, and annually on September 10[c]	yes	50
Pennsylvania	sixth Tuesday & second Friday	30 and January 31	yes	0
Utah	7	December 31	no	0
Washington	none	December 10[e]	no	25
Wisconsin	8 to 14	semiannually	no	20
Wyoming	—	10	yes	25

[a] Entries are the number of days prior to the election that reports must be filed unless otherwise specified.

[b] Entries are the number of days after the election that reports must be filed.

[c] Supplemental reports are due on this date if significant activity took place after the initial postelection filing.

[d] Candidates defeated in the primaries must file ten days postelection.

[e] Supplemental reports are required on the tenth day of every month if activity exceeds $200.

Source: Council of State Governments, *COGEL Blue Book,* 8th ed., 1990; *The Book of the States, 1992–1993.*

port their revenues and expenditures twelve days prior to an election and thirty after the election. In the states, practices vary widely with regard to preelection filing. California requires two preelection reports and others at the end of July and at the end of the year. Idaho requires reports seven days before elections. New Jersey requires reports twenty-nine and eleven days before the election. The postelection filings also vary—usually between twenty and sixty days after the election—but they are consistent in that they all require supplemental or year-end reports to insure all election activity is reported.

When government agencies choose to aggregate individual reports into a single publication, the reports vary in the time period each covers and whether the reports contain separate figures for the primaries. Reports issued by the FEC contain data on activities for the entire two-year election cycle, with no distinction between primary and general election activity. Idaho follows a similar practice. Wisconsin issues reports that cover two calendar years. California's highly detailed reports (prior to 1990) also cover a two-year cycle (calendar year), but they include separate reports for primary and general elections. Minnesota's Ethical Practices Board produces annual reports. Washington and Oregon issue reports that include all election-related activity.

Do these differences in reporting practices have an impact on our ability to conduct comparative research on campaign finance? The answer, I think, is no. The differences in preelection reports are not a problem for most campaign finance research questions since most analysts rely on the final reports of activity for the election. The practice of requiring supplemental or annual reports ensures that all election-related expenditures will be included for each of the states, minimizing any potential problems caused by different postelection filing dates.

The inability to separate primary and general election campaign finance activity in all cases does not pose a significant problem for most comparative work. We need only combine the data from the two cycles, proceeding on the assumptions that have been well accepted among scholars of congressional elections: that spending in primary elections helps win votes for the general election as well. If we are interested, however, in examining the role of money in primary elections (as we have done in chapter 5), the failure of states to separate such data limits the number of states that can be examined and weakens our ability to generalize.

Itemization Requirements

Campaign finance laws also vary in terms of the requirements for itemizing contributions. Table A-1 reports the level at which contributions must be itemized—that is, identified by source—for congressional and state legislative candidates. In Pennsylvania and Utah all contributions must be itemized; in California only contributions in excess of $250 must be itemized. There is quite a bit of variation in the states between these extremes.

These different reporting practices are most likely to hamper comparative analyses of candidates' sources of money. Small contributions—those under the limit—are most likely to come from individual contributors. If a substantial proportion of those contributions are not itemized, analyses of candidate receipts will likely underestimate contributions from individuals, distorting comparative analysis. A mitigating factor for some of the states, however, is the apparent relationship between costs of campaigns and the level at which contributions must be itemized: the states with the most expensive campaigns seem to have set higher amounts for itemizing. If the level required for itemizing is relative to the overall costs of campaigns, the type of contributions excluded from the analysis will be similar for each state. For high-cost states with low itemization levels, it may be possible to make the data more comparable by excluding some of the smaller contributions.

Classification of Contributors

An important data issue is the classification of contributors to candidates' campaigns. This issue arises from the fact that some campaign finance reports have already classified contributors and from the need of the researcher to classify contributors in order to analyze campaign finance data.

The Federal Election Commission assigns candidate revenues to seven categories: individuals, the candidate, party, business political action committees (PACs), labor PACs, professional/trade association PACs, and nonconnected PACs. Missouri has a similar classification scheme but includes categories for corporations, business, and associations (which is not necessary for federal campaigns since such contributions are illegal). There is no nonconnected PAC category in the Missouri classification system; instead, they have a category labeled "other continuing committees." Wisconsin also aggregates contributions in their biennial reports but classifies contributions by interest, mixing PAC, non-PAC, and individual contributions together.

These classifications by campaign finance recording agencies pose problems to the researcher because, in some cases, such as Wisconsin and Missouri, the categories are different. It is also a problem because the agencies do not have a standardized set of decision rules for classifying contributors.

The ideal would be to allow the researcher to categorize contributions for the special purposes of their analysis. The practical issues involved in building data sets, however, forced us to establish some categories. We decided to classify contributions first by type (PAC versus direct contributions from the organizations) and interest (e.g., business, labor, etc.). Our coding categories include:

- the candidates themselves
- individuals
- parties (separating local, state, legislative, and national party organization contributions where possible)
- businesses and corporations

- business or corporate PACs
- labor organizations (including public employees)
- labor PACs
- professionals (professional organizations and professions, e.g., doctors, and lawyers)
- professional PACs
- agriculture interests
- agriculture PACs
- ideological or single-interest groups and/or PACs

Totals

Care must be taken when utilizing totals on campaign finance reports. One area that could lead to a significant distortion of results in a few states is the inclusion of transfers to other candidates in the total expenditures. While these activities represent expenditures, they do not represent money spent for the purpose of securing more votes. Consequently, we have collected information on transfers so we can subtract such transfers when calculating how much candidates spend on their own campaigns.

Requirements Versus Reality of Campaign Finance Records

The final issue that researchers interested in comparative analysis of campaign finance must be aware of is the potential gap between the campaign finance reporting laws and how well they are followed. The knowledge of such possible problems comes from the experience of the researchers whose work appears in this book as well as from the work done by Huckshorn (1985). While many states have good reporting laws, they have not provided well for the enforcement of those laws. Most agencies maintaining the records are understaffed and underfunded (including the Federal Election Commission). Detailed documentation of irregularities in reporting accompanying data sets is the only means of addressing this problem.

REFERENCES

Elazar, Daniel J. 1984. *American Federalism: A View From the States*, 3rd ed. New York: Harper and Row.

Huckshorn, Robert J. 1985. "Who Gave It? Who Got It?: The Enforcement of Campaign Finance Laws in the States." *Journal of Politics* 47: 773–789.

Index

Access, 5–6, 159–160, 161, 171, 173, 181*n*1
Accountability, 210
Advertising, 68
Alaska, 82
Alexander, Herbert, 37, 71, 158
Arizona, 141, 158

Basnight, Marc, 4
Berch, Neil, 123
Bibby, John F., 85
Blacks. *See* Racial issues
Breaux, David, 80–98, 99–114, 117, 185–205, 215
Brown, Willie, 142, 145, 156*n*3
Budget, 14, 15*t*
Bullock, C., 141
Burrell, Barbara, 119

California
    campaign spending, 38, 43, 47, 54, 55, 56, 63, 64
    challenger fund raising, 212
    cost of competing as a challenger, 109, 110
    cost of elections, 9, 59, 60, 100–101
    districts, 19, 24
    expenditures, 91, 105
    fund raising in, 87, 88
    gender bias, 123, 126, 129–130, 132, 137*n*2
    incumbency expenditures, 103, 214
    legislature, 82, 120
    minority political participation, 141
    money and votes, 94
    political action committees, 162, 163, 166, 168–169, 171, 219
    political parties, 86, 187, 188, 193, 221, 222, 223
    population, 14, 60, 144
    primary elections, 82, 83, 84, 85, 86
    Proposition 73, 84, 193, 195
California Commission on Campaign Financing, 220
Campaign committees, 84
Campaign finance laws. *See* Legislation, campaign finance
Campaign finance systems
    constants of, 27–29
    electoral factors, 25–27
    environmental factors, 19–24
    gender bias in, 121–130
    model of, 19, 20
    rational actors in, 29
    by selected states, 12–13
    structural factors, 24–25
    study of, 18, 27–30, 38–56, 230
        data sets, 61, 80, 120, 144, 233–238
        lack of data, 37
        measurement issues, 39–42, 234–238
        regression analyses, 94, 130, 136–137
Campaigning, 24
Campaign spending
    additive effects on district-level spending, 73–76

Campaign spending *(continued)*
  campaign finance laws and, 71–72
  per candidate, by state, 43
  competitiveness and, 108–110
  constitutional issues, 212–213, 215
  district level spending per voter, 63–66, 69, 72–73, 74*f,* 75, 147–148
  electoral factors, 66–68
  gender bias, 123
  gubernatorial election cycles and, 50–52, 56
  increases in, 38–39, 56–57
  independent, 42, 205*n*3, 231*n*3
  inflation and, 47–48
  limits on, 23
  measurement of, 41–42
  money and the vote, 92–98, 99, 101–113, 117, 143
  patterns and predictors, 48–50, 74
  in state legislative races, 42–46
  studies of, 38–56
  trends over time, 47–50
  variation, at the district level, 59–79, 147–148
Candidates. *See also* Campaign spending; Elections
  campaign financing, 121–130
  effects on campaign spending, 67, 68, 76
  minority candidates, 142–143
  political action committees and, 160–161
  political parties and, 189, 191*t*
  in primary elections, 67
Cassie, William E., 99–114, 117, 158–184, 209–231
Census, 1980, 86
Center for American Women and Politics, 117
Center for Responsive Politics, 7
Challengers
  campaign costs and, 212, 214
  campaign spending, 53, 54–56, 214–215

competitiveness of, 106–110, 111, 215, 227
effect of campaign finance laws on, 23
effect of public financing on, 106
expenditures, 91, 92*t,* 99, 104–108, 111
fund raising by, 26, 67–68, 86–88, 89, 96, 100, 112–113, 151*t*
gender bias, 119, 124, 126, 129, 130
political action committee contributions, 163, 164, 169–170, 171–172, 174, 218, 220
political party contributions, 195–198, 200–202, 204, 223
public financing, 225
racial bias, 150
Citizen legislatures (Type III). *See* Legislatures, citizen
Colorado, 81–82, 141
Competition, party
  campaign spending and, 44–47, 56, 60, 61, 67, 69, 72–73, 74–75, 77
  challenger competitiveness and, 107
  cost of elections and, 101, 102, 112, 211–212
  fund raising and, 146, 151*t,* 152, 155
  in majority-minority districts, 143, 155
  political action committee contributions, 165–166, 170–172, 179
  political party contributions, 188, 190
  primary elections, 81
  role in campaign finance, 10–11, 20, 26–27, 71
Congressional races
  minorities in, 142
  political action committees and, 160
  power and money in, 28
  spending in, 5, 38
  women in, 121

Consumer Price Index (CPI), 47
Contributions. *See* Fund raising
Corporations and unions. *See*
 Contributions
Costs
 campaigns, 166–167
 criticism of, 211–212
 data sets, 61
 to elect a state legislator, 59–79, 211
 of elections, 9–10, 100–101, 110,
  179, 180
 increases in, 5, 158, 212, 220
 political action committees and,
  166–167
 political party contributions and,
  187, 188
CPI. *See* Consumer Price Index

Daniel, George, 4
Data sets. *See* Study of campaign
 finance
Definitions
 leadership, 152
 legislative professionalism, 70
 mean or average, 62
 median, 62
 seat and district, 78n2
 standard deviation, 64
Delaware
 campaign spending, 47, 55, 64
 gender bias, 121, 123, 132
 legislature, 120
 political action committees, 168,
  178, 219
 political parties, 191, 192, 205n3
 primary elections, 81–82
Democratic Party. *See also*
 Competitiveness, party; Political
 parties
 expenditures, 91–92
 and labor groups, 178
 political action committees, 154,
  173, 174, 176–179, 180
 political party contributions,
  187–189, 190, 192, 193,
  194–203, 222

 primary election revenues, 84
 soft money, 204
 southern states, 173, 211–212
Demographics. *See* Rural areas;
 Urban areas
Districts and redistricting
 campaign spending and, 43, 44,
  46, 59–79
 competition and, 84, 100
 incumbent candidates and, 86
 minority political participation
  and, 140, 141–142, 152, 154
 multimember, 25
 preclearance provisions, 140, 141
 redistricting, 40–41, 48–50, 56, 186
 size and population, 24–25, 63–64
 state, 8
 vanishing marginals, 104–108, 111
Donnay, Patrick D., 225
Donor bias, 118. *See also* Minorities;
 Women
Donor types, 130–135

Elections
 1992, 120–121, 123, 135–136, 224
 1994, 196, 224
 1996, 204, 209, 224
 competitive and close, 41,
  196–197, 198–199, 200, 203,
  222–223, 224, 229
 contested, 41
 costs of, 9–10, 101–102, 110,
  166–167, 179, 180
 length of election season, 23
 money and the vote, 92–98, 99,
  101–113, 117, 143, 209
 policy change and, 28–29
 pool of political money, 158
Election, general
 campaign spending in, 69
 compared to primary elections, 81
 expenditures, 90–91
 financing and revenues, 83
 fund raising during, 88, 89
 primary elections and, 86, 91, 93,
  94–95

Elections, primary
  campaign spending in, 67, 69
  contested, 67, 85–86
  expenditures, 88–95
  financing and revenues, 80, 82–88
  fund raising during, 88
  general discussion, 81–82
  general elections and, 86, 91, 93,
    94–95
  incumbents in, 93–94
  timing of, 84
Expenditures. See Campaign spending

FEC. See Federal Election
    Commission
Federal Election Commission (FEC),
    80
Florida, 38, 141
Florio, James, 191
Fund raising
  by challengers, 26, 67–68, 86–88,
    89, 96, 100, 112–113
  corporate and union, 12–13,
    71–72, 130
  by incumbents, 67, 86–88, 89, 96,
    100
  by minorities, 145–155
  role of political action committees,
    158–180
  role of political parties, 185–205
  as variable in campaign costs, 9–10
  by women, 117, 118, 121–137
  limits on, 12–13, 22

Garcia, J. A., 141
Gender issues, 118–120, 121–130.
    See also Women and women
    candidates
General elections. See Elections,
    general
Gierzynski, Anthony, 18–33, 80–98,
    142–143, 161, 185–205, 215,
    233–238
Glanz, Stanton A., 160
Gopoian, J. David, 159
Green, Joanne Connor, 119

Grenzke, Janet, 160
Grier, Kevin B., 160
Grofman, B., 141
Gubernatorial races, 50, 52, 56

Hamm, Keith E., 44, 59–79,
    117–138
Hadley, C., 142
Handbook of Black Elected Officials
    (Joint Center for Political and
    Economic Studies), 144
Handley, L., 141
Hayes, Robin, 4–5
Heard, Alexander, 59
Hendrie, Paul, 7
Herrick, Rebekah, 119
Hispanics. See Racial issues
Hogan, Robert E., 44, 59–79,
    139–157
Holbrook, Thomas M., 85
House of Representatives. See
    Congressional races
Hrebenar, Ronald J., 190
Hybrid legislatures (Type II). See
    Legislatures, hybrid

Idaho
  campaign finance legislation, 72,
    130
  campaign spending, 50, 55, 64, 66
  chamber competition, 71
  cost of competing as a challenger,
    109
  districts, 78n2
  gender bias, 123, 132, 137n2
  gubernatorial candidates, 50
  legislature, 120
  partisan competition, 165
  political action committees, 132,
    175, 178, 219
  political parties, 188, 192, 222
Illinois
  campaign finance legislation, 72,
    130
  campaign spending, 43, 47, 50,
    56, 63, 64

contribution limits, 22
cost of competing as a challenger,
110
cost of elections, 9, 101
expenditures, 105
gender bias, 123, 126, 129–130,
132
legislature, 120
political action committees, 162,
166, 170, 171, 176, 219
primary elections, 81
Incumbents and incumbency
advantage of incumbency,
103–104, 213–215
campaign spending, 53, 54–56,
67–68, 214
effects on campaign finance
behavior, 25–27
expenditures, 91, 92*t*, 99, 103,
104–108, 111
fund raising by, 67, 86–88, 89, 96,
100, 151*t*
gender bias, 123, 126, 127–128,
129, 130, 132, 133
interest group contributions, 21,
22–23
political action committee
contributions, 118–119, 132,
160, 161, 163, 164, 166, 167,
169–172, 173, 174, 176,
179– 180, 218–219, 220
political party contributions, 195,
195–197, 200–202
primary elections, 86–88
professional legislatures, 21
public financing, 225
racial bias, 148–151, 154
redistricting and, 86
success of, 67
women, 121
Individual contributors, 6
Inflation, 38, 47, 49, 158, 212
Inside Campaign Finance (Sorauf),
37
Intercandidate transfers
Brown, Willie, and, 145

effects of, 220
net expenditures and, 53
prohibition of, 84
from women candidates, 137*n*1
Interest groups
accountability and, 210
incumbents and, 21, 22–23
political action committees and,
180
political parties and, 190
role in campaign finance, 20–21,
26–27
in states with professional
legislatures, 70

Jacobson, Gary C., 214
Jewell, Malcolm, 38, 209–231

Kansas
campaign spending, 55, 64
chamber competition, 71
cost of competing as a challenger,
109
gender bias, 132
legislature, 120
money and votes, 94
political action committees, 168,
170 173, 175, 180, 219
political parties, 192, 196
Kentucky, 82
Kurtz, Karl, 11, 14

Labor PACs. *See* Political action
committees
Laws. *See* Legislation, campaign
finance
Leadership
definition of, 152
of incumbents, 126
political action committees and,
162, 173, 175
status of minorities, 143,
151–152, 154
status of women, 121, 126
Legal factors, 21–24

Legislation, campaign finance
  effect on campaign spending,
    71–72, 73, 74–75, 77, 216
  effect on challenger competitive-
    ness, 112
  restrictions on political action
    committees, 168–169
  restrictions on political party con-
    tributions, 190–191, 223–224
  role in campaign financing, 11
Legislative professionalism, 10,
  46–47, 163–165
Legislatures
  citizen (Type III)
    campaign spending, 43–44, 47,
      51, 54–55, 57, 70
    characteristics, 11, 70
    cost of elections, 112
    expenditures, 105–106
    gender bias, 123, 126, 129, 135
    political action committee
      contributions, 163, 165, 166
    role in campaign financing, 10
    by state, 12–13, 15t, 71, 120
  hybrid (Type II)
    campaign spending, 43–44, 47,
      51, 57
    characteristics, 11
    expenditures, 105–106
    gender bias, 123, 126, 129, 132,
      135
    political action committee
      contributions, 163, 166
    political party contributions, 190
    by state, 12–13, 15t, 71, 120
  professional (Type I)
    campaign spending, 47, 51, 54,
      57, 70–71, 72, 74–75
    challenger disadvantage, 105
    cost of elections, 60
    characteristics, 11, 70
    cost of elections and, 101,
      111–112
    expenditures, 91, 105–106
    gender bias, 123, 126, 129, 132
    leadership positions in, 126

political action committee
  contributions, 162, 165, 179
political party contributions, 190
role in campaign financing, 10,
  14, 21
by state, 12–13, 15t, 71, 120
state, 5, 40–46, 56
elections, 8
role in policy making, 209
total expenditures per candidate,
  43
upper versus lower chambers,
  39–40
women in, 117–118, 139
Lenz, T., 141
Loftus, Tom, 37
Louisiana, 142

Madigan, Michael, 156n3
Maine
  campaign spending, 43, 55–56, 63
  chamber competition, 71
  cost of competing as a challenger,
    109
  cost of elections, 9, 101
  gender bias, 132
  legislature, 120
  money and the vote, 101
  partisan competition, 165
  political action committees, 132,
    168, 173, 219
  political parties, 188, 191, 198,
    205n3, 221, 222
Massachusetts, 119
Mayer, Kenneth R., 225
Mayhew, David, 100
Media, 4, 7
Minnesota
  campaign finance legislation, 72, 77
  campaign spending, 47, 55, 64, 66
  contribution limits, 22
  cost of competing as a challenger,
    110
  expenditures, 106
  gender bias, 123, 126, 132
  legislature, 120

political action committees, 163,
  168, 170, 175, 176, 178, 219
political parties, 191, 192, 205*n*3
primary elections, 81
public financing, 11, 72, 104, 106,
  163, 170, 225–226
regulations, 22
Minorities. *See* Racial issues
Mississippi
  campaign finance legislation, 72
  campaign spending, 55, 64
  chamber competition, 71
  cost of competing as a challenger,
    109
  Democratic Party in, 86
  district-level competitiveness, 98
  expenditures, 91, 92
  gender bias, 123, 126, 132
  fund raising in, 87–88
  legislature, 120, 166
  money and the vote, 101
  partisan competition, 165
  political action committees, 132,
    166, 168, 173, 219
  political parties, 187, 188
  primary elections, 82, 83, 84, 85,
    86, 91
Missouri
  campaign spending, 44, 50, 63
  cost of competing as a challenger,
    109
  district-level competitiveness,
    98*n*3
  expenditures, 92
  gender bias, 132
  legislature, 120
  political parties, 188, 192
  primary elections, 81, 82, 83, 84, 85
Monardi, Fred, 160
Moncrief, Gary F., 3–17, 37–58, 71,
  104, 117–138, 141, 158
Money
  power and, 27–29, 142–143, 161,
    195
  votes and, 92–98, 99, 101–113,
    117, 143, 226–227

Montana
  campaign spending, 43, 54–55,
    63
  cost of competing as a challenger,
    109
  cost of elections, 9, 101
  legislature, 120
  money and the vote, 101
  partisan competition, 165
  political action committees, 132,
    163, 168, 173, 175–176, 219
  political parties, 187
Mooney, Christopher Z., 70
Munger, Michael C., 160

*National Roster of Hispanic Elected
  Officials* (National Association
  of Latino Elected Officials), 144
Nelson, A. J., 141
New Jersey
  campaign finance legislation, 130
  campaign spending, 54, 55, 63
  chamber competition, 71, 85
  cost of competing as a challenger,
    109
  cost of elections, 101, 112
  districts, 61, 155*n*1
  expenditures, 104, 105
  gender bias, 123, 123, 126,
    129–130, 132
  interest groups, 181*n*4
  legislature, 120
  money and the vote, 101, 102
  party competition, 107, 109–110,
    112
  political action committees, 166,
    173, 175, 219
  political parties, 187, 188, 191,
    221, 222
  primary elections, 82, 83, 84–85
New Hampshire, 24
New Mexico, 141
New York, 158
Nick, R., 142
Nonincumbent candidates. *See*
  Challengers

North Carolina
    campaign spending, 47, 50, 64
    chamber competition, 71
    cost of competing as a challenger, 109
    cost of elections, 9
    contribution limits, 4
    districts, 61
    gender bias, 123, 132
    legislatures, 4–5, 6, 120, 166
    partisan competition, 107, 110, 165
    political action committees, 132, 158, 162, 173, 219
    political parties, 188, 222
    primary elections, 82, 83
    soft money, 6–7

Ohio, 141
Oklahoma, 119
Open-seat races
    campaign spending in, 67–68
    expenditures, 91
    gender bias, 119, 123, 125, 126, 129, 130
    political action committee contributions, 163, 164, 169, 171–172, 181n9
    political party contributions, 195, 196, 199–202
    racial bias, 150–151
    role in campaign finance, 10, 40–41
    term limits and, 23–24
Oregon
    campaign finance legislation, 72
    campaign spending, 46, 55–56, 63, 64
    chamber competition, 71
    cost of competing as a challenger, 110
    cost of elections, 9, 101
    gender bias, 132
    legislature, 120
    party competition, 46, 107, 110

political action committees, 163, 166, 170, 171, 178, 219
political parties, 188, 198
primary elections, 82, 83, 85

PACs. See Political action committees
Partisanship. See Competition, party
Pennsylvania
    campaign spending, 54, 55
    chamber competition, 71
    cost of competing as a challenger, 110
    expenditures, 105
    gender bias, 119, 121, 129–130, 132, 137n2
    legislature, 120
    political action committees, 166, 219
    political parties, 188, 192, 222
    population, 144
Philip Morris, 7
Policymaking, 23, 28–29
Political action committees (PACs)
    contribution limits, 6, 71–72, 219
    corporations and unions, 130
    criticism of, 217–218
    gender bias, 118, 131–132, 133
    increased number of, 158
    legal restrictions on, 168–169
    of legislative leaders, 27
    motivations and incentives, 118, 159–160, 223
    partisan bias, 171, 173
    public perception of, 5–6, 130
    racial bias, 142, 152–154
    role in campaign finance systems, 26–27, 57
    types of, 176–179
    variations in contributions, 163–179, 218–219
    women candidates and, 130
Political issues, 19–22

Political parties. *See also*
    Competition, party; Democratic
    Party; Republican Party;
    Soft money
  candidate attributes, 195–200
  criticism of, 220–221
  effect of contributions on
    legislative elections, 200–205
  gender bias, 132, 134–135
  legislative party organizations, 193
  motivations and incentives,
    221–224
  power and money in, 28–29
  party organization, 42, 186,
    192–195
  political action committees and,
    161–162, 220–221, 223
  racial bias, 152–154
  role in campaign finance, 20–21,
    26, 186–192, 229–230
  role in elections, 81, 185
  role in voter decisionmaking, 81
Poole, Keith T., 160
Population
  campaigning and, 24
  campaign costs and spending, 44,
    63–64, 76
  state budget and, 14, 15*t*
Power
  elections and, 28–29
  money and, 27–29, 142–143, 161,
    195
  political action committees and,
    160
  role in campaign finance, 21
Presidential races, 5
Professional legislatures (Type I). *See*
    Legislatures, professional
Primary elections. *See* Elections,
    primary
Pritchard, A., 141
Public financing. *See also* Reforms
  argument for, 224–225
  effects of, 23, 104, 106
  evaluation of, 225–226

  states providing, in some form, 11,
    17*n*1
Public perceptions
  campaign costs, 158, 212
  campaign finance system, 3–9,
    37–38
  cynicism about politics, 228
  gender bias, 130
  role of political parties, 186–187

Quid pro quo issues. *See* Access

Races. *See* Elections
Racial issues
  discrimination, 139
  districting and, 140
  minority candidates, 141–142,
    216–217
  political participation, 140–141,
    144
  power of minorities, 143
Ramsden, Graham P., 225
Ranney state competition index, 85,
    98*n*1, 165, 181*n*5
Refield, Kent, 41
Reform and Reality (Alexander),
    37
Reforms. *See also* Public financing
  cost of elections, 113
  fund raising, 96
  leveling the campaign playing
    field, 213–216, 226–227
  political action committee
    contributions, 180, 217–218,
    219–220, 227
  political parties, 220–221,
    223–224, 227
  public funding, 110, 112, 227–228
  soft money, 204–205
  spending limits, 77
  variability between states, 210
  women and minority candidates,
    216–217
Redistricting. *See* Districts
Republican National Committee, 5

Republican Party. *See also*
    Competitiveness, party; Political
    parties
  expenditures, 91–92
  political action committees, 154,
    173, 174, 176–179, 180
  political party contributions,
    187–189, 190, 191–192, 193,
    194–203, 222
  primary election revenues, 84
  soft money, 204
  southern states, 173, 211–212
R. J. Reynolds, 7
Romer, Thomas, 160
Rural areas, 68, 70

Schlozman, Kay, 119
Senate. *See* Congressional races
Shea, Daniel M., 193
Soft money
  definition of, 230*n*2
  effects of, 192, 221, 224
  election of 1996, 204
  increase in, 6–7, 186
  role of in campaign finance sys-
    tems, 42, 204
  use of, 4–5
Sorauf, Frank, 37, 40, 63, 64
Southern states, 120
State campaign finance systems
  perceptions of, 7–8
  state-by-state variations, 9–14
  studies of, 8–9
  what is known, 38–56
State legislatures. *See* Legislatures,
    state
States, 70–73. *See also* individual
    states
Stonecash, Jeffrey, 71
Study of campaign finance
  data sets, 61, 80, 120, 144,
    233–238
  lack of data, 37
  measurement issues, 39–42,
    234–238

need for, 230
regression analyses, 94, 130,
  136–137
as study of behavior, 18, 27–30
what is known, 38–56

Term limits, 23
Texas, 78*n*4, 142
Thaemert, Rita, 117
Theilmann, J., 142
Thomas, Clive S., 190
Thompson, Joel A., 3–17, 117–138,
  139–157, 158–184
Tobacco companies, 7, 160
Transfers, money. *See* Intercandidate
  transfers
Type I, II, III legislatures. *See*
  Legislatures

Uhlander, Carole, 119
Unions. *See* Contributions
Urban areas, 68, 70, 141
Utah
  campaign finance legislation, 72
  campaign spending, 43, 47, 50,
    54–56, 64, 66
  cost of competing as a challenger,
    109
  gender bias, 132
  incumbency expenditures, 103
  legislature, 120
  money and the vote, 101
  partisan competition, 165
  political action committees, 132,
    170, 173, 178
  political parties, 191, 192

Vanishing marginals. *See* Districts
Vermont, 19, 24, 25
Voters
  bias against female candidates, 119
  district level spending per voter,
    63–66, 69, 72–73, 74*f*, 75,
    147–148
  minority, 140

role of political parties, 81
turnout in elections, 81
Voting Rights Act of 1965, 140, 141

Washington
  campaign spending, 44, 55
  cost of competing as a challenger,
    109
  cost of elections, 101
  districts, 78n2
  elections, 9, 25
  gender bias, 123, 132
  gubernatorial candidates, 50
  legislature, 120
  money and the vote, 102
  political action committees, 163,
    166, 173, 178, 219
  political parties, 107, 110, 191
Western states, 120
Whilhite, A., 142
Whites. See Racial issues
Wisconsin
  campaign finance legislation, 72
  campaign spending, 38, 46, 47,
    55–56
  cost of competing as a challenger,
    110
  expenditures, 104, 106
  gender bias, 123, 129–130, 132,
    137n2
  legislature, 120
  party competition, 46
  political action committees, 158,
    168, 170, 173, 219
  political parties, 188, 191, 192,
    205n3, 222

public financing, 11, 46, 72, 104,
    106, 163 170, 225–226
  regulations, 22, 46
Wood, John M., 225
Women and women candidates
  as candidates and legislators,
    112–118, 120–121, 216
  contributions to, 27
  discrimination against, 139
  districting and, 141
  fund raising by, 117, 118,
    121–137
  priorities of, 117
Wyoming
  campaign finance legislation, 72,
    77
  campaign spending, 43, 47,
    54–55, 63
  challenger competitiveness, 106
  chamber competition, 71
  cost of competing as a challenger,
    109
  cost of elections, 9, 59, 60, 101
  gender bias, 132
  interest groups, 181n4
  legislature, 120
  money and the vote, 101
  partisan competition, 165
  political action committees, 132,
    168, 173, 176, 178, 219
  political parties, 191
  population, 60

Year of the Woman (1992),
    120–121, 123, 135–136. See
    also Women